W9-BUE-547

Transforming Your
Go-to-Market Strategy

Transforming Your Go-to-Market Strategy

The Three Disciplines of Channel Management

V. Kasturi Rangan

with the research assistance of
Marie Bell

HARVARD BUSINESS SCHOOL PRESS
Boston, Massachusetts

Library of Congress Cataloging-in-Publication Data
  Rangan, V. Kasturi.
    Transforming your go-to-market strategy: the three disciplines of channel
  management / V. Kasturi Rangan; with the research assistance of Marie Bell.
      p.   cm.
    Includes bibliographical references.
    ISBN 1-59139-766-9
    1. Marketing channels—Management. 2. Business logistics. 3. Physical distribution
  of goods. I. Title.
    HF5415.129.R36 2006
    658.8'7—dc22

                                                                    2005030893

The paper used in this publication meets the minimum requirements of the American
National Standard for Information Sciences—Permanence of Paper for Printed Library
Materials, ANSI Z39.48-1992.

Contents

117852

Acknowledgments

The impetus for this book came in 1997, when I started teaching a course, "Channels to Market," in the second-year MBA program at Harvard Business School and developed a shorter variation of it for the Executive Education classes. By then the Internet had permeated many facets of distribution channels, which made the topic an interesting one for study. We wrote more than a dozen new cases, and these, along with the knowledge accumulated from earlier work, became the foundation for the new ideas that have emerged here. I am grateful to the hundreds of students and executives who participated in the various courses. Through their discussions they have enriched my thinking.

The real thanks go to the managers and protagonists of the many field-based research projects and case studies. By sharing their go-to-market challenges, they gave me a rich database to drive the processes of compare and contrast and pattern recognition that form the heart of good field research. These managers include Arthur Droege and Ray Löfgren (from Atlas Copco); Kevin Rollins, Scott Eckert, and Michael Dell (Dell, Inc.); Inder Sidhu and Paul Montford (Cisco Systems); Charles Butt, Todd Piland, and Rob Price (H-E-B); Richard Schulze and Robert Anderson (Best Buy); Edward Chernoff (MARS Motors); John Elliott (GE); Launie Steffens and Allen Jones (Merrill Lynch); Bill Kozy, John Gormally, Stephen Sichak, and Paul Falkenstein (Becton Dickinson); Steve Kaufman (Arrow Electronics); Glen Meakem (FreeMarkets); Per Lofberg (Medco); Ernie Maier (3M); Gary O'Neill and Dave Edwards (Dow); John Stempeck and Michael Ruffolo (Xerox); Phillip Todd and Jeff English (Haworth); Jean Kovacs (Comergent Technologies), and many more. There are far too many to name here, but they all appear (in most cases by their real names) in the case studies and articles referenced in the selected bibliography.

For the topic of channels of distribution, I have benefited from working with three mentors, who I would especially like to acknowledge. Louis Stern and Andy Zoltners (Northwestern University) were the first to engage my interest in the topic when I entered the doctoral program there. Not only did they teach me much, but also they have continued to receive and react to my ideas and encourage my work. At Harvard, the late Ray Corey was key in further fueling my interest. He taught me the joys of field research. Under his mentorship, we wrote, with Frank Cespedes, _Going to Market: Distribution Systems for Industrial Products_ (Boston: Harvard Business School Press, 1989). Ray's meticulous approach to designing and implementing field research gave me the appropriate platform for bridging theory and practice.

At Harvard, I have been blessed by interactions with many colleagues: Benson Shapiro, Alvin Silk, Robert Dolan (Dean at Michigan Business School), Rowland Moriarty (CRA International), Patrick Kaufmann (Boston University), Tom Kosnik (Stanford University), Melvyn Menezes (Boston University), Frank Cespedes (Center for Executive Development), Jeffrey Rayport (Monitor), John Sviokla (Diamond Cluster International), the late Tom Bonoma, Jai Jaikumar, and Bob Buzzell. Jose Luis Nueno (IESE) introduced me to many new aspects of the channel literature when doing his doctoral work at Harvard. My work with Rajiv Dant (University of Miami) helped me further that understanding. Gordon Swartz (consultant at Market Bridge) and Steven Michael (University of Illinois) allowed me to participate in their doctoral studies and learning about channels. And, of course, the current members of the "channels cluster" at HBS—Rajiv Lal, Walter Salmon, and David Bell—through their frequent interactions, provided a stimulating environment. When I took over and modified the retailing course in 1997, Walter Salmon brought me in touch with many consumer goods marketers and retailers.

I am also thankful to many colleagues at Harvard who provided excellent feedback at several seminars on aspects of this work: John Gourville, John Deighton, Luc Wathieu, Joe Lassiter, Sunil Gupta, Das Narayandas, Elie Ofek, Dave Godes, Marta Wosinska, Gail McGovern, Doug Holt (now at Oxford University), Rohit Deshpande, Youngme Moon, Anita Elberse, and Tom Steenburgh, all from the marketing group, and, from the technology and operations management department, Roy Shapiro, Jan Hammond, Ananth Raman, and Stefan Thomke. At those seminars, several doctoral candidates, notably Andrea Wojnicki, Marco Bertini, Mary Caravella, Tuba Ustuner, Ozge Turut, and Jill Avery, pushed us to clarify our frameworks as did Greg Bell from CRA International.

Taking the plunge to write a book is a huge one, and Jerry Zaltman deserves the credit for nudging me along. He shared his wisdom and the potential high points and low points of the process, providing extensive feedback as we began to write. Nirmalya Kumar (London Business School), too, was instrumental in getting us to take on this project and providing valuable guidance. Stephen Greyser always had words of encouragement. Krishna Palepu, Rosabeth Moss Kanter, Warren McFarlan, John Quelch, and George Day (Wharton) were other colleagues who encouraged us.

My father was the first scholar who made a huge impact on me, but in many ways, his reach extended to my two brothers and sister as well: Bala Chakravarthy, Gopal Rathnam, and Prabha Sridhar. Each of my siblings, along with my mother, Sushila Vijayaraghavan, has been an important motivator in my life. I am thankful for their encouragement on this book project and for their lifelong support.

During the process of writing this book, I had the help of three wonderful people.

Barbara Trissel, one of the most efficient office assistants ever, endured reams of writing and rewriting; some chapters went through six or more drafts. Moreover, with drafts and attachments flying among several of us, often only she knew what was where. She kept me honest, and the contents under control. She did all this with a minimum of fuss and maximum good cheer.

Regina Fazio Maruca, a developmental editor, asked great questions, showed excellent judgment on where to add, cut, and modify, and in general provided the voice of an informed reader. More importantly, she showed us how to make changes. The book is significantly more readable because of her efforts.

Marie Bell far exceeded her role as a research associate. We wrote many cases for the channels-to-market course. But Marie was also a full-fledged intellectual partner. She discussed my interpretations of various data, offering alternative views and finding data that bolstered initial arguments. She was the sounding board for many of the integrative themes, and because she was closely involved in the original creation of the field case material, she brought her critical judgment to bear. Marie also had a major role in managing the writing project.

Many colleagues from inside and outside Harvard Business School have generously helped us with their case material, which rounded out our own field case studies. We would like to thank Bala Chakravarthy for Best Buy; Rajiv Lal for Callaway and Hewlett-Packard (along with Kirthi Kalyanaraman); Das Narayandas for Arrow Electronics; V. G. Narayanan for Owens & Minor; John Deighton for Snapple; and Pankaj Ghemawat, José Luis Nueno, and Andrew McAfee for Zara.

The folks at HBS Press, with the ever cheerful Kirsten Sandberg at the helm, deserve credit for keeping us on schedule without compromising the quality of the process. The reviews were honest, helpful, and constructive. Reviewer Paresh Shah, managing director of Forge Advisors, deserves special thanks. I sent him the manuscript, hoping for a quick read, and instead, he read the entire manuscript and offered extensive editing suggestions, many of which we have incorporated. Erin Anderson (INSEAD), Louis Stern (Northwestern University), and Ben Shapiro also read an earlier version of the book and offered encouraging feedback.

The acknowledgment of the plethora of help does not, however, rule out my own errors of omission, commission, and interpretation, and I alone bear responsibility for those failures.

Writing a book is time-consuming, even for those of us in academia. Harvard Business School's division of research under former Dean Kim Clark was generous in providing us the travel and research budget to complete the inquiry, but time is a scarce commodity and has to be carved from somewhere. And that somewhere came from many weekends during the past two years taken from my family. My mother, Sushila Vijayaraghavan, my wife, Jayanthi, and our two children, Vikram and Mallika, made the sacrifice. Our daughter, Mallika, was reaching the important milestones of ages ten and eleven during this time, and Jayanthi assumed many of the parenting responsibilities, giving me the space and freedom to pursue my passion to capture in writing what I know of channel management. For that reason, I dedicate this book to my family, without whose flexibility, tolerance, and affection, this book would never have been possible.

—V. Kasturi Rangan

Introduction

IN 1998, WE WORKED with several Xerox managers on a study of the company.[1] The Internet had become popular, and this Xerox group, divided into two teams, was working on commercializing a technology dubbed book-in-time (BIT). The initiative was quite small given the scale of Xerox's operations.

The idea was simple. When book contents were digitized, Xerox, by integrating its know-how of printing technology, would be able to produce a 300-page book for about $7 at the astonishing speed of one book per minute—an enormous business advantage in a market where such cost benefits were available only when printing lots of more than one thousand copies. With conventional offset printing technology, a 300-page book would incur an up-front fixed cost of at least $5,000, compared with $7 using BIT.

The BIT technology would immediately create demand for out-of-print books (estimated to be about 1 million books in the United States and 10 million worldwide). Of course, when cleverly configured, the technology could launch a host of other small-volume books as well.

We were intrigued by the two channels-to-market approaches devised by the two teams. One team visualized BIT as an addition to the product line for the graphic arts market; this market was well cultivated by Xerox's top-notch sales force, who were well trained in selling high-ticket Docu-Tech machines to business customers and their print shops.

In contrast, the second team envisioned the value BIT could bring to several members of the value chain. Not only the printers, but others in the channel might benefit: authors (who could publish focused offerings), publishers (many of which owned the intellectual property rights to out-of-print content), wholesalers (which could reduce their inventory of slow-moving books), and retailers (which could meet the demand for out-of-print books). This group preferred to position BIT as a service to members of the book channel value chain.

This difference between the two approaches is illustrated in figure I-1. The first approach (shown at the left) shows a clear point of entry in the channel value chain; the primary source of profitability is the margins emanating from the sales of the systems. The second approach (shown at the right) is somewhat more pervasive, having multiple entry points that create value and multiple avenues that capture value.

The first team focused on developing a plan based on selling the system (which might start at a couple of hundred thousand dollars and run up to a million), whereas the second team focused on building a plan for Xerox, by itself or in conjunction with partners, to sell BIT as a service to one or more members of the channel value chain. Xerox would enter the book channel value chain and charge its clients a fee for each copy it

FIGURE I-1

Creating and capturing value through channels

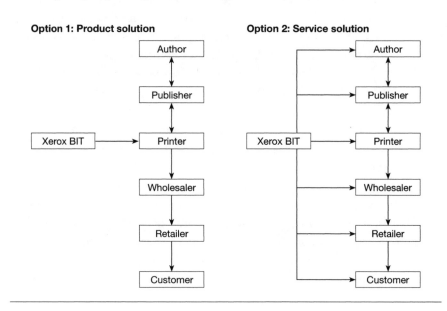

printed and sent to the retailer. This group projected revenues that were several times those of the "product" approach.

Of course, to adopt the service approach Xerox would need to reconfigure its channels, and therein lay the risk. The existing sales channels were better suited for moving high-ticket equipment to narrowly targeted customers. Ultimately, Xerox pursued a modification of the first approach.

The purpose of this illustration is not to second-guess whether the approach chosen by Xerox was right or wrong, but rather to underscore one of the key dilemmas facing managers as they design channels-to-market strategies. During twenty years of research, teaching, and consulting in this field, we encounter this same core issue again and again. Channel managers often ask the question, Should we risk a channel transformation or make do with what seems to be working fine? This question is hard to answer in the context of channels, especially because the risks seem real and imminent, whereas the rewards seem distant and ephemeral. We wrote this book to address this recurrent question. Channel managers need a framework for change, and this book attempts to provide it.

This book explains how an organization can become a successful channel steward. Our goal is to help managers understand the various forces that shape their channels and identify the barriers to channel transformation. Channel stewardship is a new way of designing and managing distribution channels to enable the transformation in an evolutionary way. This practice offers fresh approaches to designing and managing channels that will allow managers to harness those forces and fully exploit their own companies' capabilities and those of their channel partners as they go to market.

We also explain how to adapt your channel strategy systematically to address customers' best interests while driving channel profits for all productive partners, and ultimately for your own benefit. Channel stewardship is a proactive effort to manage the environment within which channel strategy is formulated and executed. The result is a robust evolution and improvement of your channels to market.

To that end, this book explores how companies can successfully navigate this complex environment via three disciplines of channel management: mapping; building and editing; and aligning and influencing. We develop and present frameworks that anchor the three disciplines, and then we show through many field examples how managers can apply these frameworks to meet the variety of challenges faced by operating managers charged with executing channel strategy.

Principles and Frameworks

In chapter 1, we present an overview of the difficulties of formulating channel strategy under a constant barrage of day-to-day channel tasks. We propose the notion of channel stewardship and its three underlying disciplines to overcome this distraction and the inertia to change.

Chapter 2 outlines the mapping framework, using the automobile industry as an illustration. Mapping provides a broad view of what others in the industry are doing and helps identify the opportunities and threats facing channel stewards. As they attempt to guide their channels to success, stewards should constantly try to read the effects of the four forces that drive channel strategy: the demand chain, channel capabilities and costs, channel power, and competitive actions.

But by the time you feel the influence of a force, sometimes it is too late to parry effectively. After all, these forces are preceded and shaped by fundamental changes in the environment. The mapping process can alert stewards to the way in which key forces are being influenced; done correctly, it reveals the unique links between cause and effect in market evolution and suggests possible avenues for change. Armed with an understanding of key forces—gained through mapping—a steward can begin to influence them by building and editing a true channel value chain, the second discipline of channel stewardship.

We develop this second discipline in chapters 3 and 4. Chapter 3 presents Dell as an exemplar of the building and editing process. Because Dell sells directly, we can illustrate the key principles cleanly before developing a methodology in chapter 4 that includes the role of the intermediary. A channel value chain is the outcome of shaping channel capabilities to address the needs of the demand chain. Such a balance requires constant calibration, and it is this task that differentiates the passive channel manager, which weathers change, from the active channel steward, which understands the forces of change, harnesses them, and profitably transforms the channel.

Chapter 4 makes a powerful statement regarding channel stewardship. The channel is not simply a conduit to reach customers; as an entity it also creates value. The six-step approach described here encourages stewards to distinguish between the roles that the channel plays and the institutions that represent those roles. Even when channel institutions do not change, by evolving their roles the steward can set in motion a process of channel transformation.

The third discipline of channel stewardship is aligning and influencing the channel value chain. This discipline complements the work begun in building and editing, and often it must be accomplished through a channel system consisting of several intermediaries. This continuous task requires a careful understanding of those intermediaries, their value-adding capabilities, and the power they wield in influencing channel behavior. This discipline is discussed in chapters 5 and 6.

Chapter 5 reviews the concept of channel power and concludes that even though it is a useful weapon, an absolute reliance on channel power as a means of editing the channel value chain misses the point of channel stewardship. The channel value chain must change from an arm's-length hand-off to a team effort, and this means that something other than power must become the primary driver of change. That something is channel value chain performance. If the overall performance of the value chain is the foundation of all the channel relationships, then even a small company with limited channel power can influence the channel to move forward in alignment with the value chain. Effective channel stewards convince all channel partners to buy into the idea that a rising tide lifts all boats. How this is done is the topic of chapter 6.

Stewardship is not about being "nice"; it requires a laserlike focus on the customer and a rigorous study of how the various partners contribute to the channel value chain. Sometimes, it also requires altering or eliminating a partner's role or making other difficult decisions. The key is that even when a steward must make a tough call, the action must not be an unexplained power play. One of the mandates of stewardship is to ensure that all partners up and down the channel understand how the channel value chain addresses customer demands. That drive for transparency, with the customer in focus, can virtually eliminate the possibility that an unpopular decision will be mistaken for a power play.

Of course, visibility up and down the channel is easy to call for; it is much harder to implement. Interestingly, information technology has made it possible to program the links and seamlessly integrate information across the channel value chain, but it can happen only if the members cooperate. They are not likely to do so unless they can readily empathize with their partners' positions. It's almost a chicken-and-egg situation. Trust comes with shared information; information won't be shared without trust. Clearly, channel partners must unite not only to improve the various processes but also to strengthen the personal relationship links between those processes.

Applications and Inferences

Having discussed the key disciplines of channel stewardship and the underlying conceptual rationale, we turn in chapters 7 and 8 to examples of actions by suppliers and intermediaries, respectively, as stewards of their channels. Channel stewardship should appeal to any organization that wants to bring a disciplined approach to channel strategy—any entity in the channel value chain that has a stake in addressing the needs of end users. The steward might be the maker of a product or service, or it might be an intermediary. Within a channel system, however, there can be only one channel steward—the one with the most accurate vision of how to create value for customers, the channel partners, and itself.

In chapter 7, we discuss the stewardship actions of five suppliers: Zara, an innovative, vertically integrated apparel maker; Cisco, a technology leader and market leader in networking gear; Atlas Copco, a manufacturer of stationary air compressors; Becton Dickinson, a medical device maker and market leader by far (in preanalytic systems); and Haworth, a maker of office furniture. Interestingly, neither Atlas Copco nor Haworth is a market share leader, and that goes to show that channel stewardship is applicable to any firm, large or small, in the value chain. It is not about which is the biggest; rather, it identifies which is willing to adapt and transform its channels in tune with customer needs.

Chapter 8 examines the evolutionary customer actions of Best Buy, the leading retailer in consumer electronics, to demonstrate how intermediaries can adapt and implement channel stewardship principles. This chapter also looks at the astute actions of grocery retailer H-E-B to maintain its market leadership position in south Texas against Wal-Mart and analyzes the actions of Arrow Electronics and Owens & Minor, two large intermediaries in the business-to-business space, as they steward their channels amid well-endowed and larger suppliers. This chapter closes with an illustration of how our stewardship principles are practiced by a smaller intermediary (of air conditioning and refrigeration components and supplies) to encourage the bigger supplier (General Electric) to assume the mantle of channel stewardship.

Having explored the concept of stewardship in a vertical channel value chain connecting a supplier to its end customers, we turn to the challenges of managing multiple channels. Suppliers often make several products or product lines and differentially support each of them to meet the different needs of customers in different market segments. Such strategies call for developing multiple channels, but as we all know they also are fraught with possibilities for horizontal conflict. Chapter 9 discusses the nature of such conflicts and offers stewardship rules for managing them. The chapter closes with an illustration of Cisco's dynamic management of its multiple channels in keeping with the evolution of its market environment.

One of the biggest changes in the past fifty years to affect a firm's channels-to-market strategy has been the rise of the Internet in the mid-1990s. The Internet was seen as a way to effect change. In many cases, however, the Internet has been thought of as a tool but applied as a weapon. In sum, despite its value as an extraordinarily powerful channel utility, the Internet has complicated the difficult task of stewarding a channel. Even though the Internet is integral to the discussion in every chapter, it is the exclusive theme of chapters 10 and 11.

In chapter 10, we offer a framework for understanding the power of the Internet as a channel and guide potential channel stewards in its deployment. We illustrate our ideas with many examples, including airline travel and business-to-business market exchanges (FreeMarkets). Chapter 11 discusses ways to integrate the Internet into a multiple-channel strategy, with suggestions for how and when to integrate it and how and when to design it as a stand-alone channel. Examples from Hewlett-Packard, Priceline, and Merrill Lynch demonstrate the framework.

For those acting as channel stewards to be able to perform to their fullest potential, the approach we advocate must be an essential part of business strategy. Many executives we have worked with make the mistake of viewing channel strategy as the implementation arm of business strategy. It is at least an integral element, and sometimes it resides at the heart of business strategy. In effect, then, channel stewardship must permeate top management's decision making. This is the topic of chapter 12.

The Scope of Channel Stewardship

Channels of distribution are ubiquitous and yet important to many things businesses do—in the consumer or business arena, in products or services. Sales through retail establishments in the United States were estimated to be about $3.9 trillion in 2005, so a good guess would put the retail industry, worldwide, at $10 trillion. This does not include the service sector, which was estimated to be at least as big.[2] A related survey estimated the sales that flowed through merchant wholesale channels at $3.3 trillion in the United States. Even though some of this includes the same goods that ultimately reach retail, this number also includes several business-to-business categories such as computers and peripherals, machinery and equipment, chemicals and allied products, and so on.[3] Again, tripling this number for a worldwide estimate, the flow through intermediaries is about $10 trillion.

The scope of channel stewardship is vast. That is one reason we have written this book at a sufficiently high level of generalization to make the principles and lessons useful in a wide array of applications. At the same time, because channel strategy often is not in the vision of top managers' strategic thinking, we have attempted to anchor our larger principles with frameworks and examples of applications to allow easy translation to the context at hand.

1

The Promise of Channel Stewardship

S ENIOR MANAGERS of most of the companies involved in moving goods or services from suppliers to end users would agree: their distribution channels are outdated and unwieldy, serving neither customers nor channel partners as well as they should.

In a few cases, distribution channels are streamlined and satisfying for all participants. In some cases, technology has improved things dramatically. But in most scenarios, distribution channels, taken as a whole, seem more like a repository of lost opportunities than an effective delivery system that appropriately serves and rewards all participants. Powerful channel members routinely impose their will; weaker participants suffer along because they see no way out; and customers . . . ? Despite much talk of customer-focused companies, customers are often ignored when it comes to distribution.

Most participants agree on the problem, but solutions have been elusive. From our decades of research, teaching, and working with top managers of companies that have tried to improve their go-to-market strategies, we have learned that almost everyone agrees it is difficult to effect significant change in distribution channels. Even though technology has made access to customers easier, transactions faster, and business processes more integrated, distribution channels tend to exhibit a strong inertia. Of all the elements of a company's marketing strategy, distribution channels are perhaps the hardest to change.

Three primary factors explain why:

1. Any change in distribution necessarily involves many different parties and is influenced by a host of factors. Intermediary relationships, institutional commitments, legal restrictions, entrenched customer behavior, and competitive practices often limit the type and extent of changes that a firm can realistically make.

2. Within companies, channels often are functions in search of a home. The various components of a channel (whether within a supplier or within a third-party vendor) may be able to improve operations by taking advantage of new technologies, but usually there is no one at the helm guiding the activities of the entire channel. CEOs typically have an overarching perspective but an insufficient grasp of the details, and CMOs (chief marketing officers) often view go-to-market decisions as being tactical. What passes for channel strategy often rests with sales divisions, but their primary motivation is to sell and they neither craft channel strategies nor lobby decision makers for change. The focus is on quantitative targets; channel tactics for effecting sales transactions are taken for strategy. No one has an eye on the go-to-market system as a whole, and no one steps back to assess the state of a channel in light of market changes, such as shifting technological capabilities, competitive actions, and customer buying behaviors.

3. As a result of this lack of leadership, a channel and its norms become deeply embedded as the primary way of reaching customers. Even when a channel gets a leader, it is hard to facilitate change in an ingrained system that has evolved without guidance and has no inherent logic. So channel management is often cosmetic and rarely affects channel design, even though channel design often contributes to the problems that require managing.

Companies need a new approach to going to market—one that we call channel stewardship. Put simply, channel stewardship is the ability of a given participant in a distribution channel—a steward—to craft a go-to-market strategy that simultaneously addresses customers' best interests and drives profits for all channel partners. A channel steward can be a manufacturer, an assembler, a service provider, an intermediary, or any other participant in the value chain to the customer. Within a company the stewardship function might reside with the CEO, a top manager, or a team of senior managers.

An effective channel steward considers the channel from the customer's point of view. With that view in mind, the steward then advocates for change among all participants, transforming disparate entities into partners having a common purpose.

When a channel has an effective steward, all participants along the way to the end customer understand, perhaps for the first time, the levers that motivate their partners up and down the line. As a result, all participants are better primed for the give-and-take required to create a value proposition that is as attractive as possible to customers and to the various channel participants.

Consider these questions:

- How does a manufacturer design channels for a new product, especially when it has an incumbent channel? It is often assumed that the incumbent channel will get the new products, but a host of problems can occur when existing distributors, although important and useful for a certain portfolio of products, are no longer appropriate for a different subset.

- How can you overcome resistance from a powerful channel partner, such as a brand-name manufacturer or a strong intermediary, over issues such as price discounting or shelf-space allocation? When are power plays appropriate? When should you exercise power? When should you give in to power? What are the consequences for partner relationships and channel performance?

- When a new channel, or a multiple-channel scenario, offers prospective market coverage, how does a supplier trade off the risks of alienating a loyal franchised retail channel against the benefits of accessing new customers? The problem is exacerbated when the new channel is a low-cost alternative such as the Internet.

Such issues are perennial in channel management. Despite the widespread use of channel partners in accomplishing go-to-market goals, two important aspects of channel management—assessing performance and setting goals—are only weakly developed and enforced. Misunderstandings of partner roles and responsibilities are common.

Many typical channel issues appear to be tactical but in fact have long-term implications. A channel steward is better positioned to have a clear perspective on these issues and is likely to foster a similarly unbiased view on the part of other participants.

Moreover, with an effective channel steward in place, all participants understand that you can seldom make dramatic improvements immediately. As a result, they gain the patience to implement changes having long-term benefits, as opposed to changes having only short-term results. Technology, for example, can facilitate major, immediate changes in a process, but only stewardship can ground those changes by ensuring that all parties truly understand why a change is necessary and how it will benefit them over the long term. Effecting change in an ingrained distribution channel—in many, if not most, existing channels—is a difficult challenge, but therein lies the opportunity.

Put another way, channel stewardship, as we define it, is anchored in the principle of evolutionary change. This should not be confused with incremental change. Stewardship means constantly guiding and directing changes in channel design and management to align the channel with customer needs while driving profit for all channel partners.

Make no mistake: what we advocate in this book is not always easy. The analyses and processes we recommend are meant to be adaptive and continuous, and they are aimed at reaching the ultimate goal in steps, with the understanding that the goal itself may continue to evolve.

The Rewards of Channel Stewardship

The concept of channel stewardship is meant to appeal to any organization in the distribution channel that wants to bring a disciplined approach to channel strategy. As mentioned, a channel steward might be the maker of the product or service (such as Procter & Gamble or American Airlines); the maker of a key component (such as microchip maker Intel); the supplier or assembler (such as Dell or Arrow Electronics); or the distributor (such as W. W. Grainger) or retailer (such as Wal-Mart). A channel steward might be any entity in the channel value chain that has a stake in addressing the needs of end users; a smaller player might not have much freedom to maneuver, but it needs a channel strategy to ensure its financial success and perhaps nudge the powerful players toward stewardship.

The examples in this book illustrate acts of stewardship by suppliers (including makers of products and providers of services) and intermediaries (distributors, agents, and retailers). Undoubtedly, effective stewards guide the course of their channel's evolutionary destiny and thus their own bottom line. That's why any member that has the opportunity should attempt to take charge.

Channel stewardship has two important outcomes. The primary (and obvious) purpose is to expand value for the steward's customers and bottom line. The main reason any partner would want to participate in a channel with an effective steward is to expand the pie for itself, perhaps by increasing the size of the market or increasing existing customers' purchases through the channel.

A second, more subtle outcome is a more tightly woven, and yet adaptable, channel. Stewardship is not a social welfare system, where all intermediaries, regardless of their role or performance, are encouraged to stay in the system. Far from it. Stewardship involves careful construction and management of channel relationships so that the valuable members are suitably rewarded and the less valuable members are weeded out.

When a channel has an effective steward, the goal is a distribution system that includes only those activities that add discernable value for customers and corresponding rewards for the channel partners. The focus is first on identifying what must be done; only then does it turn to where that work will reside.

The Consequences of Not Having a Steward

A typical channel system evolves without a channel steward. When a product is new, the sole aim of most suppliers is to get the product in the hands of users. All parties that assist in that goal are welcomed, within the broad restraints of cost. As sales revenues grow, so do channels, with many arrangements consecrated by personal relationships and the preferences of a few key decision makers. Informal rules get made on how the system operates.

Then one day when a firm has grown enough, it discovers that it has a channel footprint. Whether this organically grown, haphazardly nurtured channel is appropriate for the task at hand is not usually open for discussion. Usually, the more pressing question is how to build on what is already available to fulfill future sales goals. So appendages are built, and a maladapted structure emerges.

Now layer on the natural pressures that are brought to bear on a channel in the course of a day, a week, or a year, along with the management decisions made to deal with those pressures.

For example, suppose a product manager discovers that she is well below target on a new product launch. Her first inclination is to meet with her sales counterpart and closely reexamine the launch program. They discover that the distribution channel is not aggressively pushing the new product. Their own sales force resources are constrained. The few available salespeople must stay focused on generating and maintaining demand for the company's other product, a market leader in its category. They therefore contemplate a channel incentive program; a special promotion is planned, more trade promotion and advertising are planned, and channel margins are enhanced.

This is channel management as most of us know it, but we might as well call it "bandage" management. The manager is "managing" the channel, but because the channel wasn't carefully designed in the first place, she likely does not have any real insight into how to identify and address the root causes. The foundation of any good channel strategy is its design architecture. With a good design, day-to-day management of channels is not onerous. But when difficult management issues crop up, often they are a signal of deeper problems. If we don't address the core design issues, we don't gain much by way of channel strategy.

Rohm and Haas managers faced this kind of situation when their new Kathon MWX biocide did not achieve its launch targets.[1] They realized that a reason for the initial failure was that the company had used an existing channel. This channel was well suited to take another product—the Rohm and Haas 886 liquid biocide—to a specific set of customers: those having large coolant tanks used in metal cutting. These were sophisticated customers, and the role of the intermediary (called a formulator) was to provide outstanding maintenance services. The new product, however, was intended for operations that were supported by smaller (fifty-gallon) tanks. Customers for the new product were small and dispersed, and they were unsophisticated in understanding the properties of metal-cutting coolants. They were usually accessed by a second tier of dealers (industrial supply shops). These dealers in turn were served by the same formulators who served the large customers.

Given that both products performed the same function (extending the life of the metal-working fluid by eliminating bacteria) and both had the same channel entry point (the formulators), Rohm and Haas had used the same channel. But the end-use market for the new product was so different that the company needed to rethink its entire go-to-market strategy rather than just its channel incentive programs. Design problems usually don't get fixed by tactical actions.

Designing and Managing a Channel

In a typical arrangement, a supplier has four alternative channels to reach its customers:

1. It can go through a stocking distributor to a retail company, which then serves end users. (In the service analogy, the distributor becomes a consolidator.)

2. It can go through an agent, such as a jobber or a broker (instead of a distributor), to retail.

3. It can go directly to retailers.

4. It can go directly to end users.

Figure 1-1 illustrates these key dimensions of channel design and management. These choices are not mutually exclusive, so a combination is a viable alternative.

FIGURE 1-1

Channel strategy

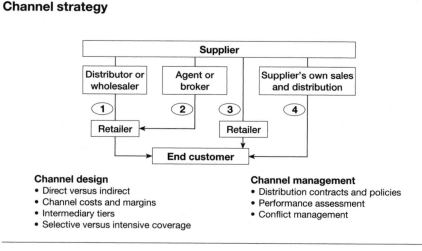

Channel design
- Direct versus indirect
- Channel costs and margins
- Intermediary tiers
- Selective versus intensive coverage

Channel management
- Distribution contracts and policies
- Performance assessment
- Conflict management

Designing channels requires answering certain questions: which channel options to choose, how many partners to include at each level, and how they should be governed. In contrast, whereas design involves structural aspects of the channel, management involves the formal or informal rules that govern the day-to-day behavior of the various channel members (including the supplier).

The two elements of channel strategy should go hand in hand. You cannot resolve design issues—such as whether to adopt a direct or an indirect channel or, if indirect, how many levels are appropriate—without a sense of how distribution policies and practices are translated. Similarly, you cannot govern the channel and set sales targets without a good handle on channel costs and margins and other operating features. When you choose multiple channels, conflict becomes a management issue. Even when you choose a single option, you may have to address questions of coverage and dealer intensity. In short, channel design and management should be interactive and integrative components of channel strategy.

Unfortunately, however, most firms—regardless of their place in a given channel—do not manage their go-to-market strategies in that inclusive way. Once they carve out a profile, channel structures slowly calcify and get cemented in place. The structural aspects of figure 1-1, captured under the heading "Channel Design," evolve only very slowly. Most firms end up using the other side—"Channel Management"—to respond to environmental changes.

But as most channel managers would readily admit, channel management, by itself, cannot be effective unless a concerted effort is made to translate much of that information into knowledge that drives long-term change in channel design. But that rarely happens. Worse, because channel management's immediate job is to facilitate the flow of products and services, often it takes on a day-to-day, tactical flavor. It may even end up doing a heroic job of achieving sales targets in a changing environment without making a dent in the channel structure. The problem is that even when an industry reaches a new equilibrium as a result of changes in its environment, you are still stuck with an unchanged underlying channel system. The system is ineffective for the new environment (in fact, it is obsolete), but the efforts of channel managers usually hold it together, continuously propping up any major breakdown.

When Management Efforts Break Down

In some cases, even extreme channel management efforts cannot overcome a flaw in channel design. Many channel managers assume that channel systems cannot be altered and therefore resort to tactical management to keep the flow of products as smooth as possible. But even if this approach seems to work in the short run, it is suboptimal and may distract managers from addressing critical long-term issues.

Consider what happened in the mid-1990s, when Dell established dominance of the direct channel to its personal computer customers. Dell's competitors, notably IBM and Compaq, wanted to emulate the Dell model and attempted to create their own built-to-order channels.[2] Those two companies, however, were beholden to their existing channel designs, so they implemented their new models through their distributor networks. Special pricing and margin arrangements were brokered to enable intermediaries to implement the built-to-order model, but the initiatives, after floundering for several years, were withdrawn.[3]

The core issue for IBM and Compaq was one of channel structure and strategy, and not incentives to motivate the middleman. For PCs, a built-to-order model simply does not work at a decentralized level because the scale is too small to smooth out uneven order flows on the production line. Dell had only one centralized factory in the United States, which it kept updating, giving it enormous supply-chain cost advantages. The result was that Dell "wielded those [manufacturing] advantages like a club, assaulting its rivals' financials while stealing their customers . . . that allowed Dell to keep making a profit on desktop PCs, while Hewlett-Packard, Compaq, IBM and Gateway [lost] money."[4] But IBM and Compaq, each holding an enormous share of the PC market, made the same mistake. Not understanding how to act as channel stewards, they attempted to solve a channel design problem with a channel management solution.

Could IBM and Compaq have approached their initiatives differently? Could channel stewardship have helped them adjust their channel designs to allow their initiatives to succeed? We know that hindsight is 20/20, but we strongly believe that any company that takes on the mantle of channel steward can spur a steady evolution and keep its channels vibrant and in tune with the changes in the environment.

When Managers Are Blindsided by Success

Lacking channel stewardship, successful companies are also more likely to be blindsided by fundamental flaws in their channel designs. Such has been the case with Callaway Golf Company, which found itself stuck in a quagmire that, much to its surprise, had slowly and steadily grown right under its nose.[5]

Callaway, founded in 1982 by entrepreneur Ely Callaway, grew by 1998 to $900 million in sales revenue and a leading market share by virtue of a string of product innovations. In 1988, for example, it introduced a revolutionary S2H2 metal wood that changed the weight distribution of the driver and offered the average golfer the opportunity to drive a longer distance. In 1991, it launched the oversized Big Bertha metal wood, which combined S2H2 technology with a redesigned sweet spot. This club made the game more productive, forgiving, and enjoyable for the average golfer. Then, in 1995, Callaway came up with a third revolutionary design in Great Big Bertha titanium drivers, which embellished and consolidated the earlier technological advantages.

Consumers flocked to Callaway products, and its market share soared. The golfing channels also soared. By 1998, about five thousand "green grass" retailers (retail stores on the golf course, also known as pro shops) and about two thousand off-course retailers (retail stores in commercial locations) enthusiastically stocked and distributed Callaway products. They loved Callaway because the products were demonstrably superior.

Not to be outdone, however, competitors like Taylor Made and Titleist followed Callaway's lead in innovation, and in 1998 they effectively caught up. That's when Callaway's sway over its retailers began to weaken. Earlier, when the environment had been favorable and its products were flying off the shelf, the company had developed a policy of offering no discounts for retailers regardless of volume; payment terms were tight, too. But with diminishing product advantage and channel policies that left them with thin margins, retailers were no longer enamored of Callaway's products.

With the changed competitive environment and a lack of major new innovations (in part because of regulations from the USGA), Callaway needed the goodwill and assistance of its retailers, especially the off-course retailers, which did the bulk of sales. Not only the margins and incentives, but also the intensity and selection of Callaway's channel coverage came under the microscope. Did it have too many retailers? Did this affect the margins and service levels of its large retailers?

Lacking channel stewardship, Callaway had not focused on these kinds of questions in the first decade, but they have become a significant driver of its second decade of channel strategy.

The company has built a close relationship with its top ten retail chains, where it is the premier preferred vendor. With these national accounts, it has special inventory arrangements and special merchandising and display agreements. At the next level, it has crafted a preferred retailer program with its off-course channel partners, offering programs for gold, silver, and bronze retailers. At the level of the pro shops, it has sought a broader and deeper coverage. In 2004, Patrice Hutin, then the company's president and COO, captured the essence of its new channel strategy: "Technology is still important, but is less differentiating. It is the channels-to-market strategy that provides a key leverage."[6]

When Managers Are Slow to Respond to Environmental Change

In 1992, Goodyear had what many experts considered a superb distribution system: some 4,400 independent distributors that were fiercely loyal to Goodyear (half did not carry competing brands, and the other half carried only one or a few other brands). But Goodyear was losing share to Michelin, which, unlike Goodyear, sold through all available channels, including mass merchandisers and warehouse clubs.[7] These channels were notorious for carrying multiple brands and often discounting branded tires. In theory, conflicts should have affected Michelin adversely, with nearly 7,000 outlets spread across four or five kinds of channels. But it was Goodyear, not Michelin, that was out of tune with new customer buying behavior.

How did it happen? For about fifteen years following the invention of radial tires, with their superior life compared with the older bias-belted tires, Goodyear had the stronger channel. The innovation required much customer education and brand building, and the way to gain share was to have a dedicated distribution system tightly administered by the supplier. But by the early 1990s, radial technology was almost fully adopted by the market, and tires had become almost commodities, at least the way consumers purchased them. Almost 75 percent of customers shopped for price one way or the other and were often influenced by what dealers had to say.

In this environment, Goodyear discovered that intensity of channels and product availability was the way to go, and it added mass merchandisers like Sears, discounters like Sam's Club, and other large tire chains to its channel mix. Undoubtedly the addition caused much conflict with Goodyear's loyal franchised dealers, but the company had little choice. It needed market share to keep its factories utilized and costs low.

The Opportunity for Improvement

Significant opportunities for channel change through stewardship have been enabled by a unique convergence of circumstances.

For example, consider automobile retailing in the United States. In 2004, 70 percent of the buyers of nearly 12 million new cars sold first searched the Internet, choosing models, features, and price ranges, before entering any store. This was unheard of only a decade ago, when consumers had to shop from store to store to compile the kind of intelligence that now takes only a fraction of that time. A similar thing happened in air travel. In 2004, some 30 percent of sales in the $100 billion air travel market were conducted online.[8] Not only was this number zero until a decade ago, but also brick-and-mortar travel agents, who accounted for almost 70 percent of all travel bookings, now have only about 45 percent of that market.[9] We could continue with this story, citing books, music CDs, and so on.

Thus, Internet technology, which became available in commercial form in the mid-1990s, changed the cost equation for certain channels of information dissemination and distribution, spawning and supporting new ways of going to market. But the Internet is only one strand of the story. Significant changes in R&D, manufacturing, and logistics technologies have also provided tremendous opportunities for channel change. Consider the following example from a specialty chemicals producer. It's about termiticides—chemicals that provide a barrier against termites eating into the wood structures of buildings.

Termiticides are handled by licensed pest control operators (PCOs) because of their training with toxic chemicals. PCOs thus make up most of the distribution chain, transporting the chemicals to the site and skillfully applying them by drilling and pumping fluid into the ground to provide the barrier. Once in place, this chemical barrier repels termites before they reach the wooden structure.

But in the early 1990s, scientists from The Dow Chemical Company discovered that termites are social creatures that like to gather food (cellulose from timber) and take it to their colony for a communal feed. The scientists learned that they could tempt the termites to gather food at strategically placed wooden stakes around the immediate perimeter of a building and, if termites were found, replace the decoy stakes with bait, which would then spell doom for entire termite colonies.

Dow launched the Sentricon product in 1995, and it has emerged as the dominant market leader, with more than a million installations. Dow owns all the product components: the stakes, the bait, and the monitoring devices. Its distributors no longer need facilities for storing and transporting liquid chemicals. They are logistics agents fulfilling demand created by PCOs. The nature of a PCO's installation and monitoring task has also changed. Enormous cost savings in materials as well as labor have been gained. Instead of getting paid for chemicals, Dow now gets a portion of the installation fee and of the annual renewal fee.[10]

Distribution channels are also affected by emerging technologies. RFID (radio frequency identification) tags, for example, unobtrusively tag every product that leaves a factory, thereby tracking its journey all the way to users. Surely this will change order fulfillment, inventory replenishment, merchandizing, and a host of other logistics systems. As we write, technologists are devising miniature sensors that continually transmit data and work in tandem with technologies (such as wireless) to organize the entire flow of information and physical goods through channels of distribution.[11]

With channel stewardship, organizations can fully embrace most of these advances and apply them successfully as integral pieces of their distribution strategies. But where does a new steward begin?

Where to Start: Understanding the Key Drivers

Reduced to its essentials, becoming a channel steward first requires a thorough understanding of the key drivers that shape and influence the channel at any given time.

As a channel steward, if you examined a snapshot of your entire distribution channel at any given moment, you would find a host of forces at work, each influencing the channel in its own way. At certain points, these forces are creating tensions; at other points, they are relieving stresses. Some forces represent the supplier; others represent the intermediaries and other organizations mediating the channel; still others represent the customer. Then there are competitors, at the supplier level and at the intermediary level, which are constantly attempting to gain and hold on to customers, including yours.

Your snapshot would catch these forces in a collective effort to advance their respective interests. Sometimes the collective effort makes progress toward its goal, and at other times it doesn't. Inevitably, however, when an active channel steward is navigating the forces and guiding the various channel members in a collective effort, there is progress, and when the forces are left unmanaged there is a steady slippage away from your interests.

The individual characteristics of these forces are unique to your industry, with the players, products, and markets coloring the context. But taken broadly, the forces are similar, or even identical, to those affecting distribution channels in other industries. In fact, the four major forces that affect the short-term ebb and flow and the long-term evolution of every channel are identical (see figure 1-2):

- Demand-chain requirements

- Channel capabilities and costs

- Channel power

- Competitive actions

These four major forces are the levers that managers must learn to harness, influence, and navigate to shape an effective, forward-looking channel strategy. When a company works with these forces in a proactive manner to benefit the interests of its customers, its channel partners, and its bottom line (its investors), that is an act of stewardship.

Demand-Chain Requirements

Traditionally, demand is often simply interpreted as being the end of the supply chain. In other words, demand is the customer need for a given

FIGURE 1-2

The forces affecting channel strategy

product or service. A supply chain, for its part, is the physical distribution and logistics support that enables the fulfillment of customer need (demand).

We think of *demand* more broadly: it is the originator of a chain of needs that encompasses the customer's desire for the product or service as well as ancillary products and services; the maintenance of the product or service; any information customers might receive as part of the search; any education they might receive as part of their purchase, and so on. We think of a *demand chain* as encompassing the transactions that occur to fulfill the customer's needs, including and surrounding the product. Thus, all complementary products and services purchased or consumed as part of the transaction become the relevant focal point.

Consider a consumer's shopping experience at a supermarket. Consumers may buy a single item, but most of the time they buy a basket of items. No doubt each individual product has an identity in the minds of shoppers, but those identities are dominated by the gestalt of the overall basket. What's more, ambience, convenience, and other aspects of service count, too. Here is where the demand chain originates—in the overall context of the search and purchase.

Traditionally, when demand is viewed as the customer end of the supply chain, managers tend to check off the aspects of customer needs that the existing channels can serve and focus on improving only those areas. The focus might be on quality, improving the sales experience, and so on—all valid pursuits. However, these pursuits fall within the narrow context of a particular product or service, when in fact the breakthrough in terms of value creation for customers might come from a complementary transaction that the focal supplier may or may not participate in.

When managers view the supply chain as a logistics network, they tend to focus only on efficiency when they try to improve performance. Recent advances in the supply-chain literature embrace the value-creation role of a firm's distribution and logistics infrastructure.[12] Still, most practitioners view the supply chain as the physical distribution component of getting product from the factory to the customer, and thus they tend to focus on its efficiency. Inevitably that focus leads to questions about what can be done to trim the costs of taking the product to market. What's more, such a view limits the supplier's notion of what is most appropriate for customers, and it may not extend to those products and services beyond the supplier's immediate purview.

Channel Capabilities and Costs

The visible part of a firm's go-to-market strategy is often represented by various entities and institutions that mediate the transaction from the point of supply to the point of consumption: sales forces, distributors, retailers, warehouses, transportation facilities, servicing centers, and so on. The role of these agents and facilities is to add value to the product or service after it leaves the point of origin, so that the ultimate user's needs and wants are duly satiated. Such activities may include provision of information, inventory, convenience, assortment, services, and so on. This range of activities defines the capabilities of a go-to-market system. It is not only the physical distribution and logistics piece of the channel; rather, it includes all the combined activities that the supplier and its intermediaries mount to generate and fulfill customer demand.

Whenever such activities are undertaken, simultaneously the supplier and its intermediaries incur costs in conceiving of and executing the activities. Thus, channel capabilities and costs go together and are important in determining the success of a firm's go-to-market strategy.

Channel Power

This third force is an acknowledgment of the distribution of power among the channel players. The more powerful parties exert a higher level of influence on the policies and procedures governing relationships among channel members.

Channel members draw their power from various sources. Power comes in two basic forms. The first consists of power associated with having a unique product or technology, and the second rests on having market access and intelligence. These two forms of power usually occur in conjunction with the other sources, such as size, scale, or legal power.

The more powerful party usually influences channel policies in its favor and allocates a greater share of the channel profits its way. But if this becomes a handicap in sustaining the cooperation of the other members and in addressing the long-term questions of channel design, it calls for an astute application of stewardship to correct the situation.

Competitive Actions

The visible and deliberate hand of competition frames the other forces. In other words, everything is relative to what the competition (both at the manufacturer's level and at the distributor's level) is doing and can do in the future. Customers always make decisions in light of alternatives. So the supplier having the channel capabilities that most closely match customers' demand-chain requirements is likely to garner a large share of business.

In response, other suppliers must match or exceed the first supplier's channel offering to have a chance of gaining share. But to do so, they need the support of their channel partners. These partners often compete with other channel systems, and sometimes among themselves. Thus, managing the other influences on channel strategy is further complicated in the face of deliberate acts by competitors to derail your efforts.

The Three Disciplines of Channel Stewardship

This book explains how to become a successful channel steward. It is intended to help managers understand the forces that shape their channels and identify the barriers that hold back channel transformation; it also offers fresh approaches to designing and managing channels that will allow managers to harness those forces and take fullest advantage of their own company's capabilities and those of their channel partners as they go to market. It is about how to adapt your channel strategy systematically for the benefit of the customer, for the benefit of your channel partners, and ultimately for your own benefit.

Instead of resigning yourself to a fate determined by the core forces, adopting the notion of channel stewardship is a proactive attempt to influence them. Simply put, channel stewardship involves the construction of a *channel value chain* that mirrors the needs of the demand chain as closely as possible. Such a construction necessarily requires remediation in some cases, and transformation in others, of the existing channel capabilities and arrangements.

What do we mean by a channel value chain? A *value chain* defines the direct and support activities that a company undertakes to produce, market, and deliver its products to the customer.[13] A value chain has an upstream component and a downstream component. "Upstream" usually refers to the network of value-added activities that precedes the arrival of the raw materials, components, parts, and supplies at the aggregation site. The manufacturer or assembler that puts together the product or service then uses the downstream value chain to move the product to the end user.

The upstream chain is widely recognized and broadly labeled as the supply chain. It would be tempting to call the downstream component the demand chain, but that would not reflect the spirit of what we mean by demand chain—the customer's, rather than the supplier's, perspective. We therefore prefer to call the downstream component the *channel* value chain.

The design of this system is in the hands of the supplier and the intermediaries (if any), which may or may not be entirely capable of addressing the end user's demand-chain needs. For those engaged in distribution or retailing, these terms are just as applicable. A retailer, for example, would consider the upstream network of suppliers to be its supply chain. On the downstream side, an intermediary's marketing, sales, and merchandising activities would constitute the channel value chain.

How does a manager become a successful channel steward? As a starting point, we offer the framework outlined in figure 1-3, which shows three disciplines:

- Mapping the industry channel

- Building and editing the channel value chain

- Aligning and influencing the channel value chain

FIGURE 1-3

The disciplines of channel stewardship

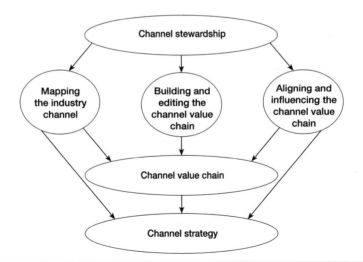

These three disciplines must be judiciously applied to create channel strategy.

We know the forces that influence channel strategy, but under our notion of stewardship, channel strategy is also meant to influence the forces themselves. It is a proactive effort to manage the environment within which channel strategy is formulated and executed. The result is a robust evolution and improvement of your channels to market. To that end, this book explores the ways in which channel stewards can successfully navigate this complex environment via the three disciplines.

Mapping the Industry Channel

Before you embark on an effort to steward your channels to market, you must understand what has caused and what can cause an evolution of the demand chain, the channel capabilities and costs, the channel power positions, and competitive actions in the first place. In studying this, you need to take an industry perspective, knowing full well that channel stewardship calls for a business-level protagonist. Understanding the big picture and its logic is crucial to formulating the action plans for the other two disciplines.

Building and Editing the Channel Value Chain

The second discipline calls for balancing the needs of customers with what the channel can offer. This requires that you enable, edit, and update the channel's capabilities to match the particulars of the demand chain, and vice versa, creating what we have called the channel value chain. This discipline animates the existing channel structure; even if immediate change is not possible, it prompts the channel structure to adapt and execute in different ways and aligns the channel steward in the right direction for long-term success.

This crucial second discipline connects the broad vision offered by the preceding mapping exercise to the reality of a firm's capabilities. It is here that a firm's strategic goals are played out. Here's where the firm establishes links to its customers' demand-chain requirements and establishes a channel system having roles and rules for the various members of the channel value chain.

Aligning and Influencing the Channel Value Chain

This final discipline calls for gaining leverage among the channel partners to alter their behavior in keeping with the needs of the "tuned" channel.

For the channel system to be healthy, vibrant, and sustaining, the rewards as a whole must be consistent with the efforts of the members. Firms like Callaway call this discipline into play as they attempt to reorganize themselves to meet the governance needs of an evolving channel environment.

This third discipline acknowledges the various channel policies, rules, and procedures that are all part of channel management tactics. It understands, however, that despite the written or unwritten rules, human managers execute channel arrangements across organizational boundaries. Thus, this channel stewardship discipline addresses channel coordination, control, and conflict resolution.

The channel steward designates the roles and responsibilities to be undertaken by the members and defines how these roles will be administered, performed, and compensated. The collective act is synonymous with channel strategy and its execution.

Our concept of channel stewardship is new, the result of a synthesis of existing research studies, our own many field case studies on channel strategy, interactions with scores of managers on the topic, and several focused consulting applications.[14] Throughout this book we offer examples and exemplars of the various components of channel stewardship, and we describe the actions of companies that are well on the way to becoming channel stewards. We present others that are taking some of the steps we advocate as well as some that seem to be floundering.

A Call to Managers

Channel stewardship is not a clarion call for blanket change or for the "flexibility" to adapt to the latest institutional or technological trend in reaching customers. Rather, our call to managers is to view channel strategy as an ongoing task and to construct mechanisms by which you consider changes, large or small, in light of their long-term viability and suitability. Channel stewardship calls for managed evolution so that, over a series of steps, stewards can make channels most suited to the environment around them. Channel stewardship is a clarion call for continuous monitoring and reasoned change.

We turn next to an in-depth look at the first discipline of channel stewardship: mapping.

2

Mapping an Industry

THE FIRST STEP in becoming an effective channel steward is to understand the key forces influencing the channel. You gain this understanding through the first discipline of channel stewardship: mapping. The art of stewarding a channel calls for a business-level perspective because an important goal is to enhance business profits. Mapping, however, is an industry-level exercise; the process reveals gaps and opportunities not apparent when a company considers only the channels in which it belongs.

Mapping provides a broader view of what others are doing and helps you identify opportunities and threats.

Mapping also acts as an early warning system. Stewards constantly try to read the effects of the four key forces (demand-chain requirements, channel capabilities and costs, channel power, and competitive actions) as they attempt to guide their channels to success. But sometimes, by the time the influence of a force is felt, it is too late to parry effectively. After all, these forces are preceded and shaped by fundamental changes in the environment. Mapping can alert stewards to the ways key forces are being influenced; done correctly, it reveals the unique links between cause and effect in market evolution, and it suggests avenues for change.

The four core forces are the immediate influences on channel strategy, and they act as a barometer of channel climate. As shown in figure 2-1, they interact and influence each other, but they are also affected by antecedent environmental influences in the industry. Mapping illuminates these other critical influences.

Regulatory changes are one good example of an antecedent influence; both deregulation and regulation have an impact on how firms go to market.

FIGURE 2-1

Mapping the forces affecting channel strategy

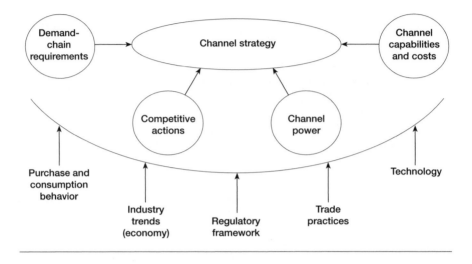

Another example is technological advances in products or channels. Having a computer chip built into an engine—an example of product technology—allows fleet operators to monitor the engine's operating characteristics and schedule maintenance to minimize breakdowns. Then it's no longer necessary to maintain intensive distribution networks to service truck fleets. The Internet—an example of channel technology—lets consumers search and buy airline tickets online, bypassing travel agents.

Another crucial external influence is a change in the culture surrounding customers' buying behaviors. Such changes may be spurred by changes in the immediate market environment; for example, the availability of the Internet prompted some investors to attempt self-directed online trading. At other times, these cultural changes happen because of seemingly unrelated changes in the business environment.

Snapple provides a good example of the latter. Many alternative soft drinks were launched in the mid-1980s, but Snapple alone seemed to latch on to an evolving offbeat yuppie culture that developed and grew with the brand. The soft drink appealed to a unique consumer culture, riding on word-of-mouth promotion on talk radio. Snapple was distributed through a network of three hundred small, predominantly family-owned distributors servicing convenience chains, pizza stores, food-service vendors, gasoline stations, and mom-and-pop stores. It was consumed one or two bottles at a time at lunch and other spontaneous meals. Clearly, Snapple did not create that consumer culture; rather, it was astute in spotting and riding the trend. This meant that the "cold" channel serving supermarket chains was less appropriate than the "warm" channels serving thousands of mom-and-pop establishments.[1]

A corollary of customer culture is *trade culture*, the set of norms and practices that define how an industry operates. Sometimes shifts in trade culture influence channel evolution; at other times, trade acts as an inertial force to resist change. For example, for decades the U.S. semiconductor distribution channel shunned Japanese semiconductors. When the Japanese entered the U.S. market in the mid-1970s, they met with resistance from distributors and manufacturers. There was nothing in the law that protected this practice—to the contrary—but that's how the rules evolved.

Another key influence is the forces of industry consolidation and fragmentation, as happened in personal computers and groceries, which we visit in later chapters.

Thus, the four core forces that influence channel strategy interact with each other as well as react to environmental forces. Figure 2-1, presented earlier, is neither exhaustive nor comprehensive; rather, it captures the essence of the key action components. Each firm in each industry faces a somewhat more customized version.

Even though a firm ultimately faces the need to evolve and transform its channel strategy through the effects of the four forces, it cannot be complacent until the pressures begin to build. A number of factors cause the pressure, many of which can be anticipated by a vigilant channel steward cognizant of the width and depth of their impact.

Mapping suggests ways in which top management can attempt to shape the environment. Regulation, trade practices—even consumer culture— are amenable to change when industry participants engage in influencing the larger policies and practices that underpin these factors.

Mapping ultimately provides an informed platform on which channel managers can start to incorporate the other two disciplines. A good mapping process gives aspiring stewards cogent insights about how to transform their own channels. Because mapping sketches the history of an industry's distribution channels, it can save stewards the time, resources, and angst associated with repeating mistakes. Stewards planning sustainable change are better off knowing at the outset why the channel operates as it does, and what the barriers to change have been in the past.

How to Think About Mapping

When you think about mapping an industry, you naturally bring to mind a certain widely used framework in competitive strategy. Formulated by Michael Porter and refined by other scholars, the five forces analysis focuses on a specific industry and maps the degree of rivalry among the participants, the threat of entry by outsiders, the threat of product substitutes, the power of buyers, and the power of suppliers.[2]

An analysis based on these five forces provides diagnostics regarding the state of an industry's channels to market. But to understand the channel clearly and to gain useful input into channel strategy making, companies must focus on what specifically influences channel strategy. In that spirit, the steward might first map the status of each of the core forces influencing channel strategy and then research how the forces came to their current positions—in other words, to know what the forces look like and why.

Companies can use the following questions to kick off the mapping process.

Demand-Chain Requirements

- What do customers buy, how do they buy, and why do they buy the products and services offered by the various players?

- How do the players segment their customer markets?

- What influences have affected customers' wants and needs? How have they shifted?

- Are customers satisfied with the output of existing channels? What are the gaps in the channel value chain?

Channel Capabilities and Costs

- Broadly, what are the industry's channel capabilities and costs? (Remember, the channel capabilities encompass activities that must occur to meet customer needs and desires.)

- How have channel capabilities evolved over time?

- How have channel costs and margins evolved?

Channel Power

- How has power shifted among the channel constituencies—vendors, manufacturers, distributors, and retailers? Why?

- Who has the power?
- Who has gained power? Who has lost?

Competitive Actions

- What has been the nature of industry competition? How has it evolved?
- Who is the dominant player? The most profitable? The most innovative? What are their channel strategies?
- What has been the nature of competition at the channel level? How has it evolved? Which is the dominant channel? The most profitable? The most innovative?

Drilling deeper to uncover the effects of the antecedents that shape the core forces, a steward might then ask these questions:

- What are the broad economic trends, and how have they affected the core forces? How will they change in the future?
- Have there been shifts in customer demographics? Psychographics? Other socioeconomic or cultural patterns? How have they affected purchase and consumption behavior?
- Have regulatory changes affected the demand chain or channel capabilities? Are future changes anticipated? How are they likely to affect the demand chain or channel capabilities and costs?
- Have there been changes in the formal and informal rules governing the trade practices of channel intermediaries? How will this likely evolve?
- How has technology affected go-to-market strategies? What is its impact on the players, including customers?

Using those two sets of questions, the steward can then construct a macro map of the industry's channels and its evolutionary patterns. Figure 2-2 shows an abbreviated version of the mapping matrix that we use later in this chapter to sketch a map of automobile industry channels.

An Example: Mapping the U.S. Auto Industry

Providing a full-scale application of mapping is beyond this chapter's scope. Instead, we look at the highlights of a map of the U.S. auto industry, as

FIGURE 2-2

Industry mapping process: An illustration from suppliers' perspective

Demand chain	Channel capabilities and costs	Channel power	Competitive actions
• 57% of consumers trade in old car as part of new-car purchase	• Dealer gross margins (13%) and net margins (1% to 2%) have stayed remarkably consistent, although departmental margins (new cars, used cars, parts and service, financing) have significantly changed	• Emergence of megadealers with multiple brands	• Attempts by U.S. automakers to rationalize dealer network

Consumer culture	Technology	Trade practices	Regulation	Environmental	Trends
• Consumers distrust car sales process	• 70% search on Internet before purchase	• National Automobile Dealers Association actively lobbies on behalf of franchised dealers	• Many state laws prohibit manufacturers from selling directly on the Internet	• Rising fuel prices	• Declining number of dealerships, down to 21,640 in 2004 from 30,842 in 1970

Opportunities	Threats
• Online ordering system, with selected customization possibilities	• Increased power of dealers

seen through the lens of the four major forces that influence channel evolution.

We selected this industry for three reasons. First, its $714 billion size in 2004 (representing dealership sales of new cars, used cars, and parts and service) makes it an important and significant sector.[3] Second, the auto industry powerfully illustrates the interplay of the four forces and their impact on channel strategy. Third, the rise of the Internet in the mid-1990s exemplifies the kind of significant environmental change that potentially spurs channel evolution.

Figure 2-3 captures a bird's-eye view of recent changes in the industry's distribution channels. In the era before the Internet, customers gathered what little information they could and visited one of twenty-five thousand new-car dealers to buy a new vehicle. List prices typically were unclear,

FIGURE 2-3

Evolution of automobile distribution channels

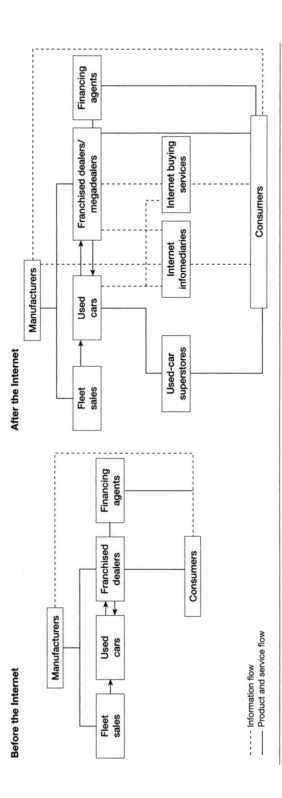

Before the Internet

After the Internet

----- Information flow
—— Product and service flow

cluttered with add-ons and special charges. Dealers treated each consumer differently, and customers often visited multiple dealers looking for the best buy. As a result, some customers paid close to the list price, but many negotiated it down. Most new-car transactions were combined with trade-in transactions that were characterized by even less reliability and customer assurance.

In the post-Internet era, many things have stayed the same, but much has changed. As of 2004, General Motors was still the market share leader, although its share had fallen from almost 35 percent in the early 1990s to 27.6 percent.[4] There were somewhat fewer dealers (21,640), but many of the remaining dealers had transitioned from independent mom and pops to megadealers such as AutoNation and United Auto Group, which owned 278 and 152 dealerships, respectively.[5] By the end of 2004, about 65 percent of new-car buyers had gone first to an electronic marketplace to gain information on models, features, and price.[6] They thereby fortified themselves for a purchase negotiation with dealers, where more than 96 percent of them purchased their vehicles.

As we map the tug of forces in the automobile industry, we have no implicit hierarchy in terms of their importance. We know that these forces are highly interactive, so it doesn't matter where we start as long as we understand their interconnections.

In the following application of mapping, we reach far back into industry history. Such a longitudinal analysis may or may not be called for in every instance. In the automobile industry, the shifts in power, demand-chain influences, and competitive actions inform the current arrangement of the industry's channels.

Channel Power in the U.S. Automobile Industry

The evolution of the channel power positions in the automobile industry is a fascinating story. As figure 2-4 illustrates, the evolution reveals an overall transfer of power in favor of the dealer network. This has been a hard-fought struggle, with the scars carried over from generation to generation of auto dealers and auto executives. Predictably, these power struggles have stymied progress toward a major redesign of distribution, even though many of the parties see the advantages of such a redesign.

The early period was characterized by absolute control by the Big Three U.S. automakers: General Motors, Ford, and Chrysler (now Daimler-

FIGURE 2-4

How channel power has evolved

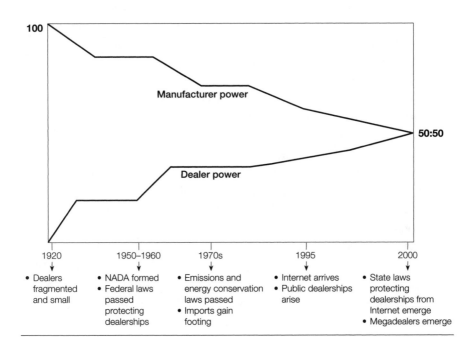

Chrysler). Dealers were restricted by market areas and prohibited from carrying and marketing competing brands. Although these early contracts heavily favored manufacturers, dealerships flourished, riding a wave of economic prosperity and rising demand for autos. In 1917, a group of thirty dealers banded together to oppose a luxury tax on autos, founding NADA (National Automobile Dealers Association). By year-end 1934, NADA had an active membership of more than thirty thousand dealers organized into independent state and local associations.

The Depression (1929–1939) brought a sharp decline in vehicle sales and a 33 percent decline in the number of dealers.[7] Dealers chafed under the tight control of the Big Three. Responding to petitions by NADA, the Federal Trade Commission (FTC) recommended that "fewer restrictions be placed on the dealers' management of their businesses; that quotas be based on mutual agreement; and that contracts be made definite as to the rights and responsibilities of both parties."[8]

Dealership resistance and NADA lobbying led to the landmark Automobile Dealers Day in Court Act in 1956. The act provided legal remedies for dealers harmed by manufacturers that had failed to act in good faith. Before long, dealers had another ally to counter the power position of the automakers. Americans had become increasingly concerned about vehicle safety and the impact of automobiles on the environment. The Big Three did not meet the stringent requirements of the Clean Air Act passed in 1970, which required a 90 percent reduction in emissions.[9] Then came the OPEC oil embargo; the resultant Energy Policy and Conservation Act of 1975 required that the average passenger car in a given automaker's line achieve at least eighteen miles per gallon. By the time of the second oil shock in 1979, the dual impact of poor quality and poor fuel economy resulted in many Americans buying reliable, fuel-efficient imported cars, and many U.S. dealers began to sell imported brands such as Honda, Volkswagen, and Toyota.

By the end of the 1980s, dealers had gained a huge degree of independence from U.S. manufacturers. Dealers could add imported car brands that were in some cases stronger than their corresponding U.S. nameplates, and dealers had made headway in creating state laws to protect them from heavy-handed franchising practices, including the termination of dealers. The automakers had significant clout at the federal level, but at the state level the dealers held significant sway. Automobile dealers accounted for only 1 to 2 percent of all retail outlets, but on average they contributed 20 percent of states' retail revenues and consequently 3 percent of all state tax revenues.[10]

As a perverse consequence of not being able to fire dealers, the only other venue open to manufacturers was to appoint more dealers at the edges of existing territories. The result was an intense distribution system, with many overdealered markets.

By the mid-1990s, when the Internet began to gain momentum, dealers had as much or more channel power than manufacturers, at least from the perspective of selling practices. And when Internet buying agents emerged and manufacturers seemed ready to sell direct to certain customers, dealers exercised their countervailing power. Why? For dealers, the heart of the issue was the importance of new-car sales, despite their declining contribution to dealer profit. As shown in table 2-1, as margins on car sales eroded, dealers placed increased emphasis on other service offerings—financing, insurance, service, and maintenance—to supplement

TABLE 2-1

Average dealer profile

	1978	1982	1986	1990	1994	1998	2002	2004
Total dealership sales ($ millions)	**$4.78**	**$6.14**	**$10.82**	**$12.89**	**$18.87**	**$24.46**	**$31.28**	**$33.01**
% of avg. dealership sales								
New vehicle dept.	64.1	61.4	67.3	60.8	60.3	59.0	59.6	60.9
Used vehicle dept.	20.9	22.8	19.9	23.9	26.9	29.4	28.6	27.5
Service and parts dept.	15.0	15.8	12.8	15.3	12.8	11.6	11.8	11.5
Total	100.0	100.0	100.0	100.0	100.0	100.0	100.0	100.0
Department gross margins %								
New vehicle dept.	N/A	9.2	10.1	8.5	7.3	7.3	7.3	7.2
Used vehicle dept.	N/A	12.9	13.7	12.0	11.8	10.7	10.9	10.9
Service and parts dept.	N/A	39.9	41.8	42.9	43.0	44.0	44.9	46.1
Total dealership gross	14.3	13.9	14.2	14.5	13.1	12.9	13.4	13.2
Department profit %								
New vehicle dept.	N/A	0.6	2.3	-0.1	0.6	0.7	0.9	0.6
Used vehicle dept.	N/A	1.8	1.5	0.8	2.2	1.1	0.9	0.6
Service and parts dept.	N/A	2.0	2.5	5.2	6.0	5.7	6.2	5.7
Net profit before tax (as a % of sales)	**2.0**	**1.3**	**2.2**	**1.0**	**1.8**	**1.7**	**1.9**	**1.7**

Source: NADA, Industry Analysis Division. Used with permission.

earning streams. But new cars remained the strategic entry point from which other revenue streams were created.

For example, in addition to any markup over the invoice price, dealers earned margin from several sources. Dealers might earn manufacturer incentives on certain models. They might also receive a *dealer holdback* of about 2 to 3 percent of dealer invoice paid by several manufacturers on the sale of a vehicle. There were also fees paid by lenders and insurers for referring finance and insurance (F&I) business as well as fees earned from the sale of extended warranties.

On a $27,000 car, a dealer might earn only $500 over invoice on the car sale but then earn $1,800–$2,000 on the trade-in and another $1,000 in service revenue over the next two years.[11] To dealers, then, the unbundling of a sale lost to a third party via the Internet was clearly a negative. Not only did they lose the admittedly modest margin on the new-car sale, but they also lost the opportunity to build a relationship with the customer and earn the larger portion of the associated revenue stream.

As a result, dealers, fearful of the new Internet-based companies and distrustful of the automakers' online initiatives, made a concerted attempt to enroll the aid of federal and state courts. The major concern was that manufacturer-owned dealerships or direct sales channels would garner a bulk of the Web-generated sales leads. Manufacturer ownership of dealerships had been an ongoing concern, with several states already prohibiting it.

So in addition to adjusting their business model—earning greater revenues from used-car sales—dealers used regulation and public policy effectively to counteract the power of manufacturers and the incursion of Internet buying agents. The swift passage of the various franchising laws established the dealers' role in automobile distribution in the Internet age.

By 1979, every state had regulated at least some aspect of automobile distribution; forty-four states required licensing of new and used dealers; license boards were often composed of license holders and local and state government officials.[12] The arrival of the Internet set off a further round of legislation. In 2000, an unprecedented 223 franchise bills on auto issues were introduced in thirty state legislatures. In September 1999, thirty-two states had laws that prohibited or restricted manufacturer ownership of new-car dealerships; by May 2000, another twelve states had passed similar rules or toughened existing legislation.[13]

This brief recap reveals that in the past several decades, franchised dealers have demonstrated a unique ability to vigorously defend against most potential threats to their business model. At the same time, the legacy of the franchised distribution system that gave manufacturers enormous power has left a mark on the expansion and contraction of the intensity of distribution. The industry, which had 47,133 outlets in 1941, had shrunk to 30,842 outlets in 1970. The trend continued, with 24,825 outlets in 1990 and 21,640 by 2004.[14]

Channel Capabilities and Costs

Now we continue to develop our map of the industry, focusing on the predominant purpose of the dealer channel: selling new cars. (The economics of the used-car and parts-and-service value chains are important, however, and we bring them into focus in the next section.)

The channel value chain for new cars, as sketched in figure 2-5, extends from the manufacturer to the retailer and then to the consumer.[15] Value is added in each step, but a cost is also associated with each value-adding activity and with the corresponding compensation for the relevant intermediary. Ultimately, the consumer price includes the margin on these intermediation activities. On average, about 25 percent of the price of a car goes for sales, distribution, and marketing value-added activities borne by the manufacturers and the dealers. Consider a new car priced at $28,000, the current average.[16] Of that, about $7,000 goes for marketing, sales, and distribution. In this value chain, manufacturers create demand through brand advertising and consumer promotions. Dealers, too, engage in sales and marketing, including advertising. They provide consumers with ready availability by holding about sixty days' worth of inventory in their lots.

In the end, after netting out the cost of all value-adding activities provided in the chain, dealers make an average net profit of about 1 to 2 percent. But the dealer's profit, as indicated in table 2-1, comes from three sources: new cars, used cars (trade-ins), and parts and service. On new cars alone, dealers have an average gross margin of 7 percent when their overall expenses of the dealership average about 12 percent. So on paper, before we account for the spillover profits from after-sale parts and service and the margin from used-car trade-ins, dealers take a loss on new-car sales. There are back-end incentives from the manufacturer as well, shown as manufacturer trade promotion in figure 2-5.

U.S. manufacturers, on average, net 5 percent on sales, but their profits vary widely with economic cycles. Their profitability ranges from –2.5 percent to nearly 10 percent (see table 2-2). Given high fixed costs (capital

FIGURE 2-5

New-car channel economics

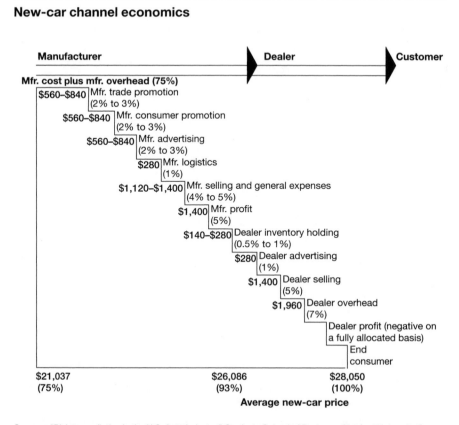

Sources: "Disintermediation in the U.S. Auto Industry," Graduate School of Business, Stanford University Case EC-10, Feb. 2000; Mark Cooper, "A Roadblock on the Information Superhighway: Anticompetitive Restrictions on Automotive Markets," Consumer Federation of America, Feb. 2001.

equipment and labor), carmakers need to sustain high production levels to break even. As of 2005, the impact of GM's fixed cost was readily apparent. The company's debt had been downgraded to junk status; it was burdened by health-care costs for current and former employees and was actively attempting to close plants and reduce fleet sales to increase plant utilization and profitability. The company lost $3 billion through November 2005.[17]

Notably, during the same period, Japanese manufacturers, while experiencing some variability in their incomes streams, were gaining share worldwide and in the United States. Toyota appeared on its way to becoming

TABLE 2-2

Auto manufacturer profile

	1992	1994	1996	1998	2000	2002	2004
GM net sales ($ million)	132,242	148,499	163,885	155,445	184,632	177,867	193,517
GM gross profit %	20.4	23.5	21.4	17.8	21.1	17.2	17.3
GM selling, general, and admin. %	8.5	7.6	9.3	10.3	12.1	11.7	10.5
GM income before tax %	−2.5	4.8	4.0	3.2	3.9	1.3	0.6
Ford net sales ($ million)	100,132	128,439	146,991	143,350	170,058	162,258	171,652
Ford gross profit %	11.3	25.3	19.3	21.4	20.2	22.9	20.8
Ford selling, general, and admin. %	9.2	9.0	10.5	9.9	9.9	15.5	13.9
Ford income before tax %	−0.1	6.8	4.6	16.9*	4.8	0.6	2.8
DaimlerChrysler net sales							
($ million 1992–1996)/(€ million 1998–2004)	35,501	52,235	61,397	131,782	162,384	147,368	142,059
Chrysler gross profit %	20.0	27.2	25.3	21.3	17.3	18.8	19.3
Chrysler selling, general, and admin. %	9.5	10.5	10.0	12.3	11.3	12.3	12.6
Chrysler income before tax %	2.6	11.2	9.9	6.2	2.8	4.0	2.5

Note: Daimler purchased Chrysler in 1998.
Percentages are a % of net sales, as reported.
*In 1998, Ford received a noncash gain of approximately $16 billion from a spinoff of The Associates, a consumer finance company.

Source: Annual reports.

the largest car manufacturer globally by establishing a reputation for vehicle reliability, technology leadership (hybrid cars as well as other improvements), and selective distribution policies that enabled its dealers to earn attractive returns.

Automobile manufacturing, then, is characterized by capital intensity as opposed to distribution, which is working capital intensive. The manufacturers' profits fluctuate widely from year to year, but dealership profits have stayed remarkably constant over the past several decades.

Most industry observers would agree that a good part of the channel for new cars, as we've just described it (and indeed as it exists today), may be unnecessary. In retailing, for example, at one time the sixty-day inventory function performed a useful role in the evolution of the distribution channel. It addressed consumer desires to drive a car off the lot, but, more importantly, it was a competitive tactic imposed by manufacturers on their franchisees to ensure that they would aggressively push car sales. Moreover, in a retailing environment characterized by intense competition among oligopolistic suppliers, it was necessary to have enough cars on the lot to ensure that consumers' needs were immediately met. A consumer walking off the lot was potentially lost to the competition, sometimes even to the same brand. All this was the consequence of scale-efficient manufacturing operations backed by fixed labor union contracts, which required manufacturers to commit to volume production regardless of consumer demand. So the cars had to be sold through aggressive distribution and marketing arrangements.

In theory, the Internet should have changed all that. Internet proponents in the mid-1990s argued that the potential direct channel they had in mind offered not only better value for customers but also significant cost savings for manufacturers. As the idea of an Internet-enabled auto industry took root, one industry analyst suggested that a fully Web-enabled auto industry that built cars to order, integrated suppliers, and engaged in online sales could save as much as $3,643 on a $26,000 car.[18]

The estimated $3,643 savings would accrue throughout the supply chain. About one-third would result from reduced sales support, freight, inventory, sales commissions, and dealer overhead. Another one-third or so would come through a reworking of the back end of the supply chain, involving better coordination and more accurate planning. The remaining one-third would result from the build-to-order process. With cars being pulled through the system, savings would arise from reduced dealer allocation issues, increased alignment between sales and manufacturing, and better material and manufacturing scheduling.[19]

Although the benefits of such cost savings are not hard to fathom, the real question is this: why have the channels not altered themselves accordingly? Part of the answer lies in the preceding discussion on channel power, and the rest lies in the following description of the evolution of the other two forces that determine channel strategy.

The Evolution of the Demand Chain

As our description of the demand chain in the automobile industry will reveal, manufacturers and retailers, in striving to keep one another in check, all but forgot the customer, especially when it came to sales tactics and selling practices.

How did this disconnect come about? According to an auto industry veteran, "In establishing their dealer network, the manufacturers put the dealerships very close to each other, ensuring that the dealers would cut each others' throats, forcing them to use clearance sales tactics."[20] Indeed, during the 1950s, customers "were subject to some of the most fraudulent bait-and-switch tactics and price gouging scams in history."[21] Although customers remained wary of the automobile purchase experience, it wasn't until the late 1970s and into the early 1980s that customers' disaffection with U.S.-built automobiles gained momentum.

Facing losses and eroding market share, U.S. automakers took remedial action. One of the first initiatives addressed vehicle quality. In the 1980s, quality became "Job 1" at Ford. GM attempted to close plants that had poor quality output. Slowly, as quality improved, focus shifted to achieving customer satisfaction, with GM's new CEO announcing in 1990 that the automaker "would become more customer and product oriented."[22]

Dealers, too, became more focused on customer satisfaction. With the quality of American cars becoming a smaller issue, they found that a customer's buying decision was increasingly affected by the sales experience both before and after the sale. Dealers attempted to make car shopping more enjoyable, offering coffee and upscale waiting areas with activities for children. Additionally, dealers clustered their franchises on one large property; this let customers shop several brands in one trip and increased the likelihood that one brand would close the sale. Automakers, too, changed their compensation systems, rewarding dealerships that had higher customer satisfaction scores.

Yet even into the mid-1990s, customers were feeling alienated. According to one study, "Industry observers generally agreed that the auto industry's push-oriented system of production and distribution, coupled with an oversupply of dealers, created the high-pressure sales environment loathed by virtually all car buyers."[23] Another study found that buying a car was "the most anxiety-provoking and least satisfying of any retail experience."[24] This attitude was reflected in customer loyalty rates; although manufacturers averaged 56.9 percent repeat business overall, only 20 percent of customers returned to the same dealer to buy a car, and the average dealership saw fewer than half its buyers ever return, whether for service or to purchase another vehicle.[25]

Why was (and is) this the case? The reality of the demand chain is that customers and dealers negotiate a complex, three-part package characterized by trade-offs and adjustments among the components of the new car, the trade-in, financing, maintenance, and repairs. Moreover, as indicated earlier, parts and service revenues are highly lucrative, enabling dealers to combine the three components to wrap up a deal.

In short, most consumers and dealers do not simply buy and sell new cars. They engage in a portfolio transaction cycle lasting several years.[26] These are the three circles in figure 2-6. Customers clearly have ideal preferences for each component, but ultimately the gestalt drives consumers' channel choices.

This is not to suggest, however, that the existing dealer-driven trade-in process is ideal. Although better information and tighter margins have re-

FIGURE 2-6

Customer needs (demand chain) analysis for new-car purchases

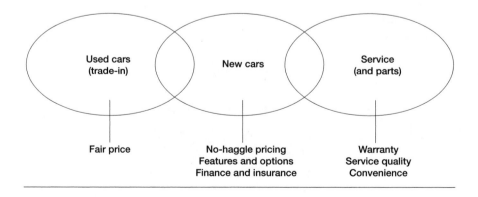

Used cars (trade-in)	New cars	Service (and parts)
Fair price	No-haggle pricing Features and options Finance and insurance	Warranty Service quality Convenience

duced price haggling on new cars, such a no-haggle policy has yet to emerge in the context of trading in used cars. CarMax, a subsidiary of Circuit City until 1992, has attempted to create confidence in the used-car market with large (60,000 square foot) lots that feature cars not more than six years old, no-haggle pricing, the ability to search inventory and prices over the Internet or through in-store kiosks, a five-day money-back guarantee, and a minimum thirty-day warranty on all vehicles. CarMax provides an appraisal that allows prospective car owners to sell their cars to CarMax at that price within seven days, whether or not they buy a vehicle at CarMax. Despite this effort and that of "certified" used-car sales by dealers, the entire used-car channel is notoriously unreliable. Even at dealerships having otherwise excellent reputations for integrity and quality of service, the price offered varies widely.

Consumers prefer to trade in their car, buy the new car, and arrange financing all at one location. Along with the new car comes a warranty that brings the customer back to the dealership for service and parts (if necessary). All this comes together at the dealership, and given the nature of the transaction, the local dealership is the preferred channel. The new-car and used-car channels work hand in hand.

In the automobile industry, Internet technology afforded consumers the chance to acquire new cars more efficiently, but this did not persuade them to switch channels, because they still did not have a good alternative for disposing of their used cars.

Competitive Actions

It was not until the early 1970s, with the oil shock and declining sales, that U.S. automakers sought to rationalize their channels. But by then the existing footprint was deeply rooted. The Big Three stood calcified and helpless in the face of the auto industry recession; at the same time, imports achieved considerable efficiency in their franchising system. Fuel-efficient designs and high-quality products meant lower service costs. It made imports attractive not only to customers but also to dealers shut out by the Big Three, or to existing dealers whose domestic sales were declining. But existing franchise agreements prevented imports from accessing some of the top-line domestic dealers that they may have wanted. The result was the development of a dispersed distribution system with fewer dealers than conceived by U.S. manufacturers.

It turned out that such a selective system was attractive to franchised dealers, because they were better able to protect their brand profitability and at the same time gain scale advantages and cost savings. These advantages persist. For example, Toyota, a Japanese car manufacturer that entered the market after the development of the major U.S. highway network, covered the entire U.S. market with about twelve hundred outlets in 1990, versus the forty-five hundred supported by Ford.[27] As a result, in 1999, the average Toyota dealership sold 1,002 cars compared with 653 for Chevrolet and 942 for Ford. In a sense, the actions of foreign cars provided the stimulus for a redesign of the decades-old U.S. franchising system. Imported cars had not only found a solid footing, but they had also founded a modified distribution infrastructure.

Coinciding with the commercialization of the Internet, in the mid-1990s each of the Big Three U.S. automakers simultaneously attempted to reduce the size of its franchise distribution system. Manufacturers surmised that an oversupply of dealerships was adversely affecting their profitability. Fewer dealers would mean reduced competition within a single brand and, with it, would reduce the use of high-pressure sales tactics. This was the manufacturers' belated admission of the consequences of a hyper-intensive dealer coverage model they had carefully structured through the 1970s and 1980s. Fewer and larger dealerships would also mean lower per-unit transportation costs from the factory to the sales floor.

The changes proposed by manufacturers were bold and significant. For example, in 1999 GM announced plans for a new subsidiary, General Motors Retail Holdings, which would buy and run dealerships from willing sellers in as many as 10 percent of its 7,700 franchised dealers in 130 markets.[28] But two months later, in January 2000, GM backed away from its consolidation plan after pressure from dealers and NADA's promise to lobby for tighter state laws regarding manufacturer ownership of dealerships. So GM approached channel rationalization by a different route. In December 2000, it announced that it would discontinue its ailing 103-year-old Oldsmobile brand and phase out 2,800 Oldsmobile dealers.

For its part, Ford planned to buy out and consolidate dealers into an Auto Collections company in as many as thirty cities. Starting with a pilot in Indianapolis in 1997, Ford asked its existing eighteen dealerships to sell their dealerships to a new company owned jointly by Ford and the dealers. The new Auto Collections company planned to operate five megastores, incorporating both Ford and Lincoln-Mercury dealerships, and would oversee the operation with a Ford-appointed manager.[29] After attempting to create Collections in five other markets (Salt Lake City; Rochester,

Minnesota; Tulsa, Oklahoma; Oklahoma City; and San Diego) and encountering dealer resistance, legal proceedings, merger difficulties, and operating obstacles, Ford, too, abandoned its strategy in December 1999.[30]

With Internet technology now available, manufacturers began to investigate its potential to reach customers. By the late 1990s, almost every manufacturer had its own Web site featuring its products and services, with varying levels of functionality. In addition, manufacturers signed co-marketing agreements with major online portals. In January 2000, GM and Ford signed with America Online and Yahoo!, respectively.[31]

Competitive Dealer Activity

As described earlier, automobile retailing is highly fragmented, with the top ten dealers accounting for less than 10 percent of the industry's sales. Sensing an opportunity to gain scale, in the mid-1990s several auto dealerships launched initial public offerings (IPOs) to gain public funds for expansion. United Auto, AutoNation (formerly part of Republic Industries), and CarMax were among the half-dozen that took the public route.[32] The drive was toward scale; hopefully, if that could be achieved over several brands, the industry would see for the first time a multibrand retail outlet. Even if the brands were not carried next to each other, they would be carried at sites next door to each other.

Moreover, there was a sense that with size would come purchasing power. The auto industry has been unique in not offering quantity discounts to its retailers; a dealer selling a hundred cars gets the same price as one selling a thousand. Dealerships like AutoNation began to openly speculate about offering a private-label car. But from a manufacturer's perspective, there was a downside as well. Publicly held dealer groups such as AutoNation and United Auto were rapidly acquiring franchises, and manufacturers were concerned about the power that these new groups might gain.[33]

The new megadealer channel faced selective resistance from automakers. Some saw possible advantages of scale, but others saw it as a power play. The resistance was especially stiff from import manufacturers like Honda and Toyota, which did not relish the prospect of a consolidated dealer base with more bargaining power. They also did not want their comparative distribution advantage over the Big Three mitigated by a channel such as AutoNation effectively engineering a selective distribution system for domestic automakers. Such trends also were not desirable to most auto dealers, which are small and fragmented. In fact, many franchising laws and other federal laws (such as the Robinson-Patman Act) are designed to protect small dealers.

Although U.S. automakers were intrigued by the notion of an alternative megachannel, franchised dealers were taking a dim view of these efforts, especially with the simultaneous availability of the Internet as a way of directly reaching consumers. Rather than use the Internet as a value-creating mechanism for customers, dealers perceived that manufacturers were using it to further consolidate dealerships and siphon away dealer sales and profits.

What This Map Suggests to a Channel Steward

The purpose of mapping is to understand how the four core forces tangle in shaping the business environment within which suppliers and intermediaries plot and execute their go-to-market strategies. But a channel steward must also attempt to understand the antecedent forces that shape the core forces. Strategic insight often comes from knowing these influences and trends.

A channel steward, on completing a map of the auto industry, might summarize it as follows:

- Manufacturers could realize significant savings—more than $3,500 on an average car. Industry pipeline inventory levels could be reduced by $80 billion. Using the Internet, automakers could rationalize the size of the dealership network.

- Dealer profitability is much more robust than that of automakers. Ultimately, therefore, the saving in supply-chain costs from a revamped channel could moderate fluctuations in manufacturers' return on investments.

- Channel power has swung to the dealers; they believe that the Internet can disintermediate them from new-car sales and therefore adversely affect their ability to capture the higher-margin components of the customer demand chain.

- The forces of the demand chain are mixed. Customers are intrigued by the notion of buying new cars online and creating a more level playing field in the purchase process. However, online models do not fulfill all the customer's needs. Buying a new car is only one component of the demand chain, which also includes old car trade-in and ongoing service. Thus, the demand chain is moderate in its support of channel restructuring.

Armed with this knowledge, the steward might then begin to plot a course of action (shaped by the steward's own position in the channel). From an industry perspective, the following kinds of initiatives would address some of the issues framed by our mapping analysis. They are only a sampling of a wide array of possibilities.

Manufacturers could focus on the development of a skilled dealership base; dealers in the top quartile sell three to four times as many vehicles as dealers in the bottom quartile. Automakers could aim for sufficient geographic distribution to serve customers without intrabrand rivalry and with a mix of brands to provide dealers with sufficient sustainable volumes and in formats that meet customers' needs.[34] But automakers could not simply impose these changes; they would have to collaborate with dealers to ensure that the evolution takes a progressive direction.

Using the Internet to inform customers and manage a demand-driven system, the industry could realize a 7 to 10 percent savings on the cost of a car.[35] Dealers would have a useful role to play in the new system; it would, however, be a different role than the traditional "stock and sell." In addition, rationalizing and consolidating distribution intensity could achieve other hidden savings.

To date, fearful of their futures, dealers have simply refused to go along, instead fortifying themselves with amendments to state franchising laws. The savings in supply-chain cost could certainly moderate the wild swings in manufacturer profitability, but that would call for the manufacturers to reengineer the financing arms of their business.

Together, manufacturers and dealers could find a solution to rationalize the dealer network. Pure Internet intermediaries, deprived of transaction margins, are not viable in this marketplace. Dealers have realized that information hoarding and differential customer pricing are no longer viable strategies, so every manufacturer's channel system needs to be transparent regarding the price of new cars. In other words, the Internet will evolve to become an integrated and inseparable part of every distribution system.

Given the bundled nature of the consumer transaction, a reliable and rational channel for used-car trade-in transactions will have to emerge before consumers will be willing to change their behavior. That remains another key stumbling block to an accelerated transformation of automobile retailing. More channel systems and intermediaries will have to take on the role of certifying credible used-car trade-in values so that customers will uncouple new-car purchases from trade-in transactions. When that happens, a new-car channel will have to stand on its own, and a selective, large-trading-area model would help.

None of our suggestions is illogical, given our mapping of the industry's evolution, but such changes will not arrive quickly because of the interconnected nature of the four forces underlying the channel system. But the ability of a manufacturer or a dealer to foster and facilitate such changes is real. The issue is whether the changes would happen through negotiation and discussions, with a steward at the helm, or through the force of law and legal battles.

A Vision for the Future

We can easily envision an optimal channel structure for automobiles, at least from the customer's point of view. If we indulged in a clean-slate projection of the demand chain, the following scenario might be a possibility, albeit an extreme one: most cars would be built to order.

That's not likely to happen soon. However, we will likely see a few significant changes that can be facilitated only with a stewardship approach. For example, we will likely see a reduction in car inventories; as a result, not only will supply-chain costs be reduced, but so will the rental costs of the vast amounts of real estate now borne by a typical dealership. A back-of-the-envelope estimation projects a savings of $350 per car on inventory and another $250 per car on real estate costs. Customers could test-drive a car, make their choice, and then pick options; the car would be delivered or picked up in two to three weeks.

Also, because of the ubiquity of price and availability information, the dealer's cost of advertising—about $300 per car—may be unnecessary. Consumers will be able to shop in the convenience of their homes. After all, much dealer advertising is designed to entice consumers to come into the store, where they face a limited selection of attractively priced offerings and where salespeople steer them toward cars that are not necessarily what they thought they came in for but what is available on the lot. In a new environment, much of the preselection preferences could be shaped by widely available information, so there would be less need for dealer advertising.

We can even hazard a guess regarding the network of service facilities. Although distributed facilities may be needed for routine maintenance and small repairs, major repairs could be pooled into a central facility to create scale advantages. Arrangements could be made for convenient customer pickup and drop-off from decentralized locations.

We could go on, but none of this will become reality without the stewardship of a few key players. Thus, what seems to be an attractive supply-chain solution to a customer need (the demand chain) cannot find facilitation through the traditional franchised dealer channel (channel power). But the dealer channel itself—its fragmented nature and the combined protection it enjoys under state franchising laws—was a creation of the manufacturers as well as a reaction to their past supply-chain policies and actions.

That is why channel reengineering is difficult: it requires a suitable alignment of the forces that determine channel structure. This balance between the forces of demand chain, channel capability and costs, and channel power is always open to changes in the environment. Sometimes it is technology, sometimes regulation, and sometimes the deliberate and concerted action of one or another player. Actions by manufacturers to gain control and direction have not succeeded.

Although there has been little visible change in the structure of retailing, a channel steward should consider the subtle, but important shifts in the process of how cars are bought and sold. A bundled purchasing and selling behavior characterized the previous system. In the new system, the information functions have been unbundled and do not travel with the original bundle, having far-reaching consequences. The hierarchical auto distribution system has given way to a distributed system in which all the channel functions are not transferred in bundles. Rather, different important functions required of the customer to complete the sale are performed by different members. The most visible and critical one has been the information function. The Internet has now replaced much of the upfront shopping experience in which the customer went from store to store ascertaining a price for a chosen list of model combinations. Thus, now consumers get much of their information or price negotiation functions fulfilled in advance. Such an unbundling of a critical function has automatically leveled the price of most new-car transactions.

Given the constraining forces as well as the history of any particular firm's channel arrangements, channel arrangements may not shift overnight; with a steward's guidance, however, they can slowly and steadily evolve toward a more productive form.

To that end, the next chapter begins to explore the second discipline of channel stewardship: building and editing a value chain.

3

Building and Editing the Channel Value Chain I

The Key Principles

THE FOUR CORE FORCES that shape a channel's evolution, left unchecked, rarely work in unison to advance the interests of suppliers, customers, and intermediaries all at the same time.

Yet those forces need not remain untamed. Armed with an understanding of the key forces—gained through mapping—a steward can begin to influence them by building and editing a true channel value chain. This is the second discipline of channel stewardship. As we said in chapter 1, a channel value chain is the outcome of shaping a distribution channel's capabilities to address the needs of the demand chain. This task requires constant calibration, and it differentiates a passive channel manager, which weathers change, from an active channel steward, which understands the forces of change, harnesses them, and profitably transforms the channel.

To introduce the core principles of the building and editing discipline of channel stewardship, we briefly examine Dell's skillful navigation of a turbulent channel environment to build a superb channel value chain. Dell is an exemplar of the building and editing process. Moreover, because Dell sells directly, we can illustrate the key principle of building and editing without the complicating force of channel power (treated in chapters 4, 5, and 6).

Dell's Position in the PC Industry

The channels in the personal computer industry have undergone a remarkable evolution. Apple, one of the original innovators of PCs, pioneered the retail format in the late 1970s (see figure 3-1). Within a few years, IBM, with its IBM PC, established the business-customer segment and, through the 1980s and early 1990s, spurred the development of new kinds of intermediaries, including business-to-business retailers, such as Businessland, and third-party VARs (value-added resellers). Compaq began to assume leadership in the early 1990s and greatly expanded the channels initiated by IBM, especially on the VAR side. Then, in the second half of the 1990s, Dell, which had entered the market in 1984, started to gain industry leadership with its innovative direct channel.

The evolution of the PC industry channels provides a graphic picture of a channel system constantly in flux. On the retail side, three successive formats emerged that mirrored the dynamics of the industry's market expansion, maturation, and margin compression. Hobbyist stores were replaced by specialty stores, which in turn were replaced by superstores, and each channel had its own unique operating model. For business customers, the VAR channel attempted to add value by providing a new portfolio of services. With Dell's entry, the direct channel became a legitimate alternative.

FIGURE 3-1

PC channel evolution

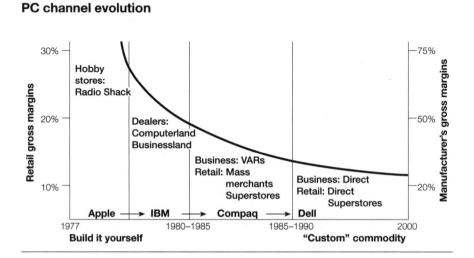

By the time the Internet entered the scene in 1995, Dell was the leader in the direct channel category, and it used the new utility to further distance itself from its competitors. By the turn of the twenty-first century, the direct channel had become the predominant way of serving business customers' PC requirements. More than half of the industry's sales were conducted through this channel (including the Internet, telephone channels, and face-to-face channels). The dealer channel (those supplying the small and medium business market) had lost its clout, with many customers preferring to buy systems directly from suppliers such as Dell. Many suppliers had begun to follow Dell's lead in connecting directly with business customers. Tables 3-1 and 3-2 indicate the influence of Dell on the industry's channels from 1984–2005.

By the close of 2004, Dell, with sales of $49 billion and a net income of $3 billion, had become the largest computer manufacturer in the United States. The company's domestic market share in personal computers (desktop and portables) was 33.1 percent, almost twice that of its closest competitor, Hewlett-Packard (HP), with a 19.5 percent market share, and far surpassing Gateway's 5.3 percent share and IBM's 4.7 percent share.[1] Dell had rewarded its investors with an average annual return on total capital (ROTC) of 40 to 50 percent in each of the preceding six years.

The U.S. PC market had exploded from $20 billion to $95 billion (from 8 million to 56 million units) from 1984 to 2004. The industry leadership had changed at least four times during that period, and a host of suppliers had entered and exited the market. PC technology and components had also dramatically evolved.[2]

TABLE 3-1

PC channel share (U.S.)

	1984	1988	1994
Direct	25%	24%	18%
Dealer/VAR/SI	70%	68%	58%
Retail	5%	8%	24%
Total units	7,700,000	9,230,000	15,602,000

Source: Adapted from John Steffens, *Computer Industry Forecasts in Newgames—Strategic Competition in the PC Revolution* (London: Pergamon Press, 1994); data in D. Narayandas and V. Kasturi Rangan, "Dell Computer Corporation," Case 596-058 (Boston: Harvard Business School, 1996).

TABLE 3-2

PC channel shipment share (U.S.)

	2001	2003	2005
Direct inbound	22.8%	18.5%	17.3%
Direct outbound	18.0%	22.7%	24.8%
Internet direct	8.0%	12.9%	12.4%
Dealer/VAR/SI	27.6%	22.1%	19.8%
Retail	18.6%	19.5%	21.4%
Others	4.9%	4.3%	4.3%
Total units	46,066,002	52,698,932	64,137,963

Source: IDC, "U.S. PC Tracker," November 2005. Used with permission.

Dell was singular in its ability to make a handsome profit in spite of the tumultuous changes in the industry. In 2004, IBM had an operating margin of 1.2 percent on sales of $12.8 billion in its personal systems group, and in December it announced the sale of the division to Lenovo Group, the largest information technology company in China. HP had earned an operating margin of 0.9 percent on revenues of $24.6 billion in its personal systems group, and Gateway a negative margin of 16.5 percent on revenues of $3.6 billion.[3] By contrast, Dell's margin was 8.6 percent on revenues of $49 billion.

More than Timing

We can attribute Dell's performance to two factors, the first of which is an uncanny ability to time the market. Dell has consistently entered markets after the technology and the product concept have been accepted by leading customers and standardization has begun.[4] As *Forbes* magazine has noted, "Dell has commoditized low end computers and had them supplant high end proprietary technology . . . Dell used this strategy almost flawlessly to dominate PCs—and, again, to attack the server business."[5]

The second factor in Dell's success has been its superb supply chain at the back end combined with its direct channel to the customer at the front end. The entire purchase process, from order to shipping, was designed to be completed in about three days. Indeed, at Dell's Optiplex factory in

FIGURE 3-2

Building and editing the Dell channel value chain

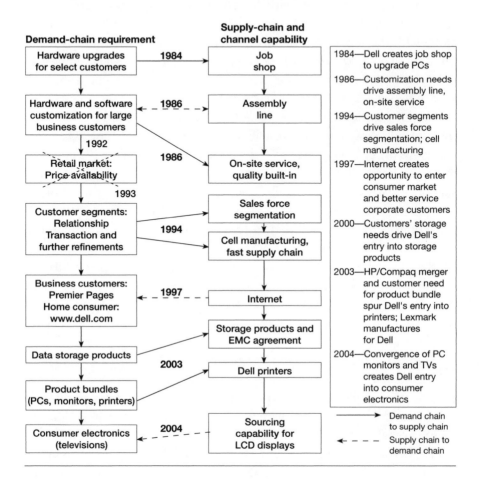

Demand-chain requirement		Supply-chain and channel capability	
Hardware upgrades for select customers	**1984** →	Job shop	1984—Dell creates job shop to upgrade PCs
Hardware and software customization for large business customers	← **1986** --→	Assembly line	1986—Customization needs drive assembly line, on-site service
1992	**1986**	On-site service, quality built-in	1994—Customer segments drive sales force segmentation; cell manufacturing
Retail market: Price availability	1993	Sales force segmentation	1997—Internet creates opportunity to enter consumer market and better service corporate customers
Customer segments: Relationship Transaction and further refinements	**1994**	Cell manufacturing, fast supply chain	2000—Customers' storage needs drive Dell's entry into storage products
Business customers: Premier Pages Home consumer: www.dell.com	← **1997** --	Internet	2003—HP/Compaq merger and customer need for product bundle spur Dell's entry into printers; Lexmark manufactures for Dell
Data storage products	**2003**	Storage products and EMC agreement	2004—Convergence of PC monitors and TVs creates Dell entry into consumer electronics
Product bundles (PCs, monitors, printers)		Dell printers	
Consumer electronics (televisions)	← **2004** --	Sourcing capability for LCD displays	

→ Demand chain to supply chain
← - - - Supply chain to demand chain

But as impressive as these achievements are, the breakthrough was Dell's mastery of the underlying continuous evolution and innovation of the channel value chain. The company's great skill is rooted not so much in the improvement of the demand chain or the channel capabilities per se, but rather in the informed interaction, or editing, between the two.

How Dell Builds and Edits the Channel Value Chain

The forces that shape any channel are dynamic; they evolve both independently and in reaction to each other. So in the real world, we often cannot craft a channel value chain as a careful flow-through from the demand chain and vice versa. Both the demand chain and the channel value chain are always evolving. This means that a channel steward must build systems that are both responsive and anticipatory. If management is well tuned to the environment, much of the anticipatory actions enhance value, giving the firm an advantage over its competition. Even if the actions are initially out of alignment, a firm having the ability to sense and respond will eventually work itself toward the mark.

In suggesting the iterative approach to building and editing, we do not overrule the time-honored marketing axiom that value building starts with the customer. Far from it. The lack of such a customer orientation, combined with lethargy in calibrating competitive offerings, has caused the failure of many channel systems. So a channel manager should certainly honor these core principles:

1. Value creation starts with the customer.

2. A company must benchmark its offerings against key competition.

These principles represent the core of competitive strategy and have been widely espoused, but they are not sufficiently practiced in the construction of go-to-market strategies. The stumbling block is the failure of strategists to recognize that channels themselves can create or diminish value. Applying a customer orientation rarely extends to the channels that carry the product to the customer, perhaps because channel decisions are perceived as tactical. But it is not sufficient to have a superior value proposition when the product leaves the factory; the value proposition must also be superior when it reaches the customer. The first two principles, then, focus our existing knowledge of competitive strategy on the channel.

Our third principle, on the other hand, is rarely recognized, let alone practiced:

3. Channel design is dynamic, and thus channel capabilities and customer requirements (the demand chain) should mutually influence each other to force channel evolution.

It might seem counterintuitive to rely on anyone other than the customer to build a future channel capability, but at times the supplier has an industry vantage point that lets it anticipate changes, especially in high-tech industries. Principle 3 may appear to be too fickle for a hard-to-change business element such as distribution channels. But you must continuously change the work of the channel to meet the needs of a changing channel environment.

Integrating these three principles provides the capability you need to transform your channel. When you undertake their application continuously and in an evolutionary manner, they circumvent resistance and create the appropriate platform for change.

Principle 1: Value Creation Starts with the Customer

The purpose of marketing is to create value for the customer, and that is why value building and editing should begin there. Channels are a means to an end, and not the other way around. It was customers who initially sought the customization that uniquely defines Dell.

In 1984, when Michael Dell started his business, he focused on solving a customer need for equipment upgrades. The company purchased the excess inventory of standard PCs from existing dealers, added disk drives and memory, and then sold them to select business customers for a profit.[6] To keep up with demand, Dell created a job shop; as he describes it, "manufacturing consisted of three guys with screwdrivers sitting at six foot tables upgrading machines."[7] In our terminology, at its outset Dell recognized the demand-chain needs of a selected group of customers and created a supply-chain capability: a job shop to fulfill those needs. This simple channel was based on the existing demand-chain needs and the supply-chain capability. But it soon evolved.

Within a few years of gaining a foothold in the business-customer segment, Dell realized that its customers needed more than hardware customization; they needed the appropriate software to unlock the power of their machines. Michael Dell recalls a visit to British Petroleum (BP) in the late 1980s when he came to this realization:

> BP's IT guy showed me a whole floor in their headquarters building that they had devoted to configuring PCs. I saw some of their people taking PCs out of the boxes, installing special features, such as job-specific software and network interface cards and removing features that they didn't use. Not only was BP spending inordinate amounts of money to configure their machines, but they were also having to do it in high-cost real estate space . . . We were watching his people custom-configure these PCs when he asked me, "Do you think you guys could do this for me?" What was both expensive and time-consuming for our customer was relatively easy for us to execute . . .

It also added a terrific opportunity for us to add the kind of value that we knew our customers in other industries would benefit from.[8]

Dell reconfigured its supply-chain capability to accommodate this customer need and increase its value for customers. It automated the process by adding a software customization step at the completion of assembling the hardware. Dell was quick to seize this advantage made possible by its built-to-order model. Admirably, Dell shared a portion of that value with its customers. As Michael Dell notes, "What happens to the money our customer is saving? They get to keep most of it . . . we make our product and service much more valuable. It also means we're not just going to be their PC vendor anymore. We're part of our customers' own information technology group."[9]

To gain a better understanding of customer needs and respond accordingly, in the early 1990s Dell segmented its customers along two dimensions. The first was by demographics: customer size, industry (such as education or government), and so on. The second dimension was customer buying behavior: either relationship or transaction. Relationship customers bought in large quantities on an ongoing basis. They sought standardized product features that were compatible with their installed base. For these reasons, price was an important buying criterion for relationship customers. On the other hand, transaction customers—mainly small and medium-sized businesses—viewed each purchase as a one-time occasion and emphasized up-to-date product features more than price.

Each segment had different demand-chain needs and also represented differing revenue potential. Dell created a sales model (part of Dell's supply-chain capability) with a differing cost to serve based on profit potential. Relationship customers bought through Dell sales representatives. The largest customers had dedicated teams, including program managers and technical support as well as sales personnel. By contrast, the transaction customer sales force was almost exclusively telephone based. Customers called Dell and received knowledgeable support from telephone sales reps. By combining buying behavior and segmentation based on size and industry, Dell was able to sense and respond to the distinct demand-chain needs of fine-grained segments.

As the Internet took hold in the 1990s, Dell not only began to use it as a channel but also understood its implications. Dell found that its customers had ever-increasing data storage needs and were seeking reliable, dependable storage alternatives. Dell entered the storage market in 1998 with its PowerVault product line, and by 2000 it had $1 billion in storage product sales, primarily at the entry level. Importantly, Dell recognized that the storage needs of its large customers were complex and varied. Rather than leave the upper end of the market to others, Dell developed a relationship with EMC (the storage market leader) to serve its customers having more sophisticated storage needs.

Principle 2: Benchmark Against Key Competitors

Initially, as a small player, Dell rarely sought to take on its competition directly; instead, it sought opportunities to differentiate itself by offering superior products and service. On the product side, Dell used high-quality components and assembled well-designed products that scored well in industry product evaluations. Additionally, in the business-customer segment, Dell priced its products very competitively.

On the service side, though, Dell lacked capability. IBM had an extensive in-house service organization, and Compaq leveraged services through its VAR network. But rather than burden itself with significant fixed costs and an army of service technicians, Dell honed its channel value chain by creating another service option. It struck agreements with a network of third-party service providers such as Honeywell and Xerox, which had a reputation for high-quality service and broad market coverage.

As Michael Dell noted, "We saw a huge opportunity to provide extraordinary service where our competitors saw none . . . In 1986 we offered the very first program in our industry for on-site service . . . Suddenly our competitor's service centers looked a little old-fashioned—and really slow."[10] Dell's relentless search for superior performance touched on every facet of its supply chain. By 2004, Dell had created a significant advantage over its competition: 4–5 points from its supply chain, some more from manufacturing and operations, and 5–10 points from its direct model (defined as information and distribution).[11]

Competitive benchmarking does not always mean that you must outsmart the competition; at times, you must honestly calibrate your capabilities and costs and adapt your channel strategy accordingly. Dell's foray into consumer channels and its subsequent withdrawal is a fine illustration of that point. When Dell entered the market in 1985, it was a small start-up with no footprint in the industry. The only benchmark available was in the consumer channel, where IBM, Compaq, Apple, and HP were the preferred vendors. But by 1991, when Dell nearly touched the $1 billion sales barrier and gained recognition for its well-built products, it attempted a foray into the consumer channels.

Dell had a solid supply chain capable of producing high volumes (for the time) of good-quality, customized PCs for business customers. Examining its supply-chain capability and eyeing the growth of the retail market, Dell began selling computers through retail channels such as Soft Warehouse (CompUSA), some office superstores (Staples), and warehouse clubs (Sam's Club). It seemed a straightforward market expansion strategy. The supply chain, Dell's internal manufacturing capacity, could handle the demand, thereby extending its reach logically to the consumer market.

But in this segment Dell's channel value chain was not tuned to the demand chain. It was not configured to profitably provide products to this market. It turned out that Dell lost about 3 percent on every retail PC it sold. In Michael Dell's words,

> We got tempted by the 20,000 odd retail storefronts that competitors like Compaq could access. But that could have meant at least 60 days of channel inventory and a similar amount of finished goods at our end to service the channels . . . Dell turns inventory 12 times, while our competitors who sell through retail only turn their inventory 6 times. Even though customization increases our manufacturing cost by about 5 percent we can get a 15 percent premium because of the upgrades and added features. But for the standard configurations we offered through retail, we were not able to get any premiums in the market. In fact, Compaq, not us, got a 10 percent price advantage.[12]

Dell quickly realized that its channel value chain was configured to create customized PCs for business customers that paid for customization. Retail customers, on the other hand, wanted low prices on PCs they could take home from the store. As a result, Dell lost money (for the first and only time in its corporate history, in 1993) and decided to exit the retail channel.[13] Although its custom assembly operation had enormous benefits for business customers, at that time Dell was unable to eke out any supply advantage at all in the consumer market.

Dell continued to aggressively extend its existing lead over its competitors in arenas where its advantages translated to bottom-line benefits. For example, in the business segment, where obsolescence occurs quickly and inventory devalues fast, excessive inventory can have severe financial consequences. As shown in figure 3-3, with its lean manufacturing systems,

FIGURE 3-3

Dell's supply-chain performance

	1990s	2002
Inventory (days of supply)	13 days	3 days
Number of suppliers	Approx. 200	Approx. 25
Units/hour	9/cell	18/cell
Order-to-ship time	36 hours	84% in 8 hours
Number of hard drive touches	8	2
PC downtime to repair	24–48 hours	8 hours
% service calls handled at time of call	N/A	75%
Return on invested capital	40%	85%
Avg. total revenue per unit	$2,700	$1,604

Sources: Dell Annual Reports; V. Kasturi Rangan and Marie Bell, "Dell Online," Case 598-116 (Boston: Harvard Business School, 1999); and V. Kasturi Rangan and Marie Bell, "Dell—New Horizons," Case 502-022 (Boston: Harvard Business School, 2002); Daniel Fisher, "Pulled in a New Direction," *Forbes*, June 10, 2002, 110.

Dell increased the effectiveness of its demand chain while simultaneously enhancing the efficiency of its supply chain.

For many years, Dell was aware that customers bundled products with their PC purchases: monitors, printers, and other peripherals. Lacking manufacturing expertise in these products, Dell had developed arrangements with other manufacturers, notably printers from market leader HP. But then in 2002, HP purchased Compaq. With a combined market share of close to 20 percent, HP became a greater threat to Dell, especially because HP could now use its printer profits to subsidize its PC sales. Dell turned to a partner (Lexmark International) to manufacture printers with a Dell label. As Dell's CEO Kevin Rollins noted, the result was to "improve the revenues and profits of our business, and at the same time put our competitors at a disadvantage."[14] By March 2005, Dell had garnered 20 percent of the ink-jet printer market in the United States.[15]

Principle 3: Channel Capabilities and the Demand Chain Influence Each Other

Popular wisdom suggests that channel capabilities should be constructed in response to the demand chain. That notion, by and large, is true, and indeed we have just made the point that value building starts with the customer. But that is not the way it always should be. Often, those that own the channel capabilities are in a position to articulate and fulfill latent demands and even create new value packets for customers. The power of much supply-chain technology is that it can anticipate and create value for customers before customers know enough to seek those attributes. In other words, the relationship between the demand chain and channel capabilities does not always go solely in one direction. They work in tandem. Dell has consistently demonstrated that it understands this duality.

By the end of 1986 Dell had reached $60 million in sales, but it realized that to grow it needed to "target large companies" and "offer them the best support in the industry."[16] To achieve its target, Dell needed scale to produce the volume of PCs required by large businesses and to provide them with the service they needed. Fortunately for Dell, Chips & Technologies had created chip sets that simplified PC design; when combined with good engineering, this technology allowed Dell to create its own PC and scale up as a manufacturer.[17] At this point, Dell redesigned its model from a job shop to that of an assembly line operation. In this instance, the editing of the channel value chain started with a technology innovation that created the opportunity for Dell to innovate its supply chain.

For example, in 1994, when Dell moved to a hybrid manufacturing design (combining cell manufacturing up front with assembly line downstream), it got the opportunity to tag each computer electronically. That was done easily in the cell. Service tagging was not an explicit customer need, but incorporating this element in the supply chain enabled Dell to offer superb service over the phone; the tags let service people easily pull up a PC's configuration before troubleshooting, making service fast and effective. It also reduced Dell's service costs.

Dell's Premier Pages are another example. Dell first approached the Internet as a means to streamline direct ordering for its core customers and as a delivery vehicle for software downloads and upgrades as well as technical support information. But Dell soon realized that it could make data available to allow its business customers to monitor and control their IT assets. Premier Pages, accessible only by authorized customer employees, let them place paperless purchase orders, select product configurations, and access corporate pricing information, real-time order tracking, purchase history, and account team information. Starting with its largest customers in 1997, Dell had more than forty thousand Premier Pages up and running by the end of 1999.

Premier Pages became an important customer communication vehicle to businesses of all sizes, including small and medium-sized accounts. For organizations whose size made it uneconomical to receive frequent visits from a Dell sales rep, Premier Pages provided a daily Dell presence, making these customers feel important—their account was sufficiently valuable to warrant a Premier Page with a direct connection to Dell.

Dell's ability to adapt Internet technology to create value for its customers is another example of how an innovation in the channel value chain can create demand-chain value. It is not a one-way street. For example, recently Dell has leveraged its supply-chain and outsourcing expertise in monitors to expand into the broader consumer electronics market, offering plasma and LCD flat-panel televisions. As an observer noted, "Teams of Dell engineers can co-develop Dell branded-TVs with suppliers of panels and other parts several of which are in-house rivals of TV makers."[18] As CEO Rollins notes, "It's flat screens, a transition technology with a new profit pool, and we leverage off our existing business."[19]

Integrating the Three Principles

Editing the value chain must be a dynamic process, because the external influences on what customers want, and competitors' capabilities, are constantly changing (albeit more so in the PC market than in some others). Because PC technology changed rapidly, it created opportunities for innovation in the channel value chain, which in turn affected how suppliers brought their products to market. As the market grew and customers learned from their experience, their expectations and requirements also evolved. Dell astutely and continuously adapted its supply chain and adapted to the demand chain, evolving its channel value chain and seizing industry leadership.

Witness how the two have played off one another to move Dell's direct channels forward: in 1985, the company was a job shop serving a handful of key corporate customers. Dell's adoption of the first 286-based chip from Chips & Technology in 1985 created the platform for scaling up its factory.[20] Although it took somewhat longer to create the assembly-line-ready version of the PC, it was Dell's awareness and willingness to adopt the new technology that allowed the company to emerge as a manufacturer.

By 1990, it was mass-assembling set configurations for business customers. Meanwhile it had added a third-party service channel to complement its own direct channel. Then by 1995, it had evolved into a well-tuned custom assembler of hardware and integrator of customer-demanded software. Simultaneously, in keeping with the evolution of its products, it developed a sophisticated installation and servicing operation for its key corporate accounts.

As Dell gained momentum in the mid-1990s, it needed to deal with the increasing volume of PC options that its burgeoning customer segments were demanding. For example, in 1989, a PC might have a hard drive, a floppy drive and some RAM, and perhaps a monitor and a keyboard. By 1995, a PC also had a CD or CD-ROM, communication hardware and software, multiple choices of monitor type and size, customized business software, and so on. Not only were there more combinations of existing products, but also customers demanded more products. The demand chain encompassed not only PCs but also laptops, workstations, and servers.

Dell found that high-volume cell production lines improved plant capacity and more easily integrated CFI (custom factory integration) components, allowing even greater customization for customers. Cell manufacturing, combined with Dell's just-in-time inventory process, cut the time required to assemble, test, and customize desktop systems in half, driven in part by a 50 percent reduction in worker handling.[21] Again, acting as an effective channel steward, Dell changed its supply-chain capabilities to meet the demand-chain requirements, and with these new capabilities it was further able to customize products.

It would be a gross oversimplification to conclude that Dell, throughout its history, merely stayed with a direct channel. The functionality of its direct channels has evolved considerably with the times. For example, Dell was among the first of the established companies to embrace the Internet as a channel. At first, a small team developed the Internet interface and began delivering online technical support and order status information. Dell built on that initial success and rapidly developed its online capability to address the needs of its corporate customers, simultaneously opening a direct channel for its "home market" consumers.

Even as Dell demonstrated its agility in seizing technology opportunities to enhance its demand chain and channel value chain, it also demonstrated its adaptability in being able to detach itself from failed channel experiments. When its foray into retail channels did not match its supply-chain economics, it retrenched quickly and decisively. Channel stewardship demands an agile and active engagement with the opportunities offered by the business environment, and at the same time a timely withdrawal when there is a mismatch between the business environment and its channel strategies. An effective channel steward must be dynamic on the upside as well as on the downside.

Translating the Principles

We have taken the perspective that Dell, as a supplier, astutely and dynamically adapted its channel value chain to the changes wrought by evolving demand and supply chains. But it can just as easily be argued that Dell is a masterful retailer. The company connects with customers directly and gives them the product selection and services they need. After all, Dell spends less than 2 percent on R&D and 10 percent on sales, marketing, and administrative expenses.[22] Or perhaps viewed another way, Dell is a value-added reseller that also chooses to assemble hardware. Most of Dell's supply chain lies on the upstream side, with its vendors. To that extent, Dell is no different from a department store assembling an assortment for its customers.

If a company is directly connected to customers, it overcomes the frictions that arise from having to handle intermediaries, and a nimble operator like Dell can successfully (brilliantly, in Dell's case) steward its channels. But what happens if you are not in direct control of your customer base? The same principle applies. Chapter 6 explores the notion of building and editing the channel value chain in intermediated channels. The point here is to highlight the absolute need to connect with customers to undertake this key discipline of channel stewardship. Some businesses, at times, make the cardinal error of addressing their intermediaries as customers. But intermediaries are partners and coproducers in the value function that targets customers. There is only one customer, and that is the end user.

Channel stewardship requires that a firm master the discipline of building and editing the channel value chain so that there is harmony between the demand-chain requirements of customers and the supply-chain capabilities of the supplying firm. Of course, and this is a big "of course," firms must then implement their channel architecture in collaboration with their channel partners, and that requires considerable expertise in the art of gaining channel leverage.

Even as a supplier attempts to achieve such harmony with its customers and channel partners, its competitors will aim for a similar coordination. They do this sometimes through overlapping channel partners, and at other times through other intermediaries, in either case creating a fierce rivalry for customers' attention. If you are to follow the discipline of building the channel value chain on customer requirements and then dynamically editing it to reflect changes in the customer as well as the supply environment, you must effect two important and interrelated embellishments. First, you must counter competitors' offerings and aspirations, and, second, you must gain channel partners' collaboration. These are part of a six-step framework offered in chapter 4.

4

Building and Editing the Channel Value Chain II

A Framework for Getting Started

U SING DELL as an illustration, chapter 3 identified three important principles that underpin the building and editing discipline of channel stewardship. Here, we offer a six-step framework to translate those principles into action.[1] The six steps are as follows:

1. Start from the perspective of the end-user customer.

2. Prioritize and segment by demand-chain needs.

3. Measure the channel's capability to serve those needs.

4. Benchmark key competitors that serve roughly the same customer segment.

5. Configure and evaluate new capabilities that address customers' latent needs.

6. Evaluate channel options and shape one that best fits the insights revealed in steps 1 through 5.

As a precursor to formulating channel strategy, this methodology makes a powerful statement regarding channel stewardship. The channel as an entity creates value. It is not simply a conduit to reach customers. The six-step approach encourages stewards to distinguish between the *roles* that the channel plays and the *institutions* that represent those roles. Even when channel institutions do not change, by evolving their roles the steward sets in motion a process of channel transformation.

That is why it is important not to view the framework as a one-off exercise. A steward, having developed a frame of reference, must continue to assess and edit the channel value chain to ensure that it is always at the leading edge and poised for change. Whereas the mapping discipline culminates in the identification of opportunities and threats in light of industry dynamics, the building and editing discipline brings the mapping analyses closer to home by identifying the strengths, weaknesses, and gaps in a company's channels.

A Sample Application

The outcomes of implementing channel stewardship are many; the channel structure that emerges as a result of our six-step framework will differ on a case-by-case basis, depending on the market context, the capabilities of the supplier and its channel partners, and the choices the suppliers make along the way.

We use a disguised case study—Alpha Company—to illustrate the key concepts underlying the six steps and show how they translate in practice. To emphasize the core logic of this important discipline, we do not delve into a detailed elaboration and quantitative analysis. Rather, we present the bare-bones architecture, knowing that different protagonists in different industries would want to adapt the proposed framework to suit their needs and flesh out the details.[2] Our purpose here is to provide an overview.

A Snapshot of Alpha Company

A leading equipment manufacturer, Alpha, with several billion dollars in sales, had slipped recently in overall market share. Pressed by competition, it was attempting to redefine its position in the marketplace. It had once been the industry leader in product innovation, selling its line of equipment through value-added resellers (VARs). Its product range was similar to telecommunications switches or midrange computer hardware. Even though important parts of the functionality were built into the product as software, there remained significant enhancements to be made before the equipment could be truly functional from the end user's perspective. Portions of this value-adding function were provided by suppliers, and other portions, by a network of resellers.

Alpha's go-to-market strategy relied on its select network of VARs, many of which had grown with the firm. For nearly two decades, the only change in Alpha's distribution policy was the steady expansion of its VAR channel to improve market coverage. Some of its VARs were authorized to sell through a second tier of resellers to gain market penetration. The industry had seen some ups and downs, but more recently had seen an increase in product innovation driven by more sophisticated customer requirements. Customers in other industries, too, were undertaking new applications of the technology; hence the overall market for the equipment was expected to grow.

Several new competitors had entered the market, and one of them had broken through the stranglehold of the top few, gaining as much as a 10 percent share in selected customer segments. With the arrival of new competition, equipment margins had been sliced by almost one-fourth. The top two or three players had almost equal market share of around 20 to 25 percent, and the market was growing in healthy single digits.

Alpha initiated the six-step process because its market share and margins were eroding. The company's once exclusive value-added partners had also suffered margin compressions, and a number of them had taken on competing lines.

Alpha Company Takes Step 1

Start with the perspective of the end-user customer. Alpha managers began by considering end users' demand-chain requirements and their perception of the existing channel value chain. For convenience, the company defined its two customer groups as large and small; they were regarded as proxies for the ways the products and services were bought and used. Large customers used the equipment mostly as the central component of the services they provided to outside customers, whereas small customers usually bought the lower end of the product line and used it directly for their own internal use.

It is crucial to segment customers by demand-chain characteristics, as Alpha did. Customer benefit segments or their demographic proxies are useful but not comprehensive for channel design, because they do not capture the nuances of the product's purchase and use dimensions, which are crucial for determining go-to-market alternatives. In other words, you must know who your customers are, what they buy, and why they buy your products. In addition, you must know how they buy the products and their complements *and* how they put their purchases to use.

Some firms have a clearly targeted customer segment, and that can streamline this step. Other companies, however, have only a general outline of customer groups. Even if the market segmentation is not completely refined, it is worthwhile to identify tentative customer segments, which can be sharpened later as the analysis proceeds.

It is also helpful to remember that a channel intermediary is rarely a customer. Firms serving business customers, for example, usually have difficulty in keying in on their end users because they often view the entity they are selling to as the customer. To gain the correct customer view, stewards must keep their eye on the importance of the product from the customer's perspective. Producers of agricultural chemicals, for example, should target farmers and not dealers. Producers of engineering plastics (pellets) for automobile bumpers, on the other hand, should focus on the automobile manufacturer and not the consumer, *because that is where the product has value in the eyes of the end user*. At the consumer level, other features and aspects of the automobile (not bumpers) are more salient in their choice.

Our emphasis on the end user may appear obvious, but in our experience, many firms make the cardinal mistake of stopping short of the end user. Business marketers in particular have long looked upon their distribution channels as "customers" and rarely look beyond them. Yet the primary purpose of the distribution channel is to satisfy end-user needs, and intermediaries are conduits to attain that goal. Intermediaries are a means to an end and not an end in themselves. They are partners and collaborators in the larger goal of anticipating and serving end users' needs. So step 1 is about defining who your end users are and then developing approximate customer segmentation schemes that broadly identify customer buying and usage behaviors.

Alpha Takes Step 2

Identify and prioritize your customers' demand-chain requirements. Each product and market context is unique; channel requirements that best represent your customers' reality are most likely to lead to effective solutions. In our notion of the demand chain, customers' needs are envisioned in the context of their overall purchasing decisions; that is, their need for complementary and supplementary products and services should form an important part of the channel value chain analysis.

In that spirit, in addition to the buying behavior questions posed in step 1 (Why do customers buy? What benefits do they seek?), Alpha managers asked customers these questions: What are your minimal requirements? What are your desired requirements? How do you prioritize your various requirements?

As figure 4-1 illustrates, the priorities and needs of the two major customer segments were quite different. Large customers ranked integration, software customization, technical support, life-cycle cost, and training support as their top five needs, whereas small customers prioritized product modularity, software upgrades, service availability, financing arrangements, and system cost as their top five. Given the natures of their respective business models, this is not surprising.

Integration of Alpha's hardware and equipment with their own was critical to the service platform on which the large customers built their business. For the same reason it was important for them to have Alpha customize parts of the software to dovetail with their existing system capabilities. Ongoing technical support was crucial because of the potential losses from equipment downtime for them and their customers. They seemed to care about the life-cycle costs of the system rather than the up-front price, and they were wedded to seeking out the least costly vendor on that score. They also sought training support for their internal maintenance crew.

FIGURE 4-1

Assessing Alpha's channel value chain

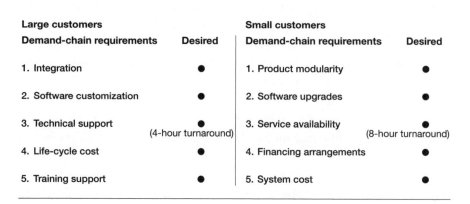

In contrast, small customers desired a high level of modularity in product design so that they could replace outdated modules without having to invest in a new system. The same reasoning applied to their need for software upgrades. Because these customers could not afford in-house maintenance, it was important for their suppliers to offer superb service availability to avoid downtime. Financing arrangements were a little more important than the ultimate system cost, because most of these small customers bought on credit.

For illustration, we have indexed customers' priorities on a scale of 1 to 5. In reality, each of those preferences would have a contextually specific meaning and an appropriate scale. For example, in the context of this product situation, the best level of technical support that Alpha could guarantee its large customers was the services of two on-site engineers, who would oversee the system implementation and scale-up and then remain on call for a four-hour turnaround. Keeping the engineers on site permanently would be too expensive and infeasible. The industry best practice at that time was an eight-hour turnaround after the phase-in period. So even the four-hour turnaround was considered challenging and would require considerable engineering investment. Nonetheless, because that level of performance was worth striving for, it brought up the anchor at the top end of the scale, shown in figure 4-2 under the heading "Desired requirement," with 5 representing the most desired state of that requirement.

Keep in mind that figure 4-2 presents only the top end of the scale. For narrowly defined segments, many customers might require the same high level of the activity. For other segments, there might be a wider variation in customers' desired requirements. Such variations indicate the need for more refined segments. In this illustration, the variations in buying and usage behavior were captured by the two-segment classification, and for simplicity we calibrate both segments' needs on a 1 to 5 scale.

The lower end of the scale represents a minimum acceptable standard rather than the worst fulfillment of it. Thus, in some instances, large customers had put up with a twenty-four-hour turnaround, which was acceptable under certain trade-off conditions but certainly not desired. It made sense, therefore, to calibrate the low end of the scale at a twelve-hour turnaround time, the minimum promised by major suppliers in this industry.

For small customers, their need for service most closely resembled the technical support requirement of large customers. The two ends of the scale were calibrated at eight-hour and twenty-four-hour turnaround,

FIGURE 4-2

Calibrating channel capabilities

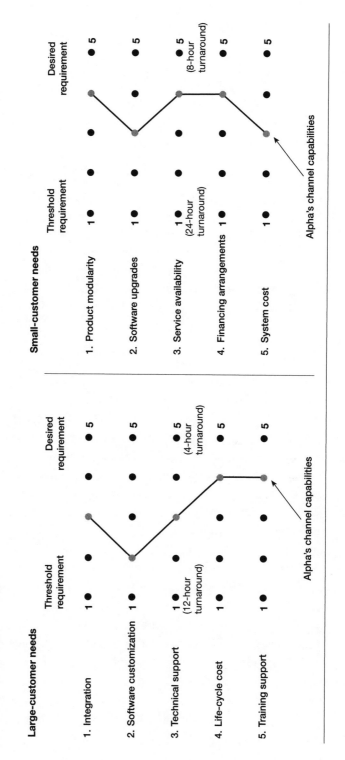

Large-customer needs

	Threshold requirement				Desired requirement
1. Integration	1				5
2. Software customization	1				5
3. Technical support	1 (12-hour turnaround)				5 (4-hour turnaround)
4. Life-cycle cost	1				5
5. Training support	1				5

Alpha's channel capabilities

Small-customer needs

	Threshold requirement				Desired requirement
1. Product modularity	1				5
2. Software upgrades	1				5
3. Service availability	1 (24-hour turnaround)				5 (8-hour turnaround)
4. Financing arrangements	1				5
5. System cost	1				5

Alpha's channel capabilities

respectively. Similar pragmatic anchor points were established for each of the demand-chain requirements.

Step 3: What Would the Alpha Channel Provide?

Get a handle on the capabilities of your channel. Armed with an understanding of demand-chain requirements and their relative importance, Alpha managers turned to their channel's existing strengths and weaknesses. They asked, what are the channel capabilities and costs? More importantly, what are those capabilities as seen from the demand-chain perspective? This critical step led managers to identify the gaps between what customers thought they needed and what the channel was providing.

Alpha sold its products to large and small customers through VARs, and this is how its customers experienced its offerings. So the products and the accompanying package of software, its installation and maintenance, and upgrades were all packaged by VARs. It would be hard, if not impossible, for a customer to parcel out the contributions of the manufacturer versus that of its value-added partner. The customer experienced it all together.

Figure 4-2, presented earlier, shows Alpha's channel capabilities in light of the demand-chain requirements. Depending on the market area, the unique needs of customers, competitive activity, and the capability of the local VAR, this calibration chart could take on different profiles. The chart reflects the output from an important market area for the firm.

Clearly, there were gaps in the channel value chain. Alpha was way off its large customers' desired demand-chain requirements in the top three attributes. These results do not mean that Alpha necessarily registered a poor market share with respect to large customers. That would depend on competitive offerings and activities. However, Alpha managers now understood that there was much room for improvement in addressing large customers' needs. There was something to be desired in its service of small customers as well, especially with respect to software upgrades and system cost. There was much to do in editing the channel value chain.

As Alpha managers found, assessing channel capabilities against the demand chain required consideration of coverage and reach issues. Were there pockets of customers that were not being reached at all? If so, how extensive was this lack of coverage? The company had one major VAR systems integrator for each major geographic area, with enough reach to cover all the large accounts. As for the small and medium accounts, the primary VARs as well as a number of local ones catered to their needs. Given Alpha's market share goals, however, there was a clear deficit in coverage for the small and medium accounts. Figure 4-2 captures the channel fulfillment only in the areas where Alpha had representation.

It is important to separate the coverage and reach issues from the capability assessment part of the exercise. Both are needed. Smaller firms—or even larger firms with smaller market share goals (for reasons of strategy)—need not cover the full range of the market, but in their chosen segments they must come out on top with respect to their chosen customers. Firms seeking broader market share will need to broaden their channel coverage, but only as a follow-up of the demand-chain exercise. You must know what the channel value chain should look like before deciding which organizations should fulfill it.

Step 4: Customers' Other Options

Benchmark your key competitors. Alpha managers had identified what their customers wanted. But what were the competitors' channels offering? A channel need not necessarily close all the gaps identified in step 3. Indeed, doing so might be too expensive. What's important is to know what the strongest competitors are doing and to identify what the channel might viably counter with.

Beyond direct competitors, at times it may be worthwhile to consider "best of show" channels. Is another manufacturer, distributor, or channel in the broader context performing better? The product supplied may not be a direct equivalent, but as long as it is serving a similar function—raw material, production supply, or critical component—you can gain much by including such alternatives as part of your benchmarking.

Figure 4-3 illustrates the channel capabilities of one of Alpha's competitors. For a long time, this competitor had been third in terms of market share, despite having products widely considered to be as good as those of the market leaders. Recently, however, this company had overhauled its go-to-market strategy by expanding its sales force and addressing the market directly.

It is clear that Alpha's channel value chain was severely handicapped with respect to large customers. This aggressive competitor came much closer to meeting customers' requirements on the top three attributes than Alpha's existing channel capabilities. This competitor had gone to market with its own team of field engineers, account managers, and dedicated

FIGURE 4-3

Competitor benchmarking

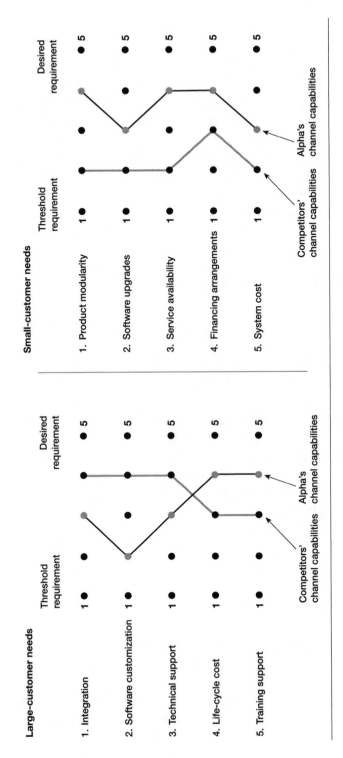

service facilities. It owned its channels and access to customers, and so it was able to offer a consistently high level of engineering contact and service.

With respect to small customers, Alpha was in a better situation, although there still were gaps in meeting customer requirements. This was not a surprise to Alpha managers because Alpha, with local VARs, was better able to address customers' service and financing needs. (Other competitors that sold through VARs were generally smaller and did not have the technology strengths of the top three suppliers.) Moreover, because Alpha was one of the few companies that had had a long history of working with the VAR channel, its market coverage was better than that of the benchmarked competitor. Despite this advantage, though, Alpha noticed a deficit on this score, because its goal was to be the overall market share leader. Several pockets of customers had inadequate VAR coverage.

Be it large or small accounts, bridging the gap between your demand chain and your channel capabilities comes at a cost, and so you must trade off the potential revenue gains before embarking on channel reengineering. More on this in step 6.

Step 5: Acting on the Findings

Configure and assess channel solutions to customers' latent needs. Steps 1 through 4 capture the "voice of customer" data and the position of the channel protagonist with respect to benchmarked competitors. Sometimes, competitor offerings can alert the channel protagonist, in this case Alpha, to build certain channel services that it has overlooked. At other times, customers' needs may be latent and unarticulated, and it is the channel steward's responsibility to tap in to and surface those requirements. As pointed out in the Dell illustration in chapter 3, suppliers often have a better vantage point for assessing new technologies and services, along with their channel economics, and thus have a better vision of potential value that can be created for customers.

Alpha did not unearth any hidden need via large-customer focus groups. For the small-customer segment, internal brainstorming generated the possibility of altering the focus from product to service. In other words, by undertaking to install, upgrade, and maintain the equipment at customers' premises, Alpha might change customers' mind-set from one of up-front investment to one of contracting for ongoing services. Thus, attributes such as modularization and software upgrades would become less consequential to customers, because they would now be part of the overall service package.

When the exercise anticipates the creation of specific new channel capabilities, you must assess its impact on new value created for customers. In this case, Alpha ended up creating an entirely new channel option for the small and medium customer segment.

Step 6: Honing Solutions

Generate, evaluate, and select options. Sometimes, this step results in the channel steward bridging gaps by taking on more functions. Often, however, what's needed is for channel partners to work together to edit and update their offerings. This means discussing channel capabilities and customers' needs. These are healthy conversations, but they are not easy. The steward's task is to keep the discussions centered on the channel value chain and its various components, and on what the various parties must do to enhance that package for customers.

At this stage it is also important to ask two fundamental questions: Is there a product problem? Is there a quality issue? That's because no amount of channel excellence can overcome fundamental weaknesses in the product. Channel stewardship is built on providing acceptable products for the appropriate segments; they need not be best-in-class products, but they cannot be subpar. Independent engineering tests revealed that Alpha's products and its performance in the field were at the top, either first or second, and even in the few exceptions, the performance gaps were within striking distance of the company's engineering capabilities. So the attention turned to channel design issues.

When managers are confronted with data such as this, often their first impulse is to mimic the competition, so an obvious next step for Alpha would have been to contemplate replacing the firm's current distribution channel with a direct sales force along the lines of its benchmarked competitor. But Alpha managers understood that doing so would involve a major transition, along with all the downside that accompanies such decisions. For example, they understood that many suppliers suffer from the "bird-in-hand" syndrome. That is, they prefer to work with the existing system rather than risk switching to a new channel because of the unknown and hidden costs involved. They also knew to ask, How much will the sales force cost? Who will bear the credit risk? Will our exit from the distribution channel provide an opening to another competitor? How will the distributor retaliate? What happens if customers refuse to switch?

Clearly, the company had to do something. Resisting change is the surest way of losing one's hold in the market. When a competitor has a superior go-to-market capability, it is only a matter of time before key customers are wooed away. But here is where the idea of stewardship was brought to bear: the main purpose of stewardship, and its attendant disciplines and frameworks, is to get there in steps rather than in a big leap.

The key stewardship idea for Alpha, then, as shown in figure 4-4, was to move the channel capabilities frontier as close as possible to customers' desired requirements. By definition, Alpha would have to exceed the benchmarked competitor's offering. The greater Alpha's advantage over the competition and the closer it was to meeting customers' desired demand-chain requirements, the better it would be from the perspective of gaining customers' confidence. There are two ways of doing this, and we shift perspective to consider these from the point of view of Alpha's managers.

The two options indicated for Alpha were taken from a larger pool. Some options were eliminated because they were considered infeasible. Others were rejected after a rigorous cost-benefit analysis indicated that they were inferior to the two under consideration. The two remaining options were put through a sensitivity analysis to judge the robustness of their

FIGURE 4-4

Building the channel value chain

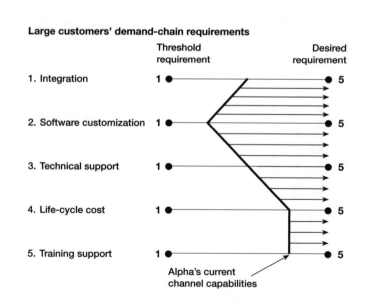

economic projections. Management felt comfortable that, if implemented well, either of the scenarios could work to enhance the bottom line.[3]

The first approach was to address those activities that the distributors were performing poorly. In this case, they were the first three: integration, software customization, and technical support for the large customers. Alpha could construct its own solution to those three needs and leave the VAR to fulfill on-site training and education. This avenue is presented as option 1 in figure 4-5.

This would be a viable solution as long as its costs did not exceed the benefits gained. Taking this path, however, might increase the price of the offering because of the additional investments and costs entailed in setting up the needed systems. It would certainly also involve a conversation with the VARs on adjusting their compensation, because they no longer would perform certain activities. This approach might also cause channel conflict, with the VARs refusing to accept the changed scenario.

The alternative was to attempt to motivate and persuade the VARs to upgrade their fulfillment of the top three attributes, as shown in option 2 in figure 4-5. In this scenario, VARs might rightly counter that issues of

FIGURE 4-5

Alternative channel configurations

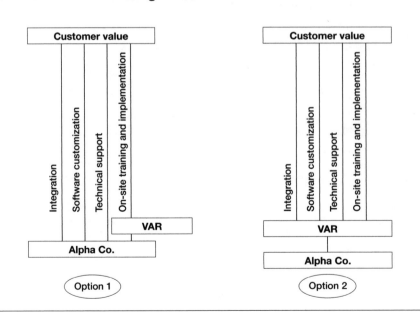

equipment integration with a customer's existing network were really a supplier issue, because there was very little a distributor could do regarding hardware; moreover, even software customization would depend on the design hooks offered by Alpha. So even if VARs took the initiative, Alpha would have to actively engage in improving these aspects of its offering.

Of course, VARs would then package the embellished offering from the supplier. But that's not all. Alpha might counter that technical support was indeed a VAR responsibility and the VAR would have to enhance its capabilities and investments, because customers seemed to be suffering dramatically there. Alpha might insist that VARs hire and train several technical people and invest in upgrading their local engineering facilities. VARs in turn might ask Alpha for technical and financial assistance to establish such a superior technical support capability.

In effect, the conversation between Alpha and its intermediaries would now take on the tone recorded in figure 4-6, which is what channel stewardship is all about. The customer is at the center of the conversation. With this approach, the supplier and distributor are talking about what makes their combined offering superior to competitors' offerings and closer to customers' desired requirements. No doubt, this would involve tough conversations on activities and effort, costs and investments, margins and their allocation. Refreshingly, however, the dialogue is not about how Alpha and its VARs attempt to manipulate each other. It is less about exercising channel power, and more about winning customers and keeping competition at bay.

FIGURE 4-6

Supplier-distributor conversations

Alpha Co.	**Value-added resellers**
• We need to better integrate our equipment with customers' legacy systems.	• We have been telling you that for some time. Only you can build the appropriate design into the equipment to make it work.
• If only your field engineers would get involved early in the selling process, they could give us customer feedback to enable us to build appropriate hooks for customization.	• We'll involve our software engineers early in the process so that we can feed your design team customer information.
• You need to get a higher-caliber staff and train them in the latest technology to satisfy customer requests.	• We will do our part, but we will need your technical and financial assistance to upgrade our training program.

The idea is to enhance the value delivered to customers through collaborative action among the channel partners. If the partners can agree on how to pull it off, and indeed accomplish their redefined tasks, they would undoubtedly change the nature of the channel arrangements.

Keep in mind that channel capability issues often are intertwined with channel coverage issues. Too large a customer territory may be the root cause of lower levels of service, so the solution may be a quantitative adjustment of the territory as a way of upgrading the qualitative abilities of the channel. At other times, as in Alpha's case, it expanded the coverage of its small accounts by appointing more dealers in the uncovered territories.

In the end, the Alpha company took a two-pronged approach. With respect to large customers, it engaged with its primary VARs to upgrade their capabilities on activities that were crucial to customers. First, to gain feedback on customers' hardware integration and software customization requirements, the Alpha sales force played a much more active role in the front end of the selling process. In addition, Alpha implemented several programs to upgrade its distributors' technical support capabilities. With respect to the small and medium-sized accounts, the company expanded coverage by providing incentives and encouraging its primary VARs to appoint secondary distributors in a number of areas lacking coverage. For these customers, the innovative option of transforming its product business to one of offering service solutions, as developed in step 5, was refined and launched on an experimental basis in one key market, with the regional VAR playing the role of an agent. Subsequently the program was modified for national launch.

The New Work of Channel Stewardship: From Analysis to Action

Based on Alpha's investigation, specifically the lack of stewardship in the large-customer segment, the company had several alternatives in addition to the ones shown in figure 4-5. These might involve other intermediaries to take on customers' demand-chain needs. In generating the options, Alpha managers might have come up with creative alternatives, outside the existing network of intermediaries, that could more effectively address the demand-chain needs of Alpha's customers. Here is where it's useful to have the output from the earlier mapping exercise. Some of the forward-looking channel options developed there should become active candidates for consideration here.

Which of the options is the best suited for the channel steward? That question is answered by the effectiveness versus cost trade-offs implied by each of these alternatives, along with their long-term viability. Assessing the impact of these trade-offs calls for consideration of alternative scenarios and extensive economic analyses, because the managers may not have had much experience operating any of these alternative systems.

But despite the difficulties, the process we've described has the huge advantage of being driven by the demand chain. Moreover, it brings a discipline to evaluating the alternative channel configurations. Undoubtedly some of the revenue-cost trade-offs involve judgments, especially when it comes to assessing the consequences of altering intermediary arrangements and the power they wield. But the very fact of knowing which channel functions are being performed by whom, and at what cost, is a big advantage in assessing the channel power positions.

Interestingly, different players in the same industry serving the same market segment often do not choose to go to market through a similar channel structure. That is because each firm has different skills, capabilities, and costs that determine which option is optimal. What we have is different systems competing with each other, each attempting to put together a channel bundle that will effectively and efficiently address the needs of its chosen customers and channel partners. That's why channel systems are strategic; they pit one firm against the other. The more effective channel value chain will win more customers and revenues, and the more efficient channel value chain will deliver it and its channel partners a higher return. For strategic reasons you may forgo a short-term, profit-maximizing alternative for a chance to create a robust long-term channel arrangement.

The six-step framework is a way to negotiate and incorporate the core forces described in chapter 2, and it is cast from the perch of the channel steward. It involves industry analyses from the mapping discipline as well as firm-level channel strategy making.[4]

Our framework is most useful when you start with a clean slate. Thus, you should put major new products through such an assessment exercise. This approach would be a big improvement over the predominant existing practice in most industries: giving in to extant channels. Unless a systematic assessment is made of the channel value chain requirements, it is impossible to develop an effective distribution support plan for new products.

The six-step framework is just as useful as an editing exercise for existing products or markets. Here is where the gaps in requirements should be actively managed. Conversations such as the one indicated in figure 4-6 are rare. Typically, channel deficits are resolved through adjustments in incentives or compensation. Rarely is there much discussion regarding the specific ways those monies should be invested. Such a general approach is wonderful for stoking existing relationships with channel partners, but it is not useful for enhancing channel performance. In general, it is this lack of accountability that interrupts the feedback loop from management to design.

Even if the decision is to retain the existing arrangements, the proposed framework gives a potential steward an estimate of the costs and benefits of the alternative. Such conscious attempts to see outside the system provide the fodder for channel transformation.

For firms that are not market share leaders, it is crucial to realize that customers buy their products and services because, in their estimation, the firm's offering is indeed the best among alternatives. So it is not as though such firms can afford to have a weaker capability profile. They should strive to be the best in their chosen market segment. They should realize that their smaller share is attributable to a narrower market focus, and therefore they should use the build and edit exercise as a way of refining their segmentation strategy simultaneously with their channel strategy.

Two Types of Channel Systems

Channel systems are often cast into one of two categories:

- *Vertically integrated.* The supplier performs all the value chain functions itself, from demand generation to fulfillment. In this scenario, the supplier has a direct connection to customers all the time.

- *Third-party delegated.* The supplier relies entirely on third-party channel members to address customers' demand-chain needs. The supplier rarely, if ever, has direct contact with customers.

Clearly, each of these systems presents a unique set of advantages—and challenges—for a supplier. Each also opens up distinct opportunities for bringing about positive and sustainable change in channel design and management.

The framework offered in this chapter suggests a third option: a partially integrated, or *composite*, channel, in which the supplier selectively performs some but not all of the value chain functions and engages channel partners to help with the rest.[5] The outcome of the building and editing discipline determines which of these three channel forms is most consistent with the notions of stewardship advocated in this book.

Key Ideas in Channel Transformation

Executing the six-step process of stewarding your channels cannot be a static exercise left to a consultancy once every blue moon. Rather, it is an active management exercise involving continuous adjustments and evolution. What seems optimal today may not be the case tomorrow, but what should be clear is that firms must learn how to manage a bundle of channel activities in the context of a channel system that may have a variety of intermediaries to execute specialized parts of that system.

Figure 4-7 demonstrates the power of the model. The starting point is the customer, and the customer's demand-chain requirements. The channel is constructed to meet this core need. Roles, responsibilities, and rewards are allocated as a consequence of this need, and not the other way around.

Channel systems are usually conceived as hierarchies, with channel institutions as the focus of design. Our approach changes that notion, focusing

FIGURE 4-7

Customers drive the demand for channel functions

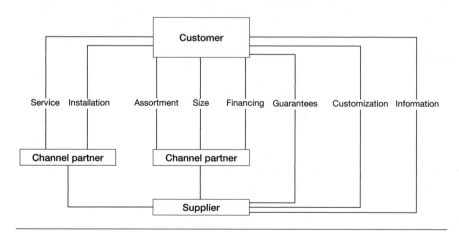

instead on customers and their bundle of needs. This fundamental break with how channels have been conceived has important implications.

Stewarding the Evolution

One important implication of the framework is that the channel configuration must change with changes in customer behaviors and competitive actions. By standing pat on your existing channel arrangements, you are exposed to the natural forces of drift. You must be proactive in navigating toward the future.

Practically speaking, however, altering distribution arrangements so frequently can be debilitating to the organization, especially because outside partners are involved. That's why the proposed framework allows channel stewards to alter channel partner's activities without changing the structure, at least not right away. Even that is a huge change from current practice, where structural changes are separated from tactical changes, and altering the former is a nonstarter in most organizations.

Moreover, the framework encourages changes in the direction of overall closeness with customers. Thus, what might look like incremental changes in fact lay the path for ultimate transformation. Remember, however, that the sweet spot triangulated by customer preferences, competitive activity, and channel capability is a moving target, and only through repeated channel editing of the kind we suggest can you approach what might look like a transformed, and yet robust, solution.

Making Coverage a Consequence of Quality of Effort

Building a channel usually involves an assessment of coverage and reach issues. Knowing the sales volume desired, channel protagonists estimate the coverage required by channels, and they plan to overcome the deficit by channel expansion. Naturally, such decisions involve questions of channel conflict and costs. Unfortunately, such actions do not change the nature of a firm's channel capabilities qualitatively; it is a quantitative solution.

In other words, adding more of the same kind of distributors or sales force will not necessarily be the perfect answer to customers' demand-chain needs. If the deficit lies in coverage and convenience, the approach will address customers' needs, but if the gaps reflect other qualitative issues, such as product design and integration or software customization, then the coverage model will not solve the problem. It is a shotgun approach to a fine-grained market need. That's why in our approach, the intensity or coverage issues are addressed as a follow-up task.

to seal that connection—and no matter which channel design a company is a party to—most successful stewards must create a channel system where the neat allocation of roles and responsibilities becomes a reality. So channel design, by itself, is not sufficient; the framework must be implemented in the field and must work in day-to-day interactions among channel partners. We explore this topic in the next two chapters.

5

Aligning and Influencing the Channel Value Chain I

The Concept of Power

T HE THIRD DISCIPLINE of channel stewardship is to align and influence the channel value chain. This discipline, a complement of the work begun in building and editing, often must be accomplished through a channel system consisting of several intermediaries. As chapter 4 indicated, this continuous task requires a careful understanding of those intermediaries, their value-adding capabilities, and the power they wield.

You must also understand how your competitors' actions exert pressure on the channel. Simply put, as figure 5-1 shows, even though the purpose of a channel is to link demand-chain requirements with channel capabilities (link A), in reality that link can be established only in light of the channel power positions and competitive actions (route B).

The challenge of channel stewardship is to navigate the more complex route without losing sight of the ultimate goal: serving customers' demand-chain needs. The steward must facilitate agreement among channel partners about the worth of the value added by each partner and must persuade them, as needed, to modify their practices for individual as well as the collective good.

But in practice, each party often has a different interpretation of the others' value-adding contributions. There is seldom a collective, reasoned agreement on how it all stacks up, and therefore all parties seldom agree

FIGURE 5-1

Channel stewardship

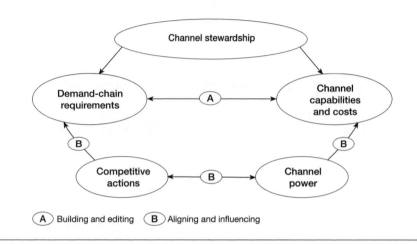

A Building and editing   B Aligning and influencing

that it is time to change for the greater good. That's why, for the channel steward, the ability to gain influence over multiple partners is a critical skill.

Channel Power

Power is the ability of one party to influence the actions of another. Even though the term is used at times in an absolute sense, its implied meaning is usually relative, involving two or more parties.[1] Moreover, in a channel context, the use of power is extensive. The word *power* usually raises images of arm-twisting, coercion, and other negatives associated with the naked use of force. In reality, however, the exertion of power in channels is much more subtle. It is more about influence than force, and you achieve influence through various means aimed at protecting and growing your business interests without necessarily vanquishing your channel partners. Gaining channel influence, as we see it, explicitly recognizes that in an effective channel value chain, all intermediaries mutually depend on one another.[2]

This chapter demonstrates that although channel power is a useful weapon in harmonizing the channel value chain, an absolute reliance on channel power to edit the value chain misses the point of channel stewardship. If the channel value chain must change from a relay to a team effort, it means that something other than power must become the primary driver

Moving from a Relay Race to a Team Sport

Channels to market have always been structured as vertical hierarchies, with flows sketched from manufacture to consumption. Inevitably the supplier occupies the top position, and customers are at the bottom. Under those circumstances, the distribution system functions like a relay race. The product package is handed off to the first-tier partner, which now owns the product—its costs as well as profits. Now the first-tier partner runs its leg of the relay as fast as possible and then hands the baton to the next, and so on.

Our framework turns this perspective on its head. We start with the customer as the driver of a firm's channels-to-market strategy, and the role of the steward is to assemble the appropriate specialists and generalists to best cater to customers. In other words, to win with customers the steward must guide the team to ensure the effective fulfillment of the demand-chain bundle. If one specialist does not perform adequately, the whole team will miss its goal.

Make no mistake about it. A team sport is no easier than a relay race; in fact, often it is far harder to achieve the needed coordination. But when it is achieved, the results for all concerned are highly satisfying.

Paying for Performance

In addition to framing the roles and responsibilities of each member of the channel team in engaging customers' demand-chain requirements, the framework provides a platform for compensation based on the effort demanded. In evaluating channel options, the potential steward must consider the various cost-versus-benefit trade-offs so that when a particular responsibility is allocated, its costs are automatically and clearly identified. This then is the starting step to construct incentive mechanisms to reflect the anticipated effort. Although this arrangement may not be perfectly synchronized with actual performance (that is known only after execution of the plan), at least it is lined up with anticipated effort. This is a major change for most channel systems, where compensation is usually based on volume and class of trade (such as wholesaler versus retailer).

The ultimate purpose of channel stewardship, however, is to integrate the efforts of the channel partners so that end customers' demand-chain needs are effectively addressed. But in doing so, stewardship also calls for an appropriate return to channel partners. The process, then, necessitates an in-depth connection to the channel value chain, end to end. In attempting

killing our margins by doing business with our long-time rival, which makes a living by calling on our customers.)

SUPPLIER: We need your active involvement in selling new products and developing new markets.

(You don't do a thing to develop new markets. All you do is serve existing markets and customers, which we develop for you.)

DISTRIBUTOR: We'd like to help, but it's expensive. How will you compensate us for the effort?

(The customer conversion cycle is so long in this business that we cannot afford to direct our commissioned salespeople anywhere near such prospects. We'll never make money in this business, nor will our salespeople.)

SUPPLIER: We must know about your customers—our customers—in greater detail; that is the only way we can develop products and services they need.

(You don't let us access valuable customers to understand how the whole value equation works, but when a customer complains we are the first ones to hear about it.)

DISTRIBUTOR: We track our customer information on an aggregate basis. We don't keep records in a way that's likely to be helpful.

(Not a chance; you'll start selling directly.)

SUPPLIER: Your channel margins are too high.

(I can't believe the overhead that you allocate to our line of business; most of it is fat, with no enduring added value.)

DISTRIBUTOR: Your prices are too high.

(You have no idea how small a quality premium you command in the market. All your key competitors make as good a product for a lower price.)

Austin, Texas, 84 percent of orders are built and shipped within eight hours. Incoming parts are pulled through the system on a just-in-time basis.

Dell seems to have a remarkable sense of timing, but its performance leverage is due largely to the unified strength of its channel value chain, along with the way it uses its direct connection with customers. Keep in mind that Dell's go-to-market strategy started as its only viable approach; only with constant attention and continuous embellishment did that approach become Dell's key competitive weapon.

We have asserted that at their outset, rarely are distribution channels thoughtfully designed; they usually emerge as an expediency. That certainly was the case with Dell. When Michael Dell entered the PC business, the market already had enough brands and enough channel coverage to support PC sales. Business retailers, such as Businessland, were not looking for a new brand, especially an unknown one like Dell. With Apple, IBM, and Compaq, there were more than enough brands. HP, too, had a presence in the market. So Dell employed the only option available: Dell Direct.

But the Dell Direct model we see today is a complex, nuanced adaptation of the original. Dell has shaped its channel to suit the changing needs of the business. It designed a superb channel value chain by blending customers' evolving demand-chain requirements with continuously enhancing supply-chain capabilities.

Figure 3-2 highlights some of the ways Dell has built and edited its channel value chain. These points are illustrative rather than comprehensive, but nonetheless they draw out the underlying aspects of channel stewardship: that value building starts with the customer, that the demand chain and channel capabilities influence each other, and that the value editing discipline is dynamic and changes with changes in the business environment.

The right side of figure 3-2 shows the familiar impressive story of Dell's evolving supply-chain capability. What began as a job shop became a well-honed assembly line, with customized cell manufacturing at the front end and software customization at the back end, fed by a just-in-time inventory system that is the envy of almost every industry.

No less impressive is the left side, which illustrates Dell's demand chain. Although it is perhaps less well known, Dell's continuously evolving ability to meet the varied product and service needs of its two types of customers—what Dell refers to as "relationship" and "transaction" customers—combined with its refined segmentation of business customers, has made Dell one of the most respected companies in the eyes of its customers.

SUPPLIER: You must improve your sales effort.

>(You run your business with a bunch of ragtag salespeople. You must bring a higher level of technical training to your sales force and greatly expand your deployment.)

DISTRIBUTOR: You must improve your sales promotion.

>(Our other suppliers, especially our more recent additions, are much more generous with their sales support programs. You could really learn a thing or two from them.)

SUPPLIER: It would help immensely if your (our) end user's order entry point would be directly linked to our order fulfillment systems—both to our factory and to your stocking locations.

>(We could save significant supply-chain costs and at the same time get a better feel for market trends in real time. You folks are still in the Stone Age.)

DISTRIBUTOR: It would not help us, because we have a half-dozen important suppliers, each with a different IT interface. It is too complicated for our customers.

>(This is yet another way to disintermediate our business. You don't seem to understand the value of our one-stop-shopping model for our customers.)

SUPPLIER: We must work together.

DISTRIBUTOR: We agree.

Both parties agree that they must work together—there's no argument there. Yet as these snippets show, their individual perspectives prevent them from seeing the other's viewpoint. Sound familiar? We wouldn't be surprised if your answer is yes. We have observed scores of such interactions between suppliers and their intermediaries.

What causes such dissonance? If manufacturers and distributors truly agree that they must act as partners, what's keeping them from it? In many cases, the answer lies in the fear that if the partner shares information or its true perspective, the other partner will use that information as power against it at some point. Power, in channels lacking stewardship, often equals distrust.

Fundamental Forms of Channel Power

For distribution channels, power comes in two basic forms.[3] The first consists of power associated with having a unique product, technology, or brand, and typically it is under the control of the supplier. Suppliers often try to gain influence through activities such as R&D, technology, engineering, product design, and branding. If they can create and demonstrate value that is uniquely attributable to their efforts, they can garner a larger share of value chain profits as the product or service winds itself through the value chain.

The second form of power rests on having market access and intelligence, which are usually in the purview of the other channel partners. Intermediaries typically try to gain influence by gaining access to hard-to-reach customers or customers who need a product or service bundle of which the target manufacturer's products are only a part. The intermediary's power and profits increase when it bundles the package for such customers.

As shown in figure 5-2, these two forms of power (in conjunction with other sources of power discussed later in this chapter) are constantly engaged in a point-counterpoint dance. For example, manufacturers want their distributors to carry a full range of their products, at least in a fo-

FIGURE 5-2

Sources of power

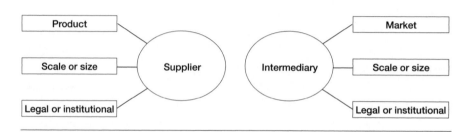

course, producers are mindful of the profit needs of their intermediaries and distribution partners. They are the first to acknowledge that a healthy partner is key to their survival. The contention is about costs of operation. Producers expect their intermediaries to operate on an aggressive cost profile. Variations in local market conditions, the scale of operations, and other factors mean that not every dealer can attain the operating cost targets explicitly or implicitly expected by suppliers.

But even if intermediaries could hold their costs within limits, it is impractical to impose a uniform margin policy. It goes against the grain of most distributors' pricing strategies. Intermediaries do not simply target a fair economic return and mark up each product across the board, a practice that would not make strategic sense. They can apply lower margins to fast-moving items because of the quicker turnover of working capital. At other times, low-margin items act as loss leaders to attract traffic or create a price image. Sometimes, items in high demand can support a higher margin to compensate for lower returns elsewhere. All in all, pricing is a complex, strategic decision for the intermediary and is best approached on a bundled basis. That's why policies set by suppliers, which usually involve product-level pricing, do not sit well with intermediaries. Suppliers that have the demand pull power may attempt to indirectly control a distributor's margins by controlling the street prices of its products.

The pricing and margin demands are reversed for high-tech and high-image products. In several instances, especially with products that require a considerable amount of value added from the channel, producers prefer their dealers to charge full margin to support the investment required to maintain the product's image, quality, and service in the field. The intermediary's role is crucial in promoting this added value, and this may require a high level of field service and technical assistance; in the case of high-image goods, it may require a superb level of local ambience and support. Such activities are likely to require significant investment by the intermediary. When some intermediaries, in their eagerness to gain a customer sale, short-change their margins, it hurts the entire channel by reducing prices and margins for all partners. As a result, full-service dealers are unable to support these investments, causing erosion for the product franchise. It is a vicious cycle. That's why suppliers want their intermediaries to uniformly uphold market prices.

Another area of contention involves gaining customer contact. To understand the customer needs in a sales territory and influence their demand, producers always seek customer information from distributors. Predictably, distributors balk, fearing loss of control of their customers, who may then be served directly by the supplier or redirected to a competing distributor. This is a distributor's greatest fear. Intermediaries like to own their customers, and they hold on to that information unless the nature of the product or the warranty forces them to part with it. In general, the less exclusivity there is on both sides, the more reluctant the distributor will be to part with customer information.

In high-tech businesses—computers, analytical instruments, industrial applications (such as chemicals and plastics), and the like—another frequent bone of contention is market development. Suppliers want their intermediaries to cultivate customer relationships and develop technology applications in their market area. Most such sales take a long lead time, and that often does not fit well with distributor sales and compensation systems, which often are based on short-term results. If distributors are assured of long-term market exclusivity and the trust of their suppliers, they may undertake such activity, but they may disagree on how long and how costly it will be and how much their suppliers should compensate them.

The Power of Scale

Large suppliers and intermediaries have another clear strength: their scale or size. Nothing else rivals size in motivating others in the channel. It directly reflects the resources used in the relationship and the opportunity cost of not having such support. Stern, El-Ansary, and Coughlan write, "To the extent that channel member A controls the resources that channel member B desires and cannot obtain elsewhere, or to the extent that A copes with or reduces uncertainties that are critical to B, then B is said to be dependent on A, and A is said to have power over B."[4]

For example, if you're dealing with Wal-Mart, the world's largest retailer with sales topping $250 billion in 2004, keep in mind that "Wal-Mart is not just Disney's biggest customer but also Procter & Gamble's and Kraft's and Revlon's and Gillette's and Campbell Soup's and RJR's and on down the list of America's famous branded manufacturers. It means, further, that the nation's biggest seller of DVDs is also its biggest seller of groceries, toys, guns, diamonds, CDs, apparel, dog-food, detergent, jewelry, sporting goods, video-games, socks, bedding, and toothpaste—not to mention it is the biggest film developer, optician, private truck-fleet operator, energy consumer, and real estate developer."[5]

Retailers such as Wal-Mart, The Home Depot, and Staples have tremendous access to customers, and that gives them unique power over their suppliers.

Similarly, many of the suppliers just named have tremendous brand pull and market coverage, as evidenced by their dominating sales positions in selected product categories. If they withhold product from certain channels, they can cause a retailer enormous financial downside. When Procter & Gamble purchased Gillette in 2005, analysts observed, "The move is a bid by two venerable consumer-products giants to strengthen their bargaining position with the likes of Wal-Mart and Aldi in Europe, which can now squeeze the largest suppliers for lower prices."[6] The new combined entity, with $60 billion in sales, gained brands such as Tide, Crest, and Pampers (with a strong franchise among women) combined with Gillette's shaving products (with a strong pull for men). The combined entity was better positioned to work with and through the $250 billion Wal-Mart.

Legal or Institutional Power

Either suppliers or intermediaries can wield legal or institutional power— power, in other words, that cannot be appropriated. The desire for this kind of power motivates technology owners to seek patent protection, product owners to seek trademark protection, and those with market access to seek legal protection. The channel power that auto dealers gained over auto manufacturers was vested in state franchising laws. NADA, the industry dealer association, ensured that automakers would find it hard to overcome the many legislative hurdles erected in their way. The main purpose was to protect dealers' exclusive access to customer markets.

A number of channel systems provide good examples of the value of institutional power. In television broadcasting, the FCC (Federal Communications Commission) controls the number of stations licensed for local broadcasting. In Boston, the FCC licensed four VHF frequencies: one public television channel and the three national networks (ABC, CBS, and NBC). In the mid-1990s, network affiliations shifted because of laws that permitted networks to own stations up to a maximum of 35 percent coverage. As a result, the owner of Channel 7 (WHDH) had two suitors for its airwaves: NBC and Fox.[7] The network that was not selected by Channel 7 would have to seek a UHF partner, automatically curtailing its reach by almost one-fourth (because UHF has a weaker signal). Not wanting to lose such a sizable audience in the country's seventh largest media market (nearly 2.25 million households), NBC agreed to pay Channel 7 nearly $95 million in affiliate fees over ten years. Until then, the norm had been about $1 million to $2 million per year.

That premium came as a surprise to many industry observers. If anything, because of the rapid increase in cable penetration in Boston (almost 67 percent at that time), it was thought that the broadcast station owners would lose power. But Channel 7 had a unique position in audience access and thus claimed a significant chunk of channel profits. It leveraged its institutional power base into an attractive business proposition.[8]

Legal protection is not the only way to institutionalize a power base. Other informal mechanisms, such as trading norms and informal business practices, often serve the purpose. The shunning of Japanese semiconductors in the United States, mentioned earlier, is one example. The traditional distributor's mentality at the time was to stick with the American manufacturers, and, from the outset, the large U.S. manufacturers imposed shelf-sharing restrictions on their distributors.[9] Only one small distributor—Marshall Industries, which had been refused distribution by the major U.S. manufacturers (Motorola, National Semiconductor, and Intel)—proved willing to distribute the unknown Japanese products.[10] Flying in the face of industry practice, Marshall provided a broad assortment of products from Europe and Japan and in 1985 became the largest U.S. distributor of Japanese semiconductors, with $265 million in sales.[11] But there was a price. U.S. chip manufacturers refused to sell to Marshall, continuing their policy of refusing to share shelf space with Japanese products.

The U.S. semiconductor industry is an example of an industry that actively sought to convert certain advantages, hard fought or otherwise, into long-term sources of power, an arrangement that benefited incumbents. In this situation, market entry becomes costly for new players. For more than twenty years, U.S. chip manufacturers effectively curtailed the broad distribution of Japanese semiconductors. One industry executive noted that this practice was often written about in the press and talked about at industry meetings, even though it was not espoused as the official industry policy.[12]

Countervailing Power

Not all environments provide the appropriate institutional platform to legitimize a company's market advantage (or to neutralize the potential advantage of the other party). In many channel situations it boils down to product power versus market power. This power is skillfully built by players that translate their market reach into a powerful customer franchise or by those that convert their customer franchise into a powerful brand relationship.

A retailer like Wal-Mart, which provides vast coverage of markets and customers, can stake a claim to its due share of the market coverage and access it provides. Its size ensures a bargaining power that delivers unsurpassed value to its customers. But a powerful supplier like Procter & Gamble, which directly influences consumer demand through brand pull, can make a similar claim. So the supplier and the retailer, in this case, will hammer out a pie-expansion and pie-allocation formula (or rather the price, volumes, and discounts characterizing their arrangements) that is in keeping with their unique sources of strength. It ultimately comes down to how each player's relative power stacks up.

If the manufacturer owns the product side and the intermediary owns the market side, it takes a great deal of coordination for the two to come together to create value. What's more, as we've said, this is not easy because a manufacturer and its distributors often have different goals and operate on different business models. The manufacturer attempts to gain returns on assets, and the distributor, returns on invested capital. The former attempts to gain volume through maximizing plant utilization, and the latter attempts to gain through working capital utilization. One is likely to emphasize economies of scale, and the other, economies of scope. What usually happens? Each uses its base of power to countervail the other's influence and to work toward a target in keeping with its own interests.

Another widely used means of gaining countervailing power is by generating alternatives. A manufacturer will seek alternative routes to market, and a distributor will seek alternative product lines. The idea is to dilute the other's unique source of value. By reducing dependence on the other, the player increases its own power. In practical terms, this means that suppliers seek alternative modes of reaching customers even if it means creating excess channel coverage. By the same token, intermediaries seek alternative sources of products, many of which form only a small portion of their portfolio (small but strategic, with the option to expand). For example, a manufacturer might dilute a retailer's market power by insisting that customers register warranties directly with it. Similarly, retailers might form an association to counter the manufacturer's sheer size advantage. The idea of countervailing power is to seek avenues of resistance to the other party's exercise of power.

Calibration of Channel Power

The primary sources of power we've described are interactive and interrelated, and, in many cases, interchangeable. A manufacturer need not own the channel (as Dell does) to have market power based on having superb market intelligence and knowledge. Similarly, many distributors and dealers own a great deal of product power. In the United States, for example, Sears (with its Craftsman tools and Kenmore appliances) has been successful in creating in-house brands with substantial product power. The same is true worldwide, with several intermediaries (such as Tesco and Carrefour) creating powerful product franchises.

Figure 5-3 provides a snapshot of a common alignment of channel power. This is a typical, but not universal, arrangement. Because the power sources are interactive, an intermediary, despite its market power, might not have the scale to adequately push back on the supplier, whose product power may be magnified by its size and scale. Depending on the nature of the product (or brand), it may be far easier for a large supplier to find market alternatives (including company-owned channels) than for the intermediary to find product alternatives.

The converse is true of large distributors or retailers such as The Home Depot or W. W. Grainger, especially when they market products or services whose availability and production they control. In that case, a key

FIGURE 5-3

Countervailing power

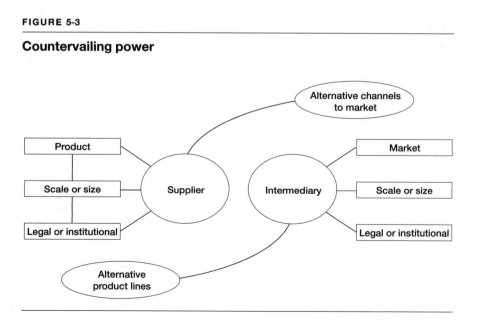

function of channel managers is to route product to market through the maze of relationships, capabilities, and power structures that constitute the channels.

How do these various sources of power play out in reality? Nike and Foot Locker provide an example.

The Case of Nike and Foot Locker

Consider the channel relationship between Nike, a $10 billion (2002 sales) athletic shoe manufacturer, and Foot Locker, its largest retailer. From their respective beginnings in the mid-1970s, Nike and Foot Locker built and enjoyed a mutually beneficial channel relationship until their head-on collision in 2002.

In 2002, Foot Locker had sales of $4.5 billion, nearly half of which were Nike shoes and apparel, and a 19 percent share of the retail athletic footwear market. For Nike, Foot Locker accounted for about 10 percent of its sales in 2002 and 27 percent of Nike's domestic revenue.[13] But in response to a highly competitive retail market, especially for higher-end sneakers, and with encroachment by discounters and sluggish sneaker sales, Foot Locker increased its promotional and discount offerings, especially its BOGO (buy one, get one-half off) sales.

Nike executives believed that such sales tactics undermined the value of Nike's brand and discouraged their retailers from using the tactics. Foot Locker reacted by canceling $200 million in Nike orders "to protest the tough terms that Nike [demanded] of its retailers."[14] Nike responded with a $175 million reduction in popular Nike products through Foot Locker's approximately fifteen hundred stores in the United States.[15] A full-blown battle had started between two powerful parties, which, until that time, had been cordial channel partners.

The Rise and Division of Power

To the surprise of many industry observers, Foot Locker was the more powerful player at the outset. A division of Woolworth, Foot Locker was founded in 1974 and grew to three hundred stores and $200 million in sales by 1981.[16] The novel idea of a specialty athletic footwear store proved successful. Foot Locker rode the growing wave of fitness and leveraged Woolworth's (and Kinney shoes') inventory management, purchasing, and marketing expertise.[17] By 1989, Foot Locker had one thousand outlets.

The fledgling Nike operation needed those attributes. Founded by Bill Bowerman (track guru at the University of Oregon, America's premier track school) and Phil Knight, a runner and entrepreneur, Nike was the antithesis of the corporate Foot Locker. In 1974, Nike introduced the Nike trainer, based on Bowerman's waffle outsole, and it became the leading training shoe in the nation. Nike was attracted to Foot Locker because it was solely devoted to athletic shoes, but Foot Locker's buyers were reluctant to take a chance on the unknown Nike, seeing the sneakers as "unbranded footwear."[18]

Thus, Foot Locker's predominant source of power lay in its market power, an understanding of its consumers' demand-chain needs. No other retailer was capable of its scale. Nike's power, in contrast, was based solely on its product power within the subcategory of running. But running was in its glory days. Oregon runner Steve Prefontaine, the holder of every distance record from 2,000 to 10,000 meters, was the first professional runner to wear Nike shoes.[19] His early demise in 1975 and the tragic lost promise increased his fame and stoked America's interest in running. Nike's running expertise gained it access to Foot Locker's distribution, and with it the scale Nike needed. By 1982, Nike had overtaken Adidas as the best-selling athletic footwear in the United States.[20]

Nike continued to grow, making performance sportswear for tennis and basketball and signing endorsement contracts with tennis star John McEnroe in 1978 and Michael Jordan in 1985.[21] Nike proved adept at moving quickly with trends and defining itself as a provider of performance shoes (such as Air Jordan) in each new arena. For its part, Foot Locker continued to expand its store base. Nike accounted for almost half of sales, but Foot Locker continued to sell other brands. By 1995, the power positions of the two players had become much more even, their mutual dependency quite large, and their individual scale significant.

Until 1985, Nike had maintained its focus on performance shoes for male athletes, but the market had expanded to aerobic and casual wear shoes popular with women. Phil Knight remarked, "Reebok came out of nowhere to dominate the aerobics market, which we completely missed. We made an aerobics shoe that was functionally superior to Reebok's but we missed the styling."[22] Foot Locker better adapted to the changing environment, maintaining its relationship with Nike but also selling Reeboks. Additionally, in 1982 Foot Locker had piloted 17 Lady Foot Locker stores; by 1985, there were 177.

Nike then broadened its positioning to include the fashion-conscious mass market, adding specialty stores to its channel.[23] The "Just Do It" advertising campaign had thoroughly permeated the American psyche by 1988, and in 1990 Nike opened Niketown, the first of its wholly owned retail stores.[24] By now Nike had expanded its product line to include apparel. In 1990, its sales had surpassed $2 billion and it had reclaimed its position as market share leader in the United States.[25] But this time its brand had a much broader reach, from the high-level performance orientation to mass-market fashion.

A Changing Relationship

By 2003, the year of the confrontation, both players had grown in power. From Foot Locker's perspective, Nike's recently released basketball shoes did not meet sales expectations, and its other product lines, many in the $100-plus range, did not move as fast. Like Nike's other channel partners, Foot Locker had been required to stock a wide range of Nike products to secure its allocation of the fast-moving items. But by then Nike had expanded its distribution to niche fashion boutiques. From Nike's point of view, "when your biggest partner, whose entire point of differentiation has been that they got your best, newest product first, decides it's a discounter, that changes the relationship."[26]

Banking on its sources of power, Foot Locker canceled orders with Nike. Nike reduced Foot Locker's allocation of merchandise and then canceled additional orders. Foot Locker sought to make up the slack with alternative brands at price points more attuned to its market and with margins more lucrative than those offered by Nike. For example, Foot Locker announced a deal to feature Adidas's Tracy McGrady merchandise in four hundred stores. These sneakers sold for $80–$90.[27]

For its part, Nike found new outlets for its products (especially the $200-plus shoes) at Foot Locker competitors Foot Star and The Finish Line. Moreover, it let it be known that "although Foot Locker will continue to receive Nike product . . . including footwear in the $90 to $120 price range, the retailer will no longer be likely to receive any product being launched at a competitor."[28]

By the end of 2003, it appeared that Nike and Foot Locker had ended their dispute. Several industry observers thought Nike had come out ahead, but neither party had emerged unscathed. In fourth quarter 2003, Nike attributed a 10 percent drop in domestic sales to the absence of Foot

Locker, its largest U.S. retailer. Foot Locker endured three quarters of declining or flat same-store sales. Foot Locker had agreed to carry Nike's Air Force One line but was also given an exclusive line called 20 Pack priced in the $80–$100 range.[29]

Indeed, the discussions look very similar to those summarized at the start of this chapter. Charitably, it can be argued that each player was attempting to perform as channel steward. Foot Locker believed that the demand chain had shifted toward less expensive shoes available at convenient (mall) locations, whereas Nike, unwilling to relent on its brand positioning, seemed to believe that the market was far from commoditized. In any case, their conversations did not appear to focus on this crucial difference regarding customers; instead, they focused on a blatant exercise of power. When two powerful parties like Nike and Foot Locker exercise their muscle, the use of power subverts the need for a disciplined focus on the customer.

The Downside of Power

Building a power base is usually a long and arduous task. In a nutshell, the idea of building power to exercise one's influence is not a realistic option in the short run. Nike was founded in 1974, and it was not until early 1992 that it consolidated its market leadership. Its power was built through products, channels, and creative brand development. Foot Locker, too, took more than two decades to build its power, but in the end, when dealing with perhaps a more powerful party, it did not have the leverage to change its supplier's behaviors. This is not to imply that the end game between Nike and Foot Locker has been played out and that Nike won. But in the short run, Nike seems to have come out somewhat ahead. The long-run implications for market coverage, and the impact of the opening this provides for Nike's competitors at Foot Locker, can be assessed only with the passage of time.

The biggest drawback to using power as a critical channel management tool is that often one might *not* have the power to influence the other party. Even the powerful Foot Locker could not sway Nike. What should a weaker party do? Obviously, those with power will attempt to use their clout to extract the desired behavior, and those without it have no choice except to conform.

Therein lies the rub. Possessing power can be intoxicating, but relations up and down the channel value chain are voluntary. Persecuted parties are not obliged to stay in the relationship and put up with the abuse. Why then do they stay? Clearly, they must see some benefit—if not in the short run, then in the long run. Something other than power must determine the nature of channel relationships and the respective economic returns. We believe that the key leverage point is channel value chain performance.

A second reason you should not bank on power as the chief means of influence is that an organization does not always gain power through its own actions. Much depends on what others in the channel are doing, and sometimes those outside the channel have a vested interest in the industry. The passage of the gas-guzzler tax in 1972 was a response to the oil price crisis facing the economy, but it had the unintended consequence of opening the door to foreign cars in the U.S. distribution system because of their superior gas mileage. That was the starting point of multibrand dealerships and further eroded the power of domestic automakers.

A similar reason enabled Boston's Channel 7 to gain power. In a unique set of musical chairs, Channel 7 fortuitously found itself on the winning side. Strangely enough, before the events leading to the megacontract with NBC, Channel 7 had been a CBS affiliate, and its relationship with the network was just fine. It so happened that Fox, an up-and-coming network, rocked the boat elsewhere by taking 20 percent ownership in a TV entity that owned twelve U.S. television stations, eight of them CBS affiliates. The new owner announced that all twelve stations would become Fox affiliates.

In response, CBS entered into a multimillion-dollar long-range agreement with another TV station entity, one whose five stations (one of them the NBC affiliate in Boston) would switch to CBS. Thus, Channel 7 found itself dumped by CBS. But Channel 4, the new CBS affiliate, had to eject its NBC franchise to accommodate its new owner. So NBC was forced to look for a partner in Channel 7. Added to this mix was Fox, which had only a UHF station in Boston. It aggressively pursued Channel 7 as a potential partner, especially because Channel 7's owner had a close relationship with Fox elsewhere in a different market. When Channel 7 leveraged its unique market position, it translated NBC's potential loss of audience, and the attendant loss of advertising revenues, into an attractive financial agreement for itself.

But such opportunities do not show up every day. More importantly, as this story illustrates, channel power is only partially under one's control, and a large part is shaped by industry conditions. Sometimes there is very little a firm can do to gain channel power, but a lot it can do to gain value chain performance.

Even assuming that a channel member can unilaterally build power through its own actions, research shows that the naked use of power usually results in negative consequences.[30] When channel members are forced to change behavior because of the threat of consequences rather than the promise of rewards, it usually leads to disaffection and dissatisfaction. Moreover, conflict levels rise. Unless power is used as a dissolution mechanism, for those dyads where relationship continuity is a requisite its exercise is not guaranteed to deliver success.

Channel Value Chain Performance Front and Center

From our perspective, the most salient influence is the benefit gained by all parties when the demand chain and channel capabilities are truly matched. As illustrated in chapter 4, there are many points in the design of a channel where the channel builds capabilities to reflect customer needs; or, alternatively, channel capabilities end up significantly shaping customer requirements. Whichever organization—either a supplier or an intermediary—performs these critical functions gains channel leverage. If it were otherwise, there would not be much value added for customers. Thus, the firm with the critical influence has more power.

Unfortunately, companies tend to misdiagnose all this and get embroiled in an exchange of product power versus market power. What product power really means is that a firm's products have a unique drawing power for a group of customers, and what market power means is that a firm's channel capabilities are uniquely attractive to a certain group of customers. So when a firm having product power combines with a distributor having market power, what emerges is a powerful combination of unique skills to serve that market segment.

But the demand chain and channel capabilities involve elements of both product and market. In other words, a supplier may have product power, but that does not give it full control of the demand chain. It may need the value-adding capabilities of the channel to fulfill customers' needs. Similarly, a distributor may have market power but not necessarily control all the channel capabilities; the product's service requirements may necessitate the producer's involvement. The integration of customer requirements and channel capabilities makes channels effective and efficient.

One of the main objectives of channel stewardship is to align the players and thereby ensure that customers receive value and channel partners make an adequate return. A firm needs power only as a means to this end, and not as an end in itself. But unfortunately, power is often executed to influence the other party to do things that are in the powerful party's interests. If the less powerful party has been forced to do things that ultimately enhance the match between the demand chain and channel capability, then it is a good thing as long as the conforming firm is rewarded. Value is created in the channel, and the profits thus generated become available for sharing among the channel participants. If the more powerful party is instrumental in creating the value, it is entitled to a higher share. No matter who gets what share of the profits, customers must receive a benefit. If power is exerted, however, merely to affect the allocation of channel profits without creating value or expanding the pie, then it is suboptimal. It becomes a zero-sum game, where there are winners and losers instead of partners that jointly work to create value for customers.

FIGURE 5-4

Coordinating channel value chain performance

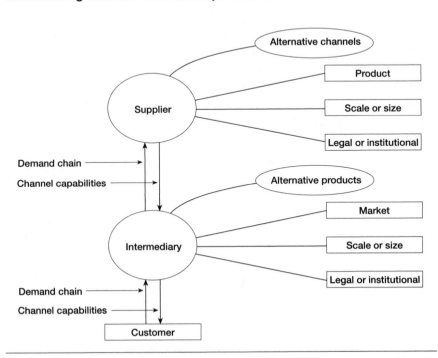

Figure 5-4 illustrates our key point regarding channel stewardship. The supplier and the various members of the channel can engage each other through their accumulated sources of power, but if that is all they do, then they are missing out on the fundamental rationale for channels of distribution: to satisfy customers' requirements. By collectively focusing on building an appropriate channel value chain, the supplier and its channel partners create value. Channel power is needed to oversee the allocation of channel profits, but when overused, it can curb value creation, which comes only from harmonizing the demand chain and channel capabilities. But to do that the supplier and its channel partners must have transparency and access to that part of the value chain that is invisible to the other.

As the figure shows, sometimes a supplier may not see the customer's demand-chain requirements, just as the channel partners might not see several aspects of the upstream value chain, especially suppliers' product-related strategies. In the absence of such information, how can channel stewardship take place? Here is where channel performance and mutual trust are proxies for information and transparency. In the next chapter, we turn to the task of putting it all together to create alignment throughout the channel.

6

Aligning and Influencing the Channel Value Chain II

Focusing on Performance

W E'VE SAID THAT STEWARDSHIP is not about being nice; it requires a laserlike focus on customers and a rigorous study of how the various partners contribute to the channel value chain. It can require altering a partner's role; it can even require eliminating a partner or making other, similarly difficult decisions.

The key is that even when a steward must make a tough call, the action must not be an unexplained power play. The attraction of using channel power is that it usually gets the job done, at least for a start. Partners generally acquiesce to the demands of powerful members. The downside, however, is that the exercise of power often leaves a bitter aftertaste, and, as a result, members of the channel value chain are not optimistic regarding the health of the relationship and its long-term viability. In such an environment, alignment is elusive.

That's why one of the mandates of stewardship is to ensure that all partners understand how the channel value chain addresses customer demand. The drive for transparency, with customers in focus, can greatly reduce the possibility that an unpopular decision will be mistaken for a power play.

Visibility is easy to call for but harder to effect. Information technology lets you program the links and seamlessly integrate information, so from a logistics standpoint, transparency isn't complicated. But it can happen only if the members cooperate, and they are not likely to do so unless they can readily empathize with their partners' positions. It's almost a chicken-and-egg situation. Trust comes with shared information; information won't be shared without trust. Clearly, channel partners must unite not only to improve channel processes but also to strengthen a channel's human relationships.

What must you overcome to establish trust among channel partners? How can a steward begin to align a channel? Answering those questions is the focus of this chapter.

A Built-In Challenge

Simply saying, "We must make our businesses transparent" is not enough. Several built-in challenges face even those channel partners most eager to effect change.

Chief among these is a disconnect between the business models at work in any given channel. As mentioned earlier, distributors' businesses usually thrive on economies of scope, and manufacturers' businesses on economies of scale. This difference often sets the stage for misunderstanding. If you begin with two business models based on different sets of assumptions and then overlay them on top of the pressures of day-to-day business, you end up with an opportunity ripe for conflict.

For example, distributors (and retailers) depend critically on efficient utilization of working capital, whereas manufacturers depend critically on best utilizing their capital investments, such as factory, R&D, or engineering capacity, and their fixed investments in human resources. Distributors and intermediaries seek a portfolio of products—some complementary, others supplementary, and still others substitutes—at varying price points to cater to the entire demand-chain needs of customers. Their pricing and margin requirements vary over the product range, and what matters is the overall bottom line, not the profitability of each item. In contrast, manufacturers need volume in their chosen product line to enhance the efficient use of their fixed assets. They need scale to drive costs down and improve quality.

Some distributors might use a supplier's brand pull and product reputation to attract customers to the store and then switch them to a more profitable product line from a different supplier. In other instances, discoordinated, customers end up facing the consequences of these gaps. By contrast, when supplier and intermediaries team up to consider the customer's point of view, great strides can be made.

JC Penney, for example, closed several of these gaps when it created a new order management system.[1] JC Penney is one of the largest retailers in the United States, with 2004 sales of $18.4 billion. It is also the country's largest retailer of hard window treatments, including blinds manufactured by industry leaders such as Hunter Douglas, Springs Window Fashion, and Levolor. In the old system, customers came into the store and ordered made-to-measure blinds. The in-store salesperson manually faxed the order to the manufacturer. The problem was that half of the store orders were incorrect or illegible, requiring an hour or more for verification. Even so, 30 percent of orders shipped were returned because the product failed to meet customer specifications, costing JC Penney half the cost of the order (the manufacturer bore the other half). No one in the channel value chain was satisfied. Customers failed to receive a satisfactory product. JC Penney invested time and effort in creating a sale but created dissatisfaction for both the customer and its channel partner.

In 2004, JC Penney installed an integrated order management solution using its data about customer satisfaction to motivate channel partners. The idea was to create a system that allowed customers to monitor the progress of their orders and, at the same time, use transparency to reduce errors in ordering and processing.

Visibility was required throughout the channel value chain. The blind manufacturers needed to upload their specifications and measurements, and JC Penney needed to provide its customer information to the manufacturers. Partners in the channel system had to make available information about prices, inventory, capacity, demand at point of sale, and so on.

But all these efforts were directed at *aligning the channel to meet customers' need for blinds that fit their windows*. The result? Order time fell to thirty minutes, and the number of wrong or illegible orders fell to zero within weeks.

The focus was on transparency, not for its own sake but for the customer's sake. But the resulting visibility gives the channel steward, JC Penney, the information and management levers it needs to initiate and implement corrective action going forward. Without transparency up and down a channel value chain, no one can construct a framework for such management action.[2] With transparency, customers, channel intermedi-

of change. That something is channel value chain performance. If overall performance is the foundation of all the channel relationships, then even a small company with limited channel power can influence the channel to move forward in alignment. Effective channel stewards convince all channel partners to buy into the idea that a rising tide lifts all boats.

Channel Conversations

Consider the following exchanges (*with unspoken thoughts in parentheses*):

SUPPLIER: You must carry our full line of products. No cherry-picking. We must be a full-line supplier to cater to the wide range of market requirements.

(Selling our specialized products is easy; they're so good that anybody can sell them. But the standardized end of our line is more difficult to sell because competitors' offerings are similar, so that's where our distributors must show their mettle.)

DISTRIBUTOR: There is no point in pushing the full line. We should concentrate on our strong points. Through hard work we have established a market leadership position for the top end of the product range. Why dilute our effort and attention?

(We make no money on the rest of your products. Besides, our other suppliers have much better programs to support their equivalent products.)

SUPPLIER: We need you to concentrate on our products; that's the only way to be true partners.

(How can you flirt with our competitors right under our noses? One day you will take on lines aimed at the core of our product range.)

DISTRIBUTOR: We need exclusive territories.

(For a company that makes such a big deal of being a "real partner," your management is highly insensitive to our needs. You are

aries, and suppliers all work together to perpetuate a virtuous cycle of improvement. No doubt this puts increased stress on the order fulfillment system, but it is good stress—the kind of stress that, when appropriately handled, can improve system efficiency and enlarge the pie.

Ideally, if various channel value chain processes are seamlessly integrated, the result is an end-to-end channel system with complete visibility and information across the pipeline. On paper, as figure 6-1 suggests, such integration may be possible if there is perfect alignment across the channel value chain regardless of the levels of intermediaries in between. You can then eliminate redundancies and gain the advantages of completely coordinating the value chain from procurement to sale.

The Deceptive Ease of Technology

Another built-in challenge facing channel partners is technology that appears to do the job but does not.

FIGURE 6-1

The channel value chain spectrum

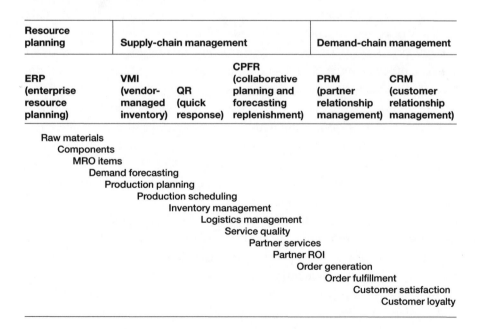

Resource planning	Supply-chain management			Demand-chain management	
ERP (enterprise resource planning)	VMI (vendor- managed inventory)	QR (quick response)	CPFR (collaborative planning and forecasting replenishment)	PRM (partner relationship management)	CRM (customer relationship management)

Raw materials
  Components
    MRO items
      Demand forecasting
        Production planning
          Production scheduling
            Inventory management
              Logistics management
                Service quality
                  Partner services
                    Partner ROI
                      Order generation
                        Order fulfillment
                          Customer satisfaction
                          Customer loyalty

Advances in technology have improved the efficiency and effectiveness of a host of processes on the demand-chain and supply-chain fronts. On the demand-chain side, we have seen the emergence of customer relationship management (CRM) and partner relationship management (PRM) tools, which are designed to help monitor and guide the demand chain. On the supply-chain side, tools such as vendor-managed inventories (VMIs), QR (quick response), collaborative planning and forecasting replenishment (CPFR), and others have brought the same level of automation to production and inventory systems that enterprise resource planning (ERP) software brought to manufacturing. As we said at the beginning of the chapter, transparency—via technology—is a real possibility now.

The issue is to ensure that channel partners do not mistake technologies that offer point solutions for true channel alignment. Just because one or another part of the channel is humming, it doesn't mean that all parties are on the same page.

With advancements in IT and the availability of real-time data, it might appear that it is not terribly difficult to implement a continuous process of editing the channel value chain, leading to channel evolution. For example, suppose that a manufacturer realizes that customer satisfaction has been eroding or that order fulfillment rates are below norm. It tweaks the channel value chain, perhaps changing the means of product fulfillment or the terms of its arrangement with channel partners. As a result, performance improves significantly for that element in the chain.

The problem is that there may not be an overall impact on the channel because other elements in the chain may move inadvertently to block the potential cumulative contribution.

For example, consider a few of the current technologies that impact the channel value chain, along with their advantages and their limits.

Demand-Chain Solutions

The combined effect of CRM and PRM is to manage the demand from sales lead to order capture and service, with the order flowing from the customer through the partner to the supplier. Fully executed, an integrated solution is meant to allow a company to see through the channel to the end customer and thereby effectively market in a complex channel environment, while at the same time enhancing partner effectiveness. Depending on its execution, the customer receives information about product, pricing, and availability directly from the supplier through the channel partner's

tributors might take advantage of a supplier's product quality to charge a premium margin to fund their other weaker products. Neither of these scenarios is attractive from the supplier's point of view. In the first case, it loses sales in spite of brand attraction, and in the second case, because of high resale prices it may not penetrate the markets as speedily as it would like. In a third variant, the distributor does not bring enough value addition to a supplier's specialty products, decreasing their worth for customers and affecting the supplier's price and margin yields.

Suppliers, too, in attempting to gain market share, may pit their own partners against each other, unmindful of how their aggression may destroy the business foundation of one or the other of their intermediaries. Suppliers may also try to bypass the channel in search of quick sales.

These practices combine to create a system riddled with conflict possibilities. The supplier and the intermediary often end up at loggerheads, as the conversations in chapter 5 illustrate.

These discussions do not represent the full range of issues channel partners discuss, but they accurately represent the tenor and quality of the interaction and, in doing so, reveal a critical piece of the solution: in the absence of channel stewardship, rarely do conversations between manufacturers and distributors center on customers' wants and needs. Making the customer the common focus is the first step in overcoming the disconnect caused by dueling business models.

The Power of Considering the Customer

Consider the channel from the customer's point of view. Customers place an order at the point where they interface with the channels of distribution; whatever else happens after that is not visible to customers, even though it affects the purchase. The order winds itself through the channel intermediary, which may fulfill it from inventory or pass it on for manufacture. If the order goes to a manufacturer, it may be a while before the customer gains information about it, and in the interim a number of things can go wrong.

Before the order is scheduled for manufacture, for example, it might have to wind its way through several internal departments: engineering, purchasing or procurement, and factory scheduling. When the product flows to the customer, either from inventory or production, it may need service, including delivery and installation. Additional departments and intermediaries may be involved. When suppliers and channel partners are not well

Web site. The benefits are increased sell-through, increased purchase conversion rates, cross-selling, and up-selling; and on the cost side, reduced operating expenses from reductions in order-entry and processing errors, improved inventory management, and fewer customer service interventions.

CRM systems and, to a lesser extent, PRM have gained a significant number of commercial applications. Their contributions to the productivity of sales force management have been impressive. But their analytics—which tend to focus on measures of customer and partner satisfaction, loyalty, and retention—have been less successful in establishing firm links to the investments or inputs that cause these behaviors. What should management do to gain customer and partner satisfaction? What should partners do to gain customer loyalty and retention? And what should suppliers and partners do together to gain market share and profits?[3]

For example, we know that in automobile retailing, customer satisfaction often can be boosted by making available the desired car and options. But that calls for an unusual bump in inventory levels. Who carries responsibility for the inventory—the dealer or the manufacturer? That is a point of debate, especially because carrying costs are involved. As one observer noted, "The theory is simple: clever software crunches data and identifies patterns of behavior that can be acted on . . . [Yet], though software lets firms identify patterns, explaining them and working out what to do about them requires human skill and marketing knowledge."[4]

Supply-Chain Solutions

Supply-chain management tools have been better able to demonstrate the tangible benefits to a firm's bottom line. In the VMI model, the distributor and the manufacturer share information about inventory levels using electronic data exchange. The manufacturer can see its distributor's inventory, often all the way to point-of-sale data. The two parties agree on an inventory plan, and the manufacturer assumes responsibility for maintenance and replenishment. The distributor gains from a reduction in inventory levels and stock outs. The manufacturer gains insight into distributor stock movements, and when a significant number of its distributors are part of VMI, the supplier understands end-user demand patterns and as a result can refine forecasting.

Just-in-time (JIT) and QR are part of the same family of supply-chain management tools that attempt to enhance performance by minimizing unwanted and slow-moving inventory. The entire production process is so programmed that parts, components, or merchandise are produced on a signal from the market and arrive quickly at the factory or retail stores without having to sit idle anywhere in the supply chain. CPFR, an even more encompassing tool, combines forecasting and planning.[5]

Notwithstanding these impressive applications, many believe that supply-chain management tools may be overly concerned with costs at the expense of effectiveness. In other words, the tools' approach to the bottom line tends to underplay the possibility of expanding the top line.

A singular focus on cost could undermine product availability and breadth, which in turn could affect sales force morale. But a corresponding decline in customer demand may not immediately follow. If anything, because of the decline in costs, the company's profits will go up, drawing further resources to the cost-cutting initiative. This vicious cycle ultimately stifles demand.

As we pointed out in chapter 1, a more enlightened view of supply-chain management views the chain as ending with customers rather than suppliers or channel partners.[6] But much of this conceptual thinking has not yet pervaded the practice of channel management.

Make no mistake: channel stewards should not discount the vast advantages that IT brings to integrating important aspects of the demand chain and the supply chain. Our view is that channel protagonists should take advantage of the win-win that IT provides to further align the channel value chain with the needs of the demand chain. But they must be wary of point solutions masquerading as alignment.

The Taproot Issue

When firms sell through intermediaries, there is a natural break between the demand side and the supply side. There are many natural gaps between the origin of the demand chain, the customer, and the steward of the channel value chain—often the producer. The ideal scenario of figure 6-1 starts to look more like the one shown in figure 6-2.

Technology also plays a role. But consider: much of what we saw as channel efficiency in the past several years focused on measurable indicators such as sales force productivity, delivery lead time, order fill rate, pipeline inventory, and so on—all very useful, and many leading to tangible improvements. But their collective efforts have not effectively nudged channel systems from their inertia. The reason is that many independent improvements in parts of the end-to-end channel value chain, by themselves, are not sufficient. The upside of these point solutions is constrained by organizational boundaries.

The players shown in figure 6-2 guard their turf to protect their long-term interests in the channel value chain. Others are not allowed the visibility and passage that might ensure a better value proposition for customers. But even though such a territorial view affects channel efficiency and effectiveness, the individual channel members are understandably worried about their own power positions and locations in the chain. In fact, each organization may not have the desired internal transparency across the various departments spanning the chain. Organizational structures, systems, and incentives often get in the way of coordination. Of course, across organizational boundaries, the reasons for a lack of coordination are only exacerbated.

Only human and organizational relationships can catalyze alignment across the entities from the supply side to the demand side. Channel alignment requires a holistic view of the channel value chain, as well as a coordinated response. The root cause of coordination difficulties is a lack of understanding or consideration of human behavior.

FIGURE 6-2

Gaps in visibility

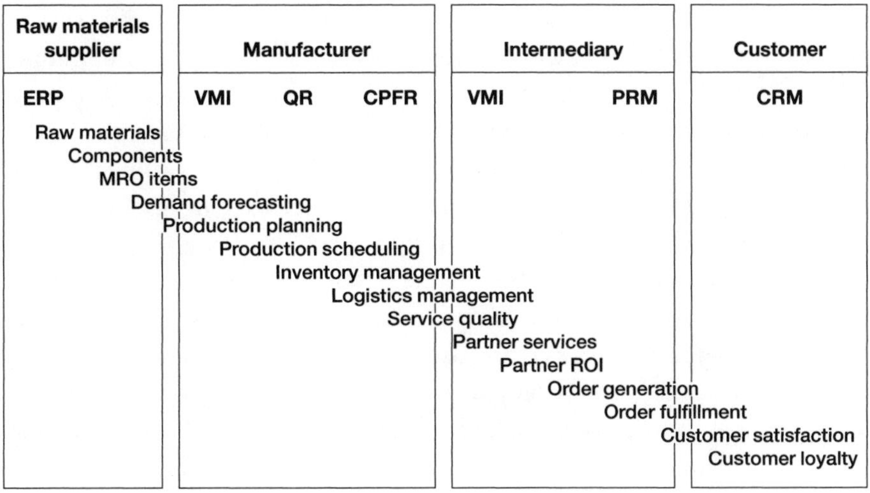

Raw materials supplier	Manufacturer			Intermediary		Customer
ERP	VMI	QR	CPFR	VMI	PRM	CRM

Raw materials
  Components
    MRO items
      Demand forecasting
        Production planning
          Production scheduling
            Inventory management
              Logistics management
                Service quality
                  Partner services
                    Partner ROI
                      Order generation
                        Order fulfillment
                          Customer satisfaction
                            Customer loyalty

Trust, Transparency, and Performance

When organizations and managers interact with each other, their behavior patterns can be summarized and synthesized through a core set of constructs: trust and commitment.[7] Even though these constructs are often used interchangeably, each has a distinct meaning.

Trust is the act of relying on the other person's words or actions as being the most likely to promote favorable outcomes for oneself. Trust involves having confidence in the other person's integrity and reliability. In other words, the partners know through their history of dealing with each other that they can be completely open and vulnerable to the other party's actions and expect the outcome to be positive.

Commitment, on the other hand, is a pledge of continuity and adoption of a long-term view, with a willingness to make investments and sacrifices to get there. Commitment, like trust, is undertaken with a view to enhancing the channel value chain as a whole, so that the result for each party is superior to what it had before. Trust is a statement of the history of the relationship, and commitment is a statement of future intentions to maintain or enhance the relationship.

Even though these constructs have meaning and applicability at the individual as well as the organizational level, we can think of trust as an interpersonal construct and commitment as an interorganizational one in the context of channel relationships.

The development of trust between individuals spurs the development of commitment between two organizations. As individuals build trust in one another, they transfer this bonding to the level of the firm. The cumulative effect of several such transfers results in an increased commitment by each firm. Trust builds commitment, and commitment in turn lays the foundation for trusting interactions. For simplicity, we broadly label this intertwined process as building trust, and we refer to it as we develop the alignment model.

Channel stewards—or for that matter any member of the channel value chain—should not think of building trust as the end goal of channel alignment. Channel *performance* is the goal. But if the first step in gaining channel performance is transparency of the channel value chain for its critical members, then trust must precede that first step. But as we've said, building trust and sharing information present a sort of chicken-and-egg issue.

Only by having a shared understanding can the team, under the guidance of the steward, start to improve its effectiveness—for the top line, for efficiency, and for the bottom line. A supplier benefits by knowing how its product is moving at retail, and the retailer benefits by knowing how its order is moving through the supply chain. A higher level of information sharing involves knowing each other's business plans and strategies as they pertain to their shared interest. If such a foundation exists, then participants can engage in trusting relationships.

Say, for example, that the supplier has a product overrun and is eager to dispose of the excess inventory. Knowing this, the retailer might offer to take it through the channel at a particular price. If the price reflects the retailer's intention to keep all the profits, then there can be no trust built with the supplier. On the other hand, if the partners have a mutual understanding and a sharing of the gains (and losses), then they create a foundation for building trust. Transparency is not the equivalent of trust; how the various players use transparency leads to or erodes trust, and they usually work in tandem, building and reinforcing each other.

This is where the importance of channel *system* performance comes in. By that we mean the performance of all the players that constitute the channel value chain. It is not a sum total of individual performances, where the upside of one member compensates for the downside of another; that is the typical zero-sum game, where the more powerful members gain a disproportionately higher share. Rather, system performance implies that every member achieves its goals.

To attain this goal, channel partners must engage in mutually trusting interactions. No doubt the goal reflects the channel power positions of each member. For example, if a supplier has unique product, brand power, or size, it is likely to attract retailers that will take on a number of supplier-led programs. Or if the retailer has enormous scale and market clout, the supplier may be willing to join in the supply chain to fulfill the retailer's bundle of products and services. In either case, it's clear that no matter how powerful the other business entity is, it will not engage in the relationship if the result is not an adequate financial return for itself.

So even as both parties engage in mutually reinforcing activities to serve customers, they must simultaneously achieve their respective business goals. When that happens, trust builds through a culture of mutual achievement. And, as they engage in repeated interactions, in spite of each having power, they'll seldom use it. Instead, each will attempt to solidify it by escalating its formal commitment to the other.[8]

The Three Steps of Alignment

The aligning and influencing discipline is the third leg of the channel stewardship model, preceded by the mapping discipline (chapter 2) and the building and editing discipline (chapters 3 and 4). Aligning and influencing go hand in hand with the building and editing step. Each affects, and is affected by, the other. Together they determine the outcome of channel stewardship.

The three steps of the alignment process (shown in figure 6-3) are straightforward:

1. Set goals for the system.

2. Assign channel roles, responsibilities, and rewards.

3. Measure and monitor channel performance.

Step 1: Set Goals for the System

Any attempt to align and influence a channel must start with clear, *quantitative* goals: sales, market penetration, market share, channel cost reduction,

FIGURE 6-3

Aligning and influencing the channel value chain

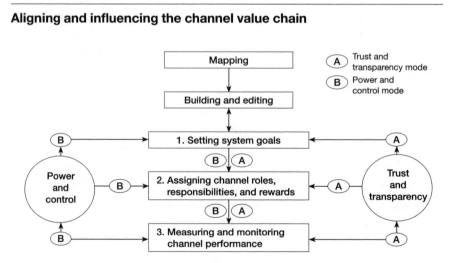

and so on. Remember that these are goals for the system. Each channel member's goals should be derived from this system goal, and not the other way around. These goals could also include the soft side of the business, such as building system loyalty, but you cannot lose sight of the central goal of improving the channel's economic performance.

These system goals may evolve from dialogues with key intermediaries or their representatives (such as a trade association), or the process may be undertaken by the channel steward unilaterally, especially if the intermediaries are fragmented, dispersed, and numerous. Under such circumstances, the steward must project individual member goals as a consequence of the system goals. The steward then builds this goal as part of a member's financial profile.

Here is where differences in perspectives may show up. The returns may be inadequate for some channel members but central for others. It may not be feasible to do such analysis for every member, but the steward should attempt to do so for classes of members. It's important to understand your channel partners' business models and know how they make a return on investment.

Step 2: Assign Channel Roles and Responsibilities

At the center of the channel relationship linking the supplier to its customers through an intermediary is the economic rationale. Products and services flow through the channel to the customer.

In the terminology of channel stewardship, this is where the demand chain and channel capabilities come together. The building and editing step provides the channel steward a road map of what to do; the alignment step implements the assignment of channel, roles, responsibilities, and rewards and determines how to implement the "what to do" analysis from the previous step. Channel stewards should realize that although there are bound to be some adjustments to the analyses suggested by the building and editing leg, they must get the assignment directionally correct.

Before assigning the channel roles, responsibilities, and rewards, the steward must carefully assess the players' power positions. A good start is to prepare an audit of the dimensions of power: product, market, scale, legal, institutional, and other countervailing sources. Of course, this assessment alone will not tell the whole story. The steward must appraise the health of the channel's mode of conduct: the level of trust among key decision makers and the level of commitment among the organizations.

This step is at the heart of channel transformation, bringing together the analytics of the building and editing discipline with the pragmatics of power distribution. Any change calls for constructive negotiation of the channel roles, but such discussions must be backed up by the design of systems that promote trust and transparency.

This is by no means an easy task. Often, the fruits of the design will manifest themselves only some time later. Nonetheless, channel stewards must invest here to ensure the long-term health and effectiveness of its channels.[9]

Step 3: Measure and Monitor Channel Performance

You align the channel to ensure that the members share an understanding of their roles and responsibilities in achieving superior system performance. This means that, for a start, there should be a clear understanding of the sales and margin goals, not only for the channel steward but also for the other members of the channel value chain.

More importantly, you need a thoughtful plan of the effort needed to reach that goal. In the past, almost all channel evaluations were based on outputs, and little attention was given to inputs; but without this knowledge, it was hard to take corrective measures. A principal task of channel stewardship, then, is to collect and share critical demand-chain and channel capability information. Thus, in addition to indicators such as sales, market share, costs, margins, and so on—all measures of output—it is important to track measures of input capacity, such as technical service, reach and coverage, order fill rate, and so on. The model's premise is that channel members make the appropriate investments in order to have a measurable impact on outcomes. Such input measures better correlate to customer attraction and to the satisfaction and loyalty such a system might engender.

So evaluations of customer satisfaction and loyalty are also very much part of the model. What's more, all these measures must be based on an assumption of how the channel effort will impact the needs of the demand chain, so you must have a clear idea of what the expected investments are and by whom. See figure 6-4 for an example. In short, a steward must monitor input, process, output, and outcome data.

Blending Power and Trust

The main idea is to encourage those channel stewards that have accumulated power to use it to build trust and transparency rather than to force

FIGURE 6-4

Performance assessment framework: An example

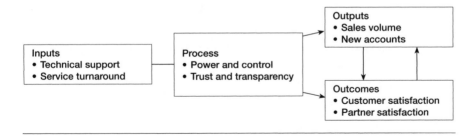

control and coercion. The idea is to trigger the virtuous, not the vicious, cycle into operation. There are two paths to achieving the channel steward's goals and objectives: one path, represented by the virtuous cycle A in figure 6-3, and the other, marked B, which we call the vicious cycle. In reality, channel stewards use a measured combination.[10]

Both paths may lead to the goals and objectives, but a judicious blend has a much better chance of attaining system performance so that the channel partners see the benefit of the value created by the channel. True, a channel member that enhances the channel value chain and the channel system's performance also gains additional power, but such power is rarely used because the other loops in the virtuous cycle play the primary role of influencing and aligning the channel.

The core of relationship development lies in the contact personnel on the two sides of a dyad. Relationship managers on both sides must foster the development of mutual trust. When trust levels increase sufficiently, these individuals will encourage their firms to invest and thereby increase commitment. Trust is built through delivering on promises made. It hinges on repeatedly achieving the agreed-to performance goals. Our research indicates that trust often is built when partners go beyond the call of duty to deliver a request. When mutual risks are taken on behalf of the partner, a culture of reciprocity sets in, ultimately expanding to increased commitment.

Interpersonal trust affects not only interorganizational commitment but also the nature of performance in a relationship. Partners become motivated not only to meet their partner's expectations under the agreement, but also to step outside agreement terms to help the other side when needed, elevating the relationship to a higher plane. Firms that invest in a relationship affect the availability of alternatives and increase their dependence levels. A more powerful party that has previously attempted to extract a disproportionate share of the surplus will now relent somewhat. In economic terms, this might be referred to as an adjustment for the lower risk that the more powerful party now perceives in the relationship. The contract (or agreement), although still not fully equitable (from one participant's perspective), will likely be more so than in the first round. These exchanges and subsequent rounds of negotiations will continue until an equitable equilibrium is obtained.

Much has been written about Wal-Mart's market power, and certainly it is not alone in wielding that kind of clout in its industry. The Home Depot in building materials, Best Buy in consumer electronics, Staples in office supplies, W. W. Grainger in electrical goods, and many others hold that type of unique position. Yet in addition to providing the shelf space and exposure for a variety of top brands, these powerful retailers have many healthy relationships with their suppliers, as the following excerpt illustrates.

> Wal-Mart also operates in a "partnering" mode, in which both sides swap information to streamline the flow of goods from raw materials to checkout counter. So while Newell Rubbermaid's "We [love] Wal-Mart" strategy can seem the ultimate in corporate vassalage, consider what Newell gets out of the deal: not only huge volume but, thanks to Everyday Low Prices, predictable volume, which lets it keep its factories running full and steady. There are no advertising costs, no "funny money." And Wal-Mart will even back up its trucks to Newell's factories. Many suppliers, including P&G, like the model so much that they've pushed it on their other customers.[11]

By contrast, in the vicious cycle, even though the channel protagonist may attain its goals and objectives, the trust among key individuals deteriorates. As a result, the channel partners experience a loss of commitment, and the channel system may unravel.

Channel Governance and Performance

If channel members are to be partners, they should share in building and accessing the data. If the data is seen as the property of only one member, it is seen as an attempt to own the customer and accumulate power in the relationship. At the same time, you cannot be oblivious to the realities of how power and control may play out in interorganizational relationships. In many channel systems, such data does not flow smoothly from end to end. Even if the members freely exchange transactional data—order generation, fulfillment, service, and pipeline inventory—they often mask crucial information on the performance of the demand chain with respect to customer needs and the real costs and margins along the supply chain.

This means that it will not be possible to successfully align a channel without active dialogue among the partners. Technology can provide useful input, but it cannot automatically monitor and guide channel performance. Each system will evolve its rules in keeping with its unique market position. There is no one-size-fits-all solution.[12] Only when a manufacturer also has a degree of influence can it be assured of gaining visibility all along the demand chain, and only then can it address customer needs and channel partners' goals at the same time.

Ultimately, channel coordination and management are a result of managers from several organizations getting together and agreeing on the rules of partnership. Especially when business is being transacted across two or more organizations, each with its own objectives, there must be mutual trust before the rules of optimization can kick in. Independent entities must agree to share data on customers, orders, and inventory transparently. When channel entities, for whatever reason, hoard and hide performance information about the demand chain and the channel value chain, they unwittingly diminish the value-enhancing capabilities of all members.

A high level of channel performance is a strong antidote to the use of power and control. Other aspects of interorganizational and interpersonal interactions take over. Trust and transparency become the key complements of a strategy to enhance the demand chain. Yet the system is anchored on clear measures of performance and mutual discussions by the players on their roles and their rewards.[13]

This does not mean that power and control, as a means of aligning the channel, will vanish, only that they will take on a secondary role. Ultimately, only those systems that are based on the logic of investments, inputs, and overall system performance will be sustainable in the long run.

7

Stewardship in Action I

Supplier Case Studies

HAVING TREATED the three key disciplines of channel steward-ship—mapping; building and editing; and aligning and influenc-ing—we now discuss case studies of several channel stewards and examine how they have attempted to implement the stewardship principles. We discuss suppliers as stewards in this chapter, followed by intermediaries as stewards in the next.

Recall the channel classification scheme offered at the end of chapter 4:

- Vertically integrated channels

- Third-party delegated channels

- Composite channels

We know that the structural outcomes of the building and editing process have many other variations and depend on the subsequent align-ing and influencing process. These three buckets enable us to analyze and discuss the disciplined ways in which skillful channel stewards, such as those discussed here, have implemented the stewardship principles. These suppliers have harmonized their demand-chain knowledge with the capa-bilities of their channels and have astutely combined the use of power with the engendering of trust to effectively align their channel partners.

Vertically Integrated Channels

In a vertically integrated system, the supplier controls all aspects of the channel value chain. The supplier may or may not own the manufacture of all components, but it must own the downstream channels. Further, even within the bounds of ownership, individual departments or divisions may have a degree of independence and separation; a supplier must coordinate these to achieve end-to-end visibility and influence.

Zara's Internal Alignment

Zara, a Spanish retail apparel chain known for its superb quick response system, provides a good example of a vertically integrated channel.[1] Zara has more than six hundred retail stores worldwide (mostly in Spain and throughout Europe), and unlike its competitors, which tend to make most of their goods overseas, Zara manufactures the bulk of its products in its home market, Spain. Only a small percentage of Zara's production is outsourced to plants in Portugal, Turkey, and other sources in Asia, but the more distant plants usually produce the less volatile items. Zara's strategy demands the flexibility and speed that only ownership can guarantee.

Zara's target customers—urban women aged eighteen to thirty-five—want fashionable merchandise but will not pay the steep prices of designer apparel from labels such as Gucci and Hermes. Yet in fashion apparel, high margins are necessary: they cover front-end design costs, support marketing efforts, and offset the steep markdowns suppliers take on goods that miss the mark.

Zara decided from the beginning that it would not try to anticipate fashion; instead, it waits for early trends to emerge and then adapts its designs. To do that effectively, its supply chain must get merchandise from design to retail counter within three to five weeks. (Top designer brands take nine to twelve months to cover the same ground.)

How does Zara's retail side, which faces the demand chain, coordinate and communicate with the manufacturing side, which makes the garments? As in most vertically integrated systems, this alignment is achieved through a merchandising group, which interprets demand and authorizes the appropriate production quantities.

Zara's merchandising group has a few unique characteristics. The group, called "the commercials," is made up of several teams, one for each major product line. These teams decide which fashions to follow, determine how to convert those sensors of the demand chain into a production plan, and decide how to allocate the merchandise to the stores. All individuals in the group work under one roof; in fact, they work side by side. In effect, the commercials group is an internal channel steward.

Here's how it works. A women's sportswear product-line team, for example, might include two designers and two product managers, who would be responsible for purchasing material, placing orders with the factories, and setting prices. Other individuals, called store product managers, serve as the main interface with the retail stores. Store product managers at Zara travel frequently, observing what customers and noncustomers in a given market wear; they also talk at length to the store managers to find out what kinds of fashions are selling (or not selling).

Retail store managers learn about newly available garments and replenishments from an offering developed and transmitted to them electronically by the commercials team. In consultation with store personnel, a retail store manager places an order, which is fulfilled by another team of product managers; these managers aggregate store orders and match them with availability at the distribution center. This information triggers a factory order for production.

Like other designers, Zara offers a winter collection and a summer collection. But the speed with which the company moves through its processes means that Zara can also introduce new items and revise existing offerings throughout the year. A consequence of Zara's approach to design, fulfillment, and manufacturing is that it does not have to predict what will be selling six months in the future; instead it needs to continually sense what customers want to buy and respond speedily.

One entity, the commercials team, is ultimately responsible for Zara's go-to-market strategy. But consider the number of steps it takes to align demand chain with supply. In a vertically integrated structure, the key alignment mechanism is the use of information; thus, at Zara, IT plays a critical role.

Just as important is the empowerment of a team that knows what to do with demand-chain information and can create a seamless connection between the demand chain and the channel value chain. Surprising as it may seem, even managers of internal departments at times feel a lack of trust or the organizational transparency needed to ensure a smooth coordination with their counterparts in an adjacent department. Internally, too, different departments are vested with different levels of power, which may come into play as the internal steward attempts to coordinate the channel value chain. That is why even in an integrated channel, the design of the human interface is key. Only when you minimize the opportunities for distortion among individuals across departments can you harness the power of information to coordinate the demand chain.

At Zara this interface has been superbly orchestrated by placing the product managers and store product managers in the same work space under a common chain of command (figure 7-1 shows the system). Zara circumvents interdepartmental miscommunication by virtually joining the store with the factory across the commercials desk. In other vertically integrated systems, such as at Dell, the integration is even more watertight because of the build-to-order system. The customer's demand chain very much commands what is needed from the channel value chain.

It would be a mistake to assume that vertical integration automatically promotes coordination. In systems like Zara's, where the two do not have such a tight fit, it is the design of the organizational and human interface that provides the integration.

Third-Party Delegated Channels

In third-party delegated systems, the supplier may not have control of the pipeline to the customer; in fact, the supplier may not even be able to see the customer from its vantage point. What's more, third-party intermedi-

FIGURE 7-1

Zara's coordination mechanisms

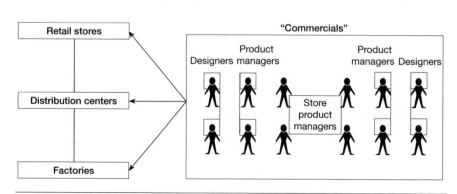

aries may or may not rely on the supplier for most of their business. The supplier, then, may or may not have the channel power to force the intermediary to fall in line with its channel policies.

Yet even in the worst case, astute channel stewards have been able to gain a measure of channel alignment *by focusing on the channel value chain.* What's needed is a careful, deliberate exercise in pooling the instruments of power: information, trust, and commitment. Examples of two suppliers' attempts to align follow. One supplier possessed significant channel power; the other did not.

Alignment in the Presence of Channel Power: Cisco

Cisco Systems, a firm that defines Internet infrastructure, illustrates the attempt to steward channels along functional lines in an ever-changing environment.[2] Indeed, Cisco's reseller program has been touted as a model for evolving an indirect sales strategy, and the firm is noted for the success of its working relationships with its supply-chain partners.

Founded in the mid-1980s, Cisco sold only 10 percent of its 1990 output (sales of $64 million) through value-added resellers. The remainder was sold through its own direct sales force. But by 2004, the company had turned this go-to-market strategy on its head. It sold nearly 90 percent of its $22 billion sales volume through value-added distributors.

It is instructive to follow the evolution of Cisco's channel strategy, especially in light of the double-digit growth it sustained for nearly ten years, which was punctuated by an abrupt slowdown in the industry beginning in 2001. When the industry slowed, Cisco began to reward its value-added partners based on their support of customers rather than on sales volume. Simultaneously, Cisco downsized its distribution intensity, unafraid to use its power to decide which organizations would continue to be part of its distribution system. Within the system, however, Cisco treated its chosen channel partners with great sensitivity and attempted to assist them in constructing business models that would boost the productivity of their working capital and their profits.

The Growth Years

Cisco's products—routers and switches—were the perfect components for the rapid growth in Internet infrastructure and for the networking boom that accompanied the golden age of information technology. Not only did thousands of new companies need technology platforms to get up and running, but also the competition from the dot-coms spurred brick-and-mortar companies to invest in Internet infrastructure.

During the sustained Internet boom of the 1990s, when healthy margins on routers and switches were assured, Cisco instituted a value-added reseller pyramid based on hardware sales volumes and other criteria, by which "Gold," "Silver," or "Premier" status was awarded to authorized resellers. Higher-status resellers received greater discounts and thus a higher profit margin. At the bottom of the pyramid, below the Premier level, was the plain and undifferentiated Authorized Reseller.

Each status level required that a reseller have a certain number of technicians and engineers who had been certified at Cisco School. Through its training facilities, both brick-and-mortar and Web-based, Cisco ran extensive courses for network professionals. On qualification, they received certifications such as CCDA (Cisco Certified Design Associate), CCNA (Cisco Certified Network Associate), and so on. VARs had to meet sales quotas to attain their status, regardless of their engineering qualifications, which were stated in terms of the FTE (full-time equivalent) of trained engineering personnel required at each level.

Within status levels, various criteria were applied so that partners at the same level received different discounts. As shown in figure 7-2, each level had to demonstrate dedicated capability, and toward that end resellers had to hire and train their people to acquire the Cisco certifications.

Cisco conducted its own sales and support operation, which supplied leads to VARs and closed and implemented deals for its own account.

Under this channel structure, Cisco quickly came to own the switch and router market. Although the company at one time had more than two thousand resellers in the United States, only about five hundred qualified for the top three categories. To grow with the rapidly exploding market for its products, the company added VARs wherever, and whenever, it made sense. Rarely was an intermediary denied product as long as it was able to justify the pull of customer demand. The higher-volume VARs were rewarded for their consistency by receiving higher discounts off list price, and this incentive, along with rapid market growth, minimized channel coordination issues.

Stewardship Changes with Market Decline

By the late 1990s, the Internet had propagated to the remote corners of the SMB (small and medium-sized business) space as well as the enter-

cused category. The idea is to leverage the strong part of the product line to gain a foothold for the weaker parts. This is particularly true of suppliers that want to expand their product or market base. The logic is straightforward: keeping competitors out makes sense, and the greater the distributor's dependence on the supplier, the greater the chance that it will promote the supplier's products and services. Even though many distributors carry complementary product lines, the supplier seldom encourages the idea of sharing the shelf with competitors.

But intermediaries have their own, equally logical agendas. Distributors prefer not to squander their investment and efforts on the weak part of a supplier's line. They would rather take on an alternative supplier's line, especially if it has strong products in the gaps left by the first supplier. Doing so not only strengthens the distributor's range and attracts customers, but it also helps it avoid overdependence on a single vendor's line (or a few vendors' lines). Just as the producer would like its distributors and dealers to be dedicated and loyal to its product line, the intermediary, too, would like its suppliers to grant it exclusive market territories.

Contentions Between Suppliers and Distributors

Now the dance begins in earnest as each party wields its market power and product power to secure an advantage. For example, because distributors are dependent on selling a variety of products, drawing the customer into the store is crucial. Sale of one product could lead to another, and so on. An intermediary needs foot traffic to give its business model a chance to work. So it must price products competitively to draw customers in. Generally, local competition hurts the margins of all intermediaries, and if this were to happen on several significant product lines, no one would profit. The manufacturer knows all this, but to increase market penetration it often tries to inject more distributors into each sales territory. From its perspective, intrabrand competition will likely lead to interbrand gains in market share. The logic rests on gaining increased attention from its intermediaries, hopefully without any of them turning sour.

Keep in mind that the one area that directly relates to the allocation of profit in the channel value chain is pricing. By that we mean discounts, rebates, holdbacks, and other allowances, along with the credits and debits that go with the list price. Producers want their products to get to the end customer with a minimal markup. From their perspective, the lower the price to the end customer, the higher the demand for their products. Of

prise space. Perhaps the best barometer of the heightened demand was the NASDAQ stock index, which rose from 1,835 in March 1998 to a high of 5,132 in March 2000. Then the bubble burst, and the NASDAQ plummeted to a low of 1,619 in April 2001.

Before the 2001 slowdown, demand for networking gear was so strong that money could be made by mere "box pushing." But after the downturn, only those resellers that could bring solutions were valued. Cisco had too many dealers to cover the significantly shrunken demand; the company knew it had to rationalize its channels.

In early 2001, Cisco announced a bold gambit. To address the needs of the changed environment, managers felt, the company had to aggressively support those intermediaries that would create demand, educate customers, and support them. So Cisco dropped volume requirements and made reseller discounts contingent on point-based specialization requirements in certain emerging technologies (see figure 7-2).

FIGURE 7-2

Cisco partners program pyramid

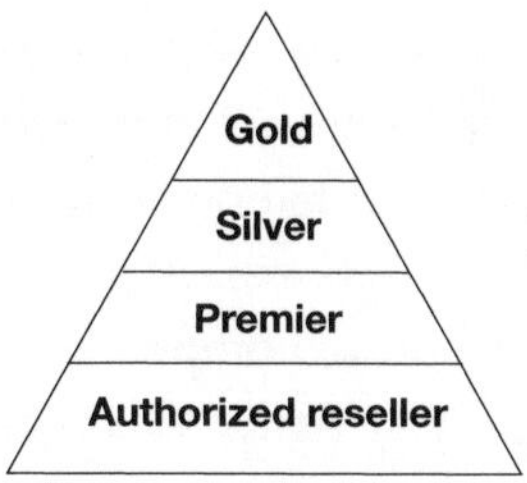

Partner program structure before 2001	Premier	Silver	Gold
Discount level	38%	40%	42%
Engineering requirements	3FTE	8FTE	16FTE
Support	8x5	8x5	24x7
Lab equipment	Demo	$40k	$100k
Volume requirements	Increasing ⟶		
Specialization	Optional	Optional	Optional

Partner program structure after 2001	Premier	Silver	Gold
Discount level	38%	40%	42%
Engineering requirements	3FTE	8FTE	16FTE
Support	8x5	8x5	24x7
Lab equipment	Demo	$40k	$100k
Volume requirements	None	None	None
Specialization	20 points	60 points	100 points

Pyramid (bottom to top): Authorized reseller / Premier / Silver / Gold

Source: Adapted from V. Rangan, "Cisco Systems: Managing the Go-to-Market Evolution," Case 505-006 (Boston: Harvard Business School, 2005). Used with permission.

Specialization points were awarded to resellers that built teams having the requisite expertise. It was a step beyond certification requirements, which applied to individuals; the specialization points applied to reseller entities. The changes affected Premier partners the most. For example, network specialization, which earned 20 points, required that the following team be in place: an account manager, a sales engineer responsible for network planning and design, and a field engineer responsible for implementation and support. IP telephony—a hot new technology for which Cisco was attempting to establish a position—earned 40 points, and so on.

Under the new system, points were awarded for exceeding the minimums. Points for customer satisfaction were awarded for exceeding numerical targets based on a customer satisfaction survey. The surveys were conducted by a third-party research house hired by Cisco. Resellers could access their results and get suggestions and training from Cisco on how to improve.

As a result of these changes and the higher degree of specialization and certification needed to qualify, nearly half of Cisco's dealers were eliminated, and only about a thousand dealers (Gold, Silver, and Premier) were retained. Before, two or three companies with a solutions approach would compete with seven or eight "ankle-biters" (those doing product fulfillment with deep discounting), but the field was now tilted toward the solutions providers, reflecting Cisco's careful approach in keeping with the new channel environment.[3]

The absence of volume requirements made Cisco's channel structure unique in the industry. The transition was to an entirely value-based system, where specialization points were weighted according to Cisco's view of future demand for a technology. Cisco's channel editing brought it closer to customers' needs and, when implemented successfully, would endear it to its customers. It was also more selective, providing opportunities for channel members to make stable margins without the fear of competition.

Initially Cisco had used its product power to gain intensive channel coverage. But it realized that this aggressive scheme destroyed value for many of its channel partners, and when the markets ceased to grow, the company pulled back to rationalize. Additionally, Cisco instituted a series of schemes to assist resellers in managing their working capital, inventory levels, and customer satisfaction. The intention was to make them more profitable. Cisco worked out elaborate models of reseller financial performance and, based on benchmarked criteria, enabled them to make changes in key operating parameters to boost performance. Cisco often had 50 percent or more of a reseller's business portfolio, and thus its management recommendations had bite and credibility.

By 2004, Cisco's dealers' return on working capital had increased by nearly 300 percent, their return on invested capital was up by about 50 percent, and their average customer satisfaction index had gone up from 4.0 to about 4.5 (on a 5-point scale). The Cisco example demonstrates the will required of channel stewards to make difficult rationalization decisions. In the end, those that remained in the system were true partners in Cisco's value enhancement scheme for customers. The partners benefited, and so did customers.

Alignment in the Absence of Channel Power: Atlas Copco

Cisco had power as the market leader. But how can smaller companies with limited power embark on channel stewardship? Atlas Copco, a worldwide leader in compressed air and hydraulics, is a case in point. Based in Sweden, Atlas Copco entered the U.S. industrial compressor market in the 1950s. During the 1980s and early 1990s, the company made great strides in gaining a respectable share from its leading competitors, especially Ingersoll-Rand, the U.S. market leader at that time.[4]

Market Entry

Atlas Copco's entry strategy was innovative. The industry norm had been to use full-line distributors with guaranteed territorial exclusivity. In return, the distributors (called air houses) focused on one primary supplier. The development of selective (and brand-exclusive) distribution was driven by the nature of the technology. Reciprocating compressors, the original and most widespread technology, required field-support facilities because the machines experienced much wear and tear, and subsequently needed spare parts and repair. Parts and service revenues were a critical component of a dealer's profit equation. Loss of territorial exclusivity would compromise after-market revenues from the installed base.

In exchange for territorial exclusivity, distributors provided brand exclusivity. An additional reason was the heavy investment required to hold compressor inventory. It would be impossible, therefore, to break into the distribution system of incumbents, especially market leaders like Ingersoll-Rand, which had close to 30 percent market share. Ingersoll-Rand had sewn up the relationship with most front-line air houses.

It was against this background that Atlas Copco went against conventional wisdom to gain entry. It focused on its strongest line of compressors, the Z series, based on rotary screw technology. This technology was most appropriate for certain kinds of plant air applications, such as in semiconductor assembly, because of the oil-free air it provided. Importantly, however, it did not give distributors the same opportunity as the reciprocating compressors to make revenues and margins on spare parts and related repair services. Atlas Copco therefore provided relatively higher margins on the original new equipment to offset the downstream loss on spare parts sales. It also encouraged its dealers to seek maintenance contracts from customers to offset the lost revenues.

Having found a foot in the door with its best product, Atlas Copco did not insist that its dealers give it exclusive representation, at least initially. Neither did the company promise its distributors selective territories. It gained a footprint of about eighty-five of nearly six hundred potential distributors for this product. Many of them did not have the scale or capability of Ingersoll-Rand's distributors, but they were the best the company could do. Until then, Atlas Copco had made no effort to manage the portfolio of functions that its channel partners brought to serve their end customers.

Consolidation

All that changed when Atlas Copco gained a respectable market share of about 10 percent. Even though Ingersoll-Rand still dominated—with about 30 percent of market share—Atlas Copco managers overhauled the distribution system to reward those dealers that provided difficult field functions. After conducting a distribution audit, the company discovered that only about one-third of its distributors, classified as A distributors, were predominant air houses. With more than 80 percent of their revenues from the compressor line, these distributors were targeted as having the potential to give Atlas Copco a larger share of their wallet.

At the same time, because so much depended on compressor revenues, these distributors could also be coached and coaxed to provide the appropriate channel effort to gain share from competitors. Yet several of them concentrated on selling what the company's managers termed "easy-to-sell" machines—the Z series compressors—without helping the company broaden its product and customer base. Those efforts were reserved for complementary products from other suppliers. Even though selling Z machines required engineering skills, the product line had earned a stellar reputation because of its demonstrated superiority and did not require the same sales intensity and coverage as the small compressors. Atlas Copco had a clear opportunity to leverage its entry and expand its share of such distributors' shelves.

At the other extreme were those dealers that worked hard to sell lower- and middle-range compressors, especially Atlas Copco's reciprocating line. These products were hard to sell because of severe competition and a lack of demonstrated superiority. Yet these distributors made the investment and the effort via intense sales support and promotion. Because many of such sales involved small compressors, distributors' revenues were smaller and their margins even tighter. Atlas Copco wanted to train, reward, and motivate these distributors to pick up the engineering skills to take on a larger (and perhaps the distinguishing) part of its product line and thus move up in revenues and profitability.

The audit also revealed that more than one-third of Atlas Copco distributors were classified as C distributors, because less than 10 percent of their sales came from compressors. The company reasoned that it would be difficult to coax these distributors into bringing specific investments to the compressor line, and therefore they would have to be replaced in the long run.

Rewarding Channel Effort

To rationalize its distribution system and reward distributors for performing tasks to generate and fulfill demand, Atlas Copco introduced a three-level franchising system (see figure 7-3). The main goal of this system was to have dealers advance through all three levels. First, they had to demonstrate their capability in selling the commercially difficult products. After that, and after they demonstrated the technical competence to sell more complex products, they earned the higher-level franchise. Ultimately, dealers could advance to an agency agreement where, for all practical purposes, they would act as the company's extended field service arm; they would derive lucrative revenues by maintaining the highly engineered and complex part of the firm's product line, many of which were sold directly by Atlas Copco. In effect, the three levels demanded growing levels of channel expertise, with different levels of rewards. The company thus used product levels as a proxy for the different levels of effort.

FIGURE 7-3

Atlas Copco's three-level product franchising policy

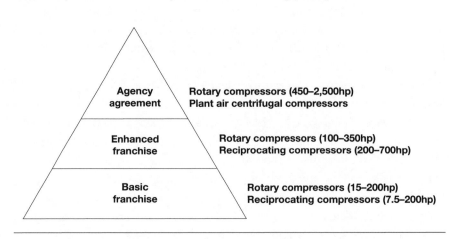

Agency agreement — Rotary compressors (450–2,500hp) / Plant air centrifugal compressors

Enhanced franchise — Rotary compressors (100–350hp) / Reciprocating compressors (200–700hp)

Basic franchise — Rotary compressors (15–200hp) / Reciprocating compressors (7.5–200hp)

Market leader Ingersoll-Rand used a variation of the product proxy idea in differentiating the value provided by the different tiers of its distribution partners. The company franchised its distributors not only by geographical territory but also by product classification. It had eight product groups, spanning a product line ranging from 5hp reciprocating compressors to 450hp rotary compressors and even larger reciprocating and centrifugal compressors. Individual distributor agreements covered one or more product classifications.[5]

Atlas Copco's distribution rationalization policy led it to part company with many of its C-level distributors. Only those distributors that provided the full line of service across a full range of products found a place in its revitalized network. As the company's distribution channel evolved, especially in the late 1990s, it increasingly began to buy out distributors that did not meet its support and service standards. By 2004, the company had consolidated its distribution channel to thirty-four distributors in fifty-seven locations; in addition, it operated eighteen company-owned distributors called compressor centers. Its own direct sales force sold and serviced all compressors above 350hp. Ray Löfgren, who became president of the North American compressor line in 2002, put it starkly: "We have steadily evolved our three-level franchising systems into a one-level policy, where every distributor is now expected to perform at the highest level."[6]

As this case shows, when a supplier does not have the power to force channels to allocate effort according to the needs of the demand chain, it can align the channel by skillfully deploying a focused source of power, in this case the Z compressor product line. Once it gains a toehold and some market access, it can use rewards to influence its partners to align with customers' needs. In Atlas Copco's case, that meant designing a franchise system that gave access to an increasingly attractive product line according to the efforts of intermediaries.

Then, when the three-level franchising policy had outlived its usefulness, Atlas Copco structured a more focused distribution policy with uniform requirements across the system. As a result, the company increased its market share to nearly 18 percent by the end of 2004.

Composite Channels

Composites, as we've said, are partially integrated channels. Suppliers work through channel intermediaries but retain the option of addressing some demand-chain requirements themselves. A supplier might directly influence customers with regard to product choice and perhaps even negotiate an appropriate price or volume arrangement, leaving the rest of the channel flows (such as delivery, installation, and repair) to its channel partners.

Whenever a supplier bypasses its intermediary, it opens the possibility of creating friction. The stewardship principles we have advocated (the building and editing principles) imply that a supplier should take on those functions that it can better perform, but such a move can convey a lack of confidence in the intermediary's capabilities.

Managing this frustration calls for a mixture of carrot and stick. The supplier must demonstrate and use its product or brand power to generate and attract customer demand, and then use its good relations with its channel partner to gain effective fulfillment through its channel capabilities. In essence, suppliers construct composite channels having some direct and some indirect elements.

Becton Dickinson's Evolution to a Composite Channel

Composite channels often can serve as an effective way to align a channel value chain. The composite channel of medical supplier Becton Dickinson (BD) provides a good example. BD's preanalytical systems division, a maker of various medical devices, had the brand pull to influence customer

FIGURE 7-4

Becton Dickinson's composite channels

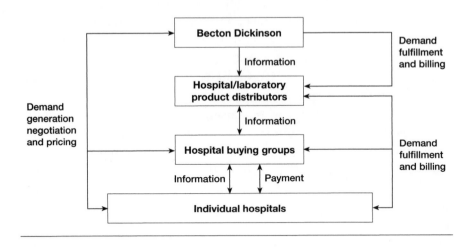

choice (see figure 7-4).[7] Its Vacutainer blood collection systems were widely regarded as high-quality innovative devices with easy-to-use color coding, and its wide variety of products covered a multitude of blood tests. The tubes that were used to collect and carry the specimen, as well as the accompanying needle systems (called "sharps"), were considered superior to anything that competitors offered. In this product category, BD had an 80 percent market share in the United States.

Market Evolution

BD's evolution to the composite channel illustrates what happens when an astute channel steward does its mapping homework to understand the interplay of the core forces in its channel environment. Until the mid-1980s, BD sold entirely through its distributors, which generated and fulfilled orders. After an upheaval in the U.S. health-care structure in the mid-1980s, BD began negotiating order quantities and prices directly with hospital buying groups, leaving its distributors to fulfill orders and collect payments. At that time there was massive pressure on health-care costs (and that pressure continues). By the mid-1980s, with health-care costs continuing to outpace inflation and comprising nearly 12 percent of the annual U.S. GDP, there were several dramatic changes in the environment.

Chief among them was that the U.S. government changed the way it reimbursed hospitals for Medicare patients (enrollees in the government insurance program for U.S. citizens older than sixty-five). Previously, hospitals had been reimbursed for all costs incurred in serving those patients. Most observers agreed that this cost-plus system did not reward hospitals for efficiency. Then federal legislation introduced a payment approach based on diagnosis-related groups (DRGs). Under the new system, payments were based on national and regional costs for each DRG, and not on the hospital's costs. Even though Medicare patients comprised only 40 percent of the patient pool, private insurers soon followed suit.

By the early 1990s, the virtual monopoly of indemnity plans in the health insurance industry was broken. The so-called managed care revolution began to take an increasing slice of the health-care pie. All this had the intended consequence of cost conservation at most hospitals. As a result, if they were not part of multihospital chains, they began to affiliate with buying groups to gain economies of scale and to reduce purchase costs.

The Composite Transition

BD chose to conduct sales negotiations directly with customers and their buying representatives rather than let its distributors advocate on its behalf. The reasons for this move are not hard to fathom. Multibrand distributors would be hard pressed to promote only one brand, especially in an environment where customers were attempting to reduce costs. It was more important for distributors to keep customers than to push a brand on a reluctant customer and face losing the entire business.

Keep in mind that once a supplier influences customer demand, it is in a position to parcel out that order to the appropriate distributor at an appropriate margin. The distributor that provides the logistics is then rewarded for its investments to support the distribution infrastructure but not for generating the demand. The revised margin represents an adequate return on the intermediary's investment, but the supplier is not obliged to overcompensate. Distributors that show they can operate effectively at that compensation level are rewarded with the bulk of the supplier's orders and thus make up the loss of higher margins with higher volumes.

The top distributors in the medical device market were powerful because of their size and market reach. For example, American Hospital Supply (AHS), then the top distributor, was about three times as large as Becton Dickinson. Through a series of mergers and acquisitions, AHS is now part of Cardinal Health, which reported revenues of $50 billion in 2003 (its Scientific Products Distribution arm distributed BD's products). In 2003, BD reported revenues of about $4 billion. In the same period, its preanalytic systems division did a little less than $1 billion.

Interestingly, the industry's buying groups are just as powerful as suppliers and distributors. For example, Premier and Novation, the two largest buying groups, reported purchases of nearly $24 billion each in 2004. With one stroke of the pen, such purchasing agents, which often control large chunks of the market (as much as 20 percent or more), can swing the fortunes of suppliers. That's why BD not only called on them for price negotiations, but also called on end customers—the hospital laboratories—to specify the product and create the pull. In this way, BD made the critical pitch to the customer and, if need be, weighed in with a price to reel in the orders. After the deal was closed with the customer and the buying group, the distributor was the most appropriate fulfillment entity because it also served customers' other needs and not just the focused items made by one supplier. Thus, needles, syringes, blood collection tubes, sutures, bandages, and other supplies could be efficiently bundled by a logistics agent for delivery every week, or sooner as needed.

In practice, there are many types of composite channels, all aiming to guide the customer's desired bundle of functions in the most efficacious manner. As noted at the beginning of this chapter, our review of composite channels to this point has been limited to channels engineered by suppliers, especially those with considerable clout in the end-customer market. When there is demand uncertainty in the end market, a powerful supplier often finds it easier to take on the critical demand-influencing functions. But because the powerful supplier in BD's case controlled more than 80 percent of the market demand, it would not be hard to get the intermediary to fall into line. From the intermediary's perspective, the relationship is not as one-sided as it may appear. The supplier needs the distributor's economies of scope: the ability to put together a product or service bundle for the customer.

What about suppliers that do not have channel power? What if their product, technology, or brand is not influential in determining customer demand? What if it is the distributor that wields the power by providing access to key customer markets? How does the notion of a composite channel work then? In such cases, the supplier typically plays a constructive role on the distributor's team. In the blood-collection needles and syringes market, smaller suppliers like Greiner are dependent on the stewardship of their distributors or buying groups.

Under careful stewardship, a composite channel is always led by the demand chain, no matter which partner ultimately fulfills customer demand. Consider the composite combination used by window coverings supplier Hunter Douglas, introduced in chapter 6. Hunter Douglas makes its product range widely available through home-construction specialty stores like The Home Depot, mass merchandisers like JC Penney, and others. At most of these locations, customers obtain product information rather than take home the product. Customers choose from a range of styles and designs and then customize their measurements. If desired, the retailer can also arrange installation. The customized order is then manufactured and shipped to the store or the installer for final installation.

This arrangement is a classic composite, where demand is generated through the combined effort of the supplier's brand pull and the retail store's convenient platform. Customers shop for window coverings in the context of complementary home decorating products and often demand a choice of brands and variety. Order entry happens at the retail interface, order fulfillment is handled by the manufacturer, and installation may involve yet another intermediary, perhaps an outside service provider.

Composite channels require considerable coordination and conversations among the channel partners. Strikingly, however, the conversations change as manufacturers and distributors together try to improve their market positions by giving customers more of what they want and need. The level and quality of customer inputs increase, and the relay race of traditional channels starts to become more of a team effort. Moreover, the structure of the channel begins to evolve proactively, driven by channel partners working in concert toward a common goal. As customer input is increasingly considered fundamental to channel design, the various members of a channels-to-market team pool their special skills to deliver a channel value chain to meet their customers' needs.

A composite channel is not a silver bullet, however, and it is important to underscore its management challenges. It is hard to spin off channel functions from distributors to yourself, and vice versa. Channels simply cannot work as an on–off switch. The channel partner must make long-term investments to support functions, and the returns may take a long time to come.

Thus, after you make a composite allocation, it makes sense to fine-tune the existing arrangements. Designing appropriate incentives is at the heart of keeping a composite channel well aligned. In a vertically integrated structure, coordination can be mandated; here it must be courted with performance rewards.

Toward Virtual Integration

The ultimate purpose of channel stewardship is to integrate the efforts of the channel partners to effectively address end customers' demand-chain needs. But in doing so, stewardship also calls for an appropriate return to channel partners. The process, then, necessitates an in-depth connection to the channel value chain, end to end. In attempting to seal that connection—and no matter which channel design a company is a party to—most successful supplier stewards attempt to create a virtually integrated channel system.[8]

In this system, channel partners act as though they are an extended arm of the supplier. A channel partner's primary role is to assist the supplier, even though the partner may also participate in creating or expanding the pie. These distributors may or may not be exclusive to the supplier and may carry competing lines. Invariably, all the intermediaries are independent entities with no supplier ownership. It is purely their drive for personal gain that motivates their buy-in to this arrangement.

The key is to build a system in which the supplier can leverage the channel to act as though it is an extension of itself. Thus, a supplier might align the channel to gain visibility on the demand-chain side, although alignment will still depend on the nature of the distribution agreements and other factors (such as intermediary size) and on the importance of complementary lines in relation to the supplier's offerings. The independent channel partners must see adequate financial returns if the system is to be viable in the long run.

Virtually integrated systems work best if the channel partners' level of mutual dependency is high. Aligning the demand chain and the channel value chain, then, is a matter of programming the various flows to ensure harmony. The critical driver of such systems is the end-to-end visibility of end customers and the commitment of all parties to each other's success.

As you know from earlier chapters, commitment by itself, without the accompanying trustworthy interactions among the individuals representing the channel entities, does not ensure success. Value chain harmonization must proceed hand in hand with building and nurturing of trust and transparency. Zara was already vertically integrated, and Cisco had the size, scale, and technology to engage in a virtually integrated channel. But that was not the case with Atlas Copco; its efforts were an attempt to get there. BD, too, because of its product power and associated brand reputation, was able to program its composite channels to yield an unclouded view of its end users. This does not mean that smaller-market-share players cannot shape virtual channels. But they must take a different approach, relying on trust and transparency first.

A Virtual Channel: Haworth Office Furniture

Consider the channels-to-market strategy of office furniture maker Haworth.[9] This $1.7 billion (2004 sales) manufacturer sold its range of office furniture through nearly three hundred independent distributors in the United States. Of these dealers, Haworth had a close relationship with about fifty "preferred" dealers, which typically carried the Haworth line exclusively along with some complementary lines (less than 25 percent of a dealer's sales).

Haworth was not the number 1, nor even the number 2, supplier in the office furniture industry. These distinctions went to Herman Miller and Steelcase, respectively. But by carefully stewarding its channel system, Haworth had gained considerable influence and coverage in the market. Its "preferred" distributors, which accounted for 80 percent of sales, did not carry a competing line, and Haworth in turn sold directly to only a limited number of end-user accounts. Everything else belonged to the dealers, no matter who generated the order. Haworth had almost four hundred sales associates generating orders. Thus, Haworth and its distributors had their goals well aligned and highly dependent on each other. For all practical purposes, Haworth's distributors acted as though they were solely representing the supplier, a case of virtual integration.

Nearly 80 percent of the company's products are built to order in its facility in Holland, Michigan. Traditionally, its dealers called on customers, discussed options, and faxed the orders. The factory communicated with the dealers about projected delivery dates as well as any order changes. Depending on dealer and order size, orders were shipped either to the dealer or to the customer site. The dealer was responsible for the assembly and installation of the furniture at the customer site (see the left side of figure 7-5).

Although the system functioned well, during the mid-1990s Haworth's large customers became involved in e-commerce and pressed Haworth to

FIGURE 7-5

Haworth: Promoting virtual integration

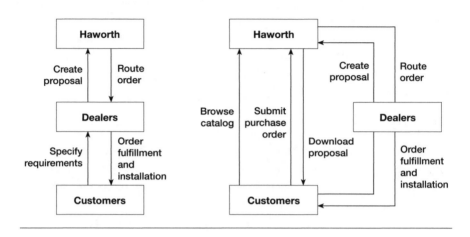

automate its channel. From the outset, Haworth brought its dealer net-work into the design of the new system, designed by Comergent Technologies, an innovative Silicon Valley start-up. Dealers played an important part in the selling and service process, which the new model attempted to capture. Beyond the pure sales effort, dealers were essential in product delivery, assembly, and after-sale service—all key components of the customer demand chain.

To improve its presale activities with customers and to be more responsive in fulfilling orders, however, Haworth needed a more direct connection to the demand chains. All key decisions in the design phase were routed through the company's twelve-member Dealer Advisory Council. Another ten senior Haworth managers attended the council deliberations. Through its past stewardship, Haworth had earned its dealers' trust, and in turn they were willing to provide the end-to-end visibility required by the e-commerce application.

Overall, the alignment of the channel provided its customers with a closed feedback loop (see the right side of figure 7-5). Customers could go directly to Haworth via its Web site, but dealers remained in the process, receiving and installing orders. Or customers could work directly with the dealers, but again Haworth stayed in the loop with its interactive catalog site and automated order entry. The selected Comergent system was hosted by a third party and required no investment from dealers, only access to an Internet browser.

Since installation of the Comergent system, Haworth's dealers spend more time actively selling to customers than managing accounts. Haworth realized a 30 percent reduction in the cost of order fulfillment, and a 50 percent reduction in sales cycle time. This channel design is a win-win for Haworth and its dealers.

Lessons of Stewardship

A channel steward must make a disciplined attempt to organize intermediaries according to their level of functional expertise and to design compensation schemes that reflect the nature of the tasks at each level. Many suppliers are guilty of using a one-dimensional quantity or volume discount scheme to discriminate between the levels. In some cases, they award points for certain investments, such as demonstration facilities, logistics facilities, and so on. These arrangements are fine if they are an outcome of a disciplined channel audit, such as the one we outlined in the six steps described in chapter 4. Lacking such a process, the channel compensation becomes a roundabout way of implementing the supplier's vision rather than being based on customers' requirements.

Nothing precludes suppliers from having a differential compensation structure for each of its product groups based on the technical and commercial effort of bringing these products to market. It may seem confusing to structure a range of incentives and discounts for a variety of product tiers that distributors may support, but if these differences are based on the different levels of specialization called for, suppliers must find ways to develop the appropriate policies to carry them through to end users.

A composite arrangement is a useful alternative, especially when a channel member seeking stewardship feels blocked from viewing and influencing customers' needs. Such a scheme not only provides an avenue for gaining visibility to end users, but it also helps motivate the other channel partners to fall in line with the team's goals. Composite channels may present an ideal opportunity to blend power with trust and transparency to promote a high level of channel performance.

Information technology, by itself, will not create the magic of a stewardship culture. Fundamental issues regarding channel value chain harmonization, compensation, and governance must be addressed first. But when these elements are in place, IT provides the platform for accelerating the goals of the channel.

Underlying all this is the pressing need to conduct periodic assessments of the channel with respect to the stewardship concepts outlined in chapter 6. Conversations should reflect a constructive attempt to address the gap between the demand chain and channel capabilities rather than the contentions you saw in chapter 5. That calls for regular, collaborative evaluations of channel performance, and these can come only if the relationship is based on trust. That will happen when all parties are aligned in the direction of enhancing the system's value and allocating the returns fairly. Such behavior promotes transparency and makes it easier to coordinate. Coordination in turn promotes performance, and the virtuous cycle kicks in.

8

Stewardship in Action II

The Intermediary's Perspective

C HAPTER 7 EXPLAINED how several suppliers orchestrated the key disciplines of stewardship to align their channel systems. Intermediaries, too, can be exemplary channel stewards. Often, the nature of the customer demand chain gives them the perfect vantage position.

Consider the arena of home construction. The top eight home improvement companies accounted for 88 percent of all sales in 2003. The Home Depot led the list with $64.8 billion in sales, followed by Lowe's with $30.8 billion.[1] In the home office and stationery sector, the top eight companies accounted for 78 percent of sales, with Staples accounting for $13.1 billion, followed by Office Depot with $12.3 billion. There are also powerful intermediaries in wholesale distribution; Arrow Electronics, Bergen Brunswig (pharmaceuticals), and Hughes Supply (construction supplies) are only a few of the many large intermediaries thriving in their respective sectors.[2]

As more intermediary companies become consolidators, selling goods from an increasingly large pool of suppliers, the list of sizable distributors wielding considerable clout continues to grow.

Even in industries that aren't consolidating, the size and reach of the dominant intermediaries make them a force to be reckoned with. In others, their size and customer reach alone make them an important force. Consider W. W. Grainger, one of the largest distributors in the United States. With $4.6 billion in sales (2003), primarily in the distribution of electrical components, parts, and supplies, Grainger had 394 branches spread across fifty states.[3]

These powerful intermediaries are natural candidates for the role of channel steward. Smaller companies, however, can also wear the mantle of steward successfully. The problem has been that most intermediaries, regardless of their size, seldom use their channel position to their greatest advantage. Historically, intermediaries were created to carry inventory, break bulk, and provide an assortment of goods, services, and credit to end customers. Now, with new technology and IT tools, much more is possible.

Many intermediaries are the only entity that sees customers at the point of purchase, but they fail to take advantage of that access. What's more, mired in strategies that address only their own needs, they often fail to recognize their potential for realigning channel capabilities to better meet customer needs and increase the size of the pie across the channel. As a result, these intermediaries are often reluctant to develop new markets and new product applications. They tend to operate on gross (and net) margin metrics rather than on ROI, and so they often lose the ability to distinguish profitable from unprofitable customers.

This chapter explores the notion that intermediaries, as well as suppliers, can make excellent channel stewards. To be sure, the opportunities we discuss are more readily apparent to large, powerful intermediaries. But the lessons are no less actionable for smaller distributors. The secret truly is not scale, but perspective.

Wal-Mart: The Classic Intermediary Steward?

Wal-Mart provides an excellent example of how an intermediary—albeit one of the most powerful—can be an effective steward in some instances and perhaps a power monger in others. The company has trained its customers to look for "everyday low prices" on products ranging from perishable groceries to housewares and apparel. In turn, it passes that expectation to suppliers, which are compelled to make steep price concessions. With $250 billion in sales in 2003, the company's clout is clear.

Wal-Mart as a Channel Steward

With some of its several supply chains, Wal-Mart conducts itself as a true steward because suppliers that play by its rules end up benefiting. Indeed, according to one report, "Operating margins of household product makers [that sell to Wal-Mart] actually grew 48% between 1992 and 2001; food processors' went up 30%; soft drink makers' rose 14%."[4]

How does Wal-Mart do it? First, the entire supply chain to Wal-Mart is automated to connect customers with factories (with buffer points in between). The company installed a retail link information network (a $4 billion IT capability) in 1991 and has since offered its suppliers point-of-scan data by store.[5] For example, Procter & Gamble, one of the most powerful consumer product brands, has EDI (electronic data interchange) links to Wal-Mart's stores. When inventory falls to a target number, product is automatically replenished from P&G warehouses and factories.

The result is immediate supply-chain cost reductions, in one case 40 cents per shipping case, split evenly between the supplier and Wal-Mart.[6] From a stewardship perspective, however, a second-order benefit is much more important: the links tell suppliers how their products are moving at different times in the different stores in the different geographical markets. Wal-Mart provides the data conveniently and freely to many of its suppliers. It wants them to be in tune with its efforts to provide customers the best fulfillment at the best price.

Wal-Mart stewards the channel in the interests of its customers, but its channel partners also benefit. In these situations, Wal-Mart exemplifies the principles of stewardship. But this does not mean that suppliers like Procter & Gamble and Coca-Cola do not have power; in fact, they have enormous power *with their consumer franchise*. But Wal-Mart customers go to its stores primarily because they trust the Wal-Mart value proposition. They may look for national brands, but that choice is secondary to the choice of the store. Without the power of the national brands at everyday low prices, however, Wal-Mart would lose its appeal to its customers. It is a symbiotic relationship. The brands and Wal-Mart need each other.

Wal-Mart as a Power Monger

A *Fast Company* article chronicles the bankruptcy of pickle maker Vlasic.[7] After market tests confirmed that gallon jars moved fast at $3, Wal-Mart forced its supplier to extend the pricing to all three thousand stores. The gallon jar of pickles at $3 became, according to the article, "a devastating success." It started to cannibalize Vlasic's sales in supermarkets, where the prorated price of its quart offering was nearly four times the price at Wal-Mart. As the company's profits from pickles started to shrink, its managers attempted to renegotiate prices with Wal-Mart but were rebuffed with veiled threats regarding Vlasic's other products being sold through Wal-Mart, and even the possibility of having a competitor replace the Vlasic shelf space. We have not talked to Wal-Mart or Vlasic to verify the *Fast Company* report, but the underlying principles are not hard to discern.

Wal-Mart's power comes from its scale and access to millions of consumers. If Wal-Mart uses its scale to bring value to its customers and fair returns to its suppliers, that is a good thing, and it epitomizes what channel stewardship is all about. If, however, that same scale is used to crush its competitors (in this case, supermarkets), and unwittingly its own suppliers, then Wal-Mart has destroyed long-term value for its consumers. It is a delicate balance and often not easy to calibrate.

As we have pointed out, in the interests of the system and its end users, channel stewards often must make tough decisions about who stays in the system and who leaves. We admire Cisco for making such a call. In the interests of its customers, Wal-Mart, too, at times may have had to squeeze its supply-chain partners for low prices. But if such behavior is chronic and untenable for the supplier, and if the intermediary's power is the only reason for its sustenance, then there is a problem. If, on the other hand, the lower price is aimed at addressing its consumers' needs, and when that goal is accompanied by an effort to keep its suppliers (of those products) healthy, then it has indeed demonstrated stewardship qualities.

How Many Cooks in the Kitchen?

The Wal-Mart case raises a valid question: can there be more than one channel steward in the same channel system, especially when there are two equally powerful entities attempting to serve customers? Could one be a supplier, and another an intermediary? The answer is an emphatic no. There can be only one steward at the helm of any given distribution channel. In some cases, the supplier is in a better position, and in other cases, the distributor or retailer is more suited to the role. (Sometimes, the supplier would be the more natural candidate but lacks the vision to step into the role.)

The steward, then, is the channel member that is most cognizant of the other partners' efforts in the channel value chain and of the need to reward them appropriately. With a steward in place, there is no incentive for another partner to jockey for a parallel stewardship or leadership position. Only when the focus changes from stewardship to power do multiple channel leaders emerge, but as you have seen, channel power battles are shortsighted and not in line with the concept of stewardship.

For improved performance over the long term, it is more important to gain and be part of an alignment that improves channel value chain performance and your own bottom line, than to be drawn into a contest of wills. Let us be clear: this does not mean that brand builders like Coca-Cola and Procter & Gamble should abandon their brand investments. Without this pull they would not gain shelf space at Wal-Mart. Moreover, it is precisely this brand power that sways consumers after they are in the store. Even more importantly, consumers have been attracted and habituated to the brand by means of the pull exerted at vending machines, other points of purchase, advertising, and a dozen other influence points. This pull spills over when they go to Wal-Mart. Without powerful brands, channel profits could dissipate away to the power retailer, as you saw in chapter 5.

How, then, should powerful suppliers work with intermediary stewards that have the scale, the customer reach, and the product scope to effectively take on the ownership of channels? If the supplier's power comes from product advantages or brand equity derived from its customers' preferences, then it's a viable alternative for the supplier to construct and administer a composite channel. This usually works if the supplier also has its own route to interacting and influencing the demand chain (recall the discussion in chapter 7 on composite channels).

If the supplier does not have access to such a resource, it is forced to work with, rather than through, the channel partner. Inevitably the dynamic of the power interchange will come into play, and either the supplier or the intermediary must rise above such skirmishes to focus on the benefits of harmonizing the demand chain with the channel value chain. Ultimately, the idea is to create an environment in which a channel steward emerges and the other parties can play constructive roles. This is what we see in Procter & Gamble's relationship with Wal-Mart.

Finally, if the supplier does not have brand power, scale, or alternative sources (legal or institutional), then it must learn to play as part of a channel stewarded by an intermediary. Even under those circumstances, however, it can play a productive role in helping a steward emerge. The same goes for an intermediary that must play as part of a system stewarded by a powerful supplier.

The Principles of Intermediary Stewardship

Large intermediaries have obvious stewardship opportunities. Such entities should distinguish between the power they have because of their size and the power they might wield as stewards. The latter is a far more nuanced strategy of understanding and orchestrating the demand chain. Scale and size are used only as instruments to gain alignment.

Smaller intermediaries should note that expertise in the channel value chain, and not size, is the key lever of stewardship. One cautionary note: it is only natural to band together with similar organizations as part of a trade association to bulk up their countervailing power. In general, however, these associations do a better job of protecting entrenched interests than of creating new value. So the onus is on the intermediaries themselves to seek and implement ways to enhance the channel value chain.

The stewardship principles for intermediaries are nearly identical to those for suppliers. Intermediaries confront the same four forces: the demand chain, channel capability (referring here to the capability of the network of suppliers), supplier power positions (referring here to the brand power exerted by suppliers), and the force of competitors' actions. These forces are impacted by the same antecedents discussed in chapter 2: regulation, trade practices, customer buying behavior, technology, and so on. Whether supplier or intermediary, an astute channel steward should first map these forces to understand the context of their evolution and then exert the appropriate influence to align the demand chain with the channel capability. Given that we build on the same framework from previous chapters, we highlight in this chapter only the key aspects to draw the parallel and underscore the nuances.

The essential principles of intermediary stewardship, then, are as follows:

1. Create offerings that address demand-chain needs and, if possible, further influence and shape it.

2. Blend channel power and channel relationships to steward and create advantages for customers and channel partners (in this case, suppliers and vendors).

3. Gain competence and expertise in those functions that add value to those already performed by the supplier, and ensure that you are appropriately compensated. Charge customers according to the level of value they gain from the channel, and tune prices and service levels accordingly.

4. Understand that not every intermediary is in the position to steward its channel, but almost everyone will have the opportunity to

guide the potential steward to accept and perform its role. This ensures a better channel system for all.

Principle 1: *Address Demand-Chain Needs*

When it comes to stewardship, distributors and retailers have one major advantage over suppliers: they are in a position to bundle all the products and services that customers need. Some infrequently purchased goods and highly valued items might draw a customer's direct attention, but customers' demand-chain needs often exceed the range of products or services offered by any one supplier.

This is true of consumer as well as industrial products. As noticed by suppliers of coated abrasives, metal-cutting fluid, medical and surgical supplies, and other MRO products (used in maintenance, repair, and operations), customers often prefer to buy these items from distributors, which aggregate such products on their behalf. This is true of not only small customers but also large customers, which value the economic advantages of outsourcing such purchases. In many industries, such as hospital supplies, the combined cost of order processing and logistics is almost as much as the product's cost. That's why, despite the distributor's margin, this option is still cheaper. When an intermediary can interpret that bundle of needs and offer a powerful value proposition, the chances are high of gaining a channel steward's vantage position.

Being at the head of the demand chain means that you must change with it. The value proposition must evolve, and for retailers that is a steep challenge.

Consider Best Buy's rise from its humble origins to the number 1 retailer in consumer electronics.[8] Like many other exemplars discussed in this book, Best Buy engineered its success by a variety of strategic moves and leadership actions. We focus here on one aspect of that complex success formula: the company's ability to respond and change with the demand-chain needs of its customers. Best Buy's actions underscore the fact that such actions affect business proposition, format, and physical assets.

Founded in 1966 as Sound of Music, the company's only store in 1967 sold $173,000 in high-quality audio electronics equipment. By 2004, reinvented as Best Buy, the company had 627 stores in North America, with revenues of nearly $25 billion. The explosive growth was the result of at least five major value chain transformations. Some were driven by the

FIGURE 8-1

Best Buy: Growth history

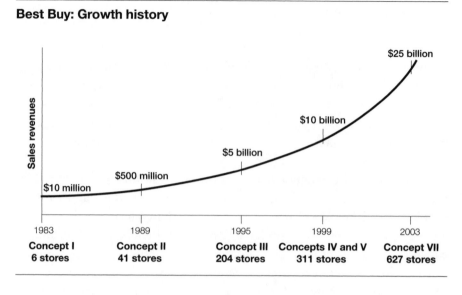

demand chain, others by the retailer's capability. All five were undertaken in the teeth of intense competition from rival retailers (see figure 8-1).

The original Sound of Music store was less than 5,000 square feet and carried high-quality audio entertainment products. Commissioned sales-people gave customers personalized service, steering them to products that best met their requirements. The predominant segment focus was male shoppers eighteen to twenty-five years of age. But the high margins supported by this format began to erode by the late 1970s, as the industry began to mature. It no longer created value for customers, and it needed to change to support customers' need for low prices.

Company founder Richard Schulze sought to transform the company into a low-cost operator and decided to adopt the superstore format. He called the new approach "Concept I." The company changed its name to Best Buy in 1982, expanded its stores to about 12,000 square feet, and began offering its consumers a large selection of products at low prices. During the next four years, Best Buy added product categories such as video equipment, microwave ovens, and major appliances, followed by cameras.

Four years into the superstore strategy, however, Best Buy's larger competitors had also adopted this format and the company faced stiff competition. Price competition was exacerbated when VCR sales tumbled in the 1980s and superstores slashed prices to shed inventory.

Change was necessary, and it started with customers. In customer interviews, Best Buy found that they had a poor image of superstores in general, Best Buy included. In fact, they saw all retail shopping as a high-pressure experience.

Again, the company transformed its channel value chain. This next iteration (Concept II) was built on the idea that customer service meant empowering customers to make the purchase they wanted. Customers would be given the information they needed to decide which products to buy and would not be steered toward items that Best Buy wanted to sell. Thus the role of the salesperson changed from pushing products to being an information resource. Salaried and hourly, rather than commissioned, product specialists were stationed in "answer centers" located in each department, ready to answer customer questions. Customers had the option of shopping and leaving the store without encountering a salesperson.

The idea was to guarantee everyday low prices and thus eliminate the need for customers to comparison shop. The company changed its logo to a yellow price tag to signify this everyday low price guarantee. The stores were redesigned as 28,000 square feet, austere offerings. With the redesign, sales took off.

As markets and customer buying behaviors evolved, Best Buy experimented with a new hybrid strategy for Concept III. Some products, such as video players, had become near commodities, whereas others—big-screen TVs, car stereos, camcorders—retained considerable brand pull and technology sway. New product categories, such as personal computers, printers, and other accessories, were rapidly gaining hold in the consumer arena, and Best Buy saw this as a natural opportunity to expand its offering.

The new strategy called for the retailer to be good at appealing to the rational and emotional sides of buyers. With its third concept, Best Buy sought again to harness the dynamic nature of the channel value chain. By remixing its supply chain to accommodate both high-margin goods in emerging technologies and low-margin commodity products, Best Buy met its customers' needs for the ready availability of high-quality, low-priced goods as well as their interest in high-margin emerging technology.

The company also sought to upgrade its product mix, focusing on stocking a broader range of brands and models within the more profitable categories while still offering price-conscious customers a focused choice of popular brands and selected models in each category. So the centers of Best Buy stores supported the "myth" products—those with the technology and brand halo—with high levels of service. The commodity products were stacked up against the walls and, true to its promise, were aggressively priced with little or no service (and interference) from a sales associate. This new approach called for roomier, more elegant stores of 45,000 to 55,000 square feet. Again, after the changes, sales took off.

Concept IV and Beyond

On the verge of a digital revolution in 1999, Best Buy saw lucrative opportunities for a range of products such as cameras, scanners, and HDTV. Broadband access, too, was becoming popular, and Best Buy saw an opportunity to participate in the Internet access business. This service would be a worthy successor to the PC, which by now had become almost completely commoditized. Again, these developments required a change in retail strategy. Each store now had a new digital imaging area. Consultants in special booths helped shoppers choose technologies and closed transactions. Clearly, more team effort was called for, and therefore team incentives were increased.

With these waves of strategy changes—in response to demand-chain needs and in anticipation of market trends—Best Buy has grown at a compounded annual rate of 17 percent in the past decade, compared with the industry rate of 4.9 percent. Currently, Best Buy, under the leadership of CEO Brad Anderson, is implementing Concept VII, Customer Centricity.

Thorough market research revealed that Best Buy customers could be classified into five major segments based on buying behavior: the family man, the suburban soccer mom, the affluent professional, the active, younger male, and the small-business customer. Each segment bought a different bundle of products and engaged in a different buying process. To cater to the varying needs of these customers, the company has decentralized aspects of its store operations and service that face the customer demand chain.[9] Stores would now have the flexibility to merchandize their offerings to mirror the predominant segments in their markets.

What is remarkable about Best Buy's evolution is that not only its merchandise, but also the format, layout, HR policy, and even configuration of its stores have continuously evolved. With every phase of its evolution, it has redesigned its channel capability. In the early phases, especially

Concept II, Best Buy had to forgo products from leading appliance makers and some consumer electronics vendors. When it regained power by virtue of its growth and customer reach, suppliers came back; but then the company's management focused on reengineering its channel for efficiency, going through a major supply-chain transformation and restricting the number of commodity items. It is this constant building and editing of the balance between demand chain and channel capability that has let Best Buy take on the stewardship of consumer electronics retailing. Other channel stewards might be able to do the same thing without reorienting their physical assets; nevertheless, every steward must evolve.

Consider luxury goods retailer Neiman Marcus. On behalf of its consumers, it is the editor of a vast array of luxury brands: Henry Dunay, Cartier, and Piaget (fine jewelry); Chanel, St. John, Armani, and Escada (women's apparel); Zegna, Brioni, Armani, and Oxxford (men's apparel); MacKenzie, Waterford, and Baccarat (gifts), and so on. As the chief interpreter and translator of its consumers' demand-chain needs and as the channel for its leading suppliers, Neiman Marcus has a unique role in tuning the match for the satisfaction of its consumers as well as its suppliers. Ultimately, all the nearly 500,000 products in its stores, most of them from brand-name suppliers, must fit into a package of needs demanded by its discerning customer base.

From a retailer's perspective, managing the supply chain is more than ensuring the availability of the appropriate products and merchandise to address the needs of the demand chain. The channel steward has to co-evolve with the demand chain. This calls for alacrity in responding to market needs. Fortunately, intermediaries have suppliers as partners, who could be very valuable allies in interpreting the customer trends, only if they were co-opted into the process. Of course in doing all this, one cannot forget that all members of the channel system must earn a return commensurate with their effort, which is the focus of our next principle.

Principle 2: Blend the Channel Value Chain and Channel Power

H. E. Butt (H-E-B), a grocery retailer based in San Antonio, Texas, offers an excellent example of how channel stewardship combines our concept of value chain performance with traditional notions of channel power.[10] Unlike Best Buy, H-E-B is a regional operator and does not have the scale and size to match the muscle of its powerful suppliers. In this industry, looming larger than any of its suppliers is Wal-Mart. Wal-Mart has more than thirty supercenters (stores of 100,000 to 200,000 square feet, combining general merchandise with groceries and other food items). Despite being sandwiched by powerful forces, however, H-E-B has parlayed its special demand-chain relationship with its customers into the appropriate level of power. In this way, it has not only countervailed its suppliers but also engaged them as allies in its own competition with Wal-Mart.

The privately held H-E-B—with 2003 sales of $11 billion, the eleventh largest grocery store chain in the United States—has long been recognized as an innovative industry leader and has consistently earned profits that put it in the industry's top quartile. In the early decades of its founding—the 1940s to the 1960s—blue-collar workers populated H-E-B's markets, such as the one in San Antonio. These customers sought value. They wanted fresh produce and well-stocked shelves at reasonable prices. Until the early 1970s, H-E-B provided that value mainly by carrying a large assortment of private-label products. But, as noted by CEO Charles Butt, over that period, especially the late 1970s, the branded goods manufacturers had gained considerable clout over H-E-B's consumers. As a result of the brand power held by marketers like Kraft, Procter & Gamble, Unilever, Nestlé, and Coca-Cola, H-E-B opportunistically and gracefully transitioned a big portion of its business to the national brands.

But recognizing the erosion of its power to manufacturers of consumer packaged goods, H-E-B undertook several critical steps to deepen its relationship with its consumers. It made special efforts to deliver on its promise of high-quality products at everyday low prices. By keeping its operating costs under 15 percent, it was able to offer national brands at attractive prices. National brands, in turn, provided marketing support for the placement of their products.

H-E-B also offered its private-label (its own brand) program. It sought out the best local produce and maintained close ties to the community. Its premium brand, H-E-B, offered products tailored to the Texas palate, such as fully cooked beef brisket and Creamy Creations ice cream. With a second brand, Hill Country Fare, it offered a lower-priced alternative to national brands. A wide range of products—nearly three thousand items, ranging from salt, sugar, and flour to frozen vegetables and ice cream— was offered under the Hill Country label. H-E-B's own brands, typically priced 10 to 30 percent below competing brands, still allowed H-E-B to earn a positive gross profit.

H-E-B's own brands accounted for nearly 20 percent of its sales revenues and provided alternatives to national brands. Interestingly, however, H-E-B had no intention of driving its own brand sales anywhere near the 50 to 60 percent achieved by leading European retailers like Tesco and Sainsbury.[11] At that level H-E-B would be seen as an adversary rather than as a collaborator by the national brands that needed its reach and access. Rather, the national brands found H-E-B a valuable ally in expanding their reach and penetration of the south Texas markets because H-E-B understood its customers' needs and offered them appropriate merchandise.

As a result of this mutual respect and effort, H-E-B's sales and market penetration grew. In its key markets, H-E-B had an estimated market share greater than 65 percent, ranging from 77 percent in Corpus Christi to 67 percent in San Antonio and 62 percent in Austin.[12] Meanwhile, in the 1990s, fueled by the expansion of the high-tech sector, H-E-B's markets in towns like Austin and San Antonio grew rapidly. National brands that might have considered it a secondary regional market were interested in the high-growth region and, with it, the welfare of the market leader, H-E-B.

Having accumulated a blend of value chain expertise and market power, H-E-B faced a major challenge in the early 1990s with the entry of Wal-Mart in its market area. In 1992, after several years of experimentation, Wal-Mart added groceries to its discount mass-merchandise stores, creating its low-price "supercenter" format.[13] Headquartered in neighboring Arkansas, Wal-Mart had the perfect distribution setup to enter Texas, and it did so, adding about 155 stores in Texas over ten years.

H-E-B's defense was based on astute channel stewardship. It had already built strong connections to its customer base and suppliers. On average, its market share exceeded 60 percent in several markets. So in terms of volume in its local markets, H-E-B still delivered more branded products to the South Texas market than Wal-Mart did. This market power secured attractive prices from suppliers, which also sought viable alternatives to offset Wal-Mart's huge market power. But H-E-B had also built a healthy relationship with national brands, one in which both parties believed they had gained. Each side built its power based on mutual gain and performance—national brands, through the pull of their brands and the scale of their operations; and H-E-B, through its regional concentration, customer loyalty, and own-brand program. This astute practice (see figure 8-2) was instrumental in tiding H-E-B over during the Wal-Mart disruption.

FIGURE 8-2

H-E-B: Gaining channel influence

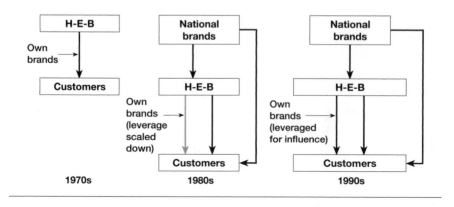

Principle 3: Leverage Your Expertise

Stewardship is not a blanket concept; it does not have to be an all-or-nothing affair. Suppliers, for example, may make exemplary stewards in one channel while playing a supporting role in another system stewarded by a distributor. The same is true of intermediaries. Because they carry a wide assortment of alliances—some with powerful brand-name suppliers, others with suppliers that seek the intermediary's market reach—intermediaries also have blended roles to play.

At one level, Arrow Electronics is a true channel steward for the small and medium market. These end customers cannot get product directly from many suppliers (because of the high cost to serve), and several of them also need design expertise, something only a distributor like Arrow can provide. At the same time, many of these customers seek the reputation of suppliers such as Intel or Motorola even though they transact through the intermediary. The supplier, too, may try to encourage such behavior in an attempt to keep its brand in front of customers and gain preference. How does an intermediary tackle this pressure and gain alignment?

Arrow is the largest distributor of electronic equipment and components to end users engaged in the manufacture of products such as computers, analytical instruments, and other devices requiring semiconductors, memory devices, and electronic hardware and software.[14] Suppliers undoubtedly acknowledge Arrow's relationship with small and medium-sized customers, but several of them, because of their size, technology, and product reputation, also attempt to influence how Arrow positions and markets their products to customers.

In the semiconductor industry, about 60 to 75 percent of chips are sold directly to original equipment manufacturers (OEMs), but one-third of the industry volume is routed through distributors for sale to small and medium-sized enterprises. Arrow Electronics, with sales revenues of about $10.4 billion in 2004, is one of the largest electronics distributors.

The Arrow line card (the set of products for which Arrow was a franchised distributor) comprised two chip categories: standardized and proprietary. Standardized chips were interchangeable and produced by multiple suppliers; proprietary chips were made by a single supplier for special applications and often included special software. Only franchised distributors could sell suppliers' standardized or proprietary products. Large suppliers like Intel usually franchised select distributors to sell their products and provided them with financial incentives such as price protection and limited return privileges.

More to the point, suppliers refused to honor warranties of products purchased through channels other than the ones they appointed. The margins were adequate for sale to small customers, but when a big quantity came up for a quote, distributors could not cut price, and if they did so it was at their own risk. However, suppliers like Intel worked a price-quote mechanism that let Arrow call the supplier and give it the details of the customer and the opportunity. The supplier would then decide how much additional discount it would offer on this request. The level of discount varied depending on whether it was a "design win" or a "jump ball" for Arrow.

It was common practice in the industry for value-added distributors like Arrow to help customers engineer end products by using specific proprietary components. When Arrow provided such presales assistance, it would register the design with the supplier. When the customer firmed up the design and placed orders, the chip manufacturer would offer differential pricing support to the multiple dealers it might have in the market area. Only the distributor that had the design registration (the design win) would be offered special discounts. This was a way of rewarding the value-adding function brought to bear on the sale.

On the other hand, for standardized products in the portfolio, there were no special concessions; it was considered a "jump ball," and all distributors were treated the same as they competed for the customer's business.

In effect, the design win award acknowledged the functional specialization brought by Arrow and its stewardship of the channel functions.

Even while carving out a unique channel role for itself, Arrow has shown remarkable ability in adapting its role as a coproducer of customer value, a win-win for itself and its suppliers in the best interests of its customers. Steve Kaufman, the company's former CEO, observed,

> Our suppliers are able to guide our destiny in many ways. In the case of jump balls, our suppliers inform the customer about the various distributors they can buy from. Suppliers usually don't exclude a distributor from the list. But they do control the order of names. This is an important factor. Being the first name on that list increases the chance of getting the sale. It is the supplier's way of rewarding one distributor over another.
>
> Another way suppliers manage demand flow is in the order in which they inform the distributors about an opportunity. Getting to know about an opportunity even a few minutes or hours before anyone else can give our sales reps all the time they need to secure the sale.
>
> Finally, suppliers can manage the flow of orders by managing the time they take in responding to a distributor's request for prices. The norm is that the supplier needs to get back within 24 hours of a request. If you have a good relationship or if the supplier wants to reward you, you might get a response a lot faster. If you are not in the good graces of the supplier, you could be the victim of an overloaded sales rep who was so busy that it took all of 24 hours for them to process your request.[15]

Powerful suppliers use these strategies to gain influence over the channel, and intermediaries like Arrow also have their countervailing power to keep suppliers honest. For example, Arrow carried lines from multiple suppliers, some with identical specifications. So when Arrow received customer orders for standard or commodity products, it usually shopped the business among its suppliers until it obtained an attractive price and therefore a higher margin.

It is not as though suppliers are not aware of this tactic, only that both supplier and distributor often display a mature understanding of each other's strengths and work out productive rules of engagement. An intermediary should be vigilant in exploiting such opportunities, without diminishing the health of the relationship with its suppliers and the value it creates for its customers.

Arrow's channel stewardship also demonstrates excellence in an area where suppliers and distributors have often struggled to gain a workable partnership model. This has to do with environments where suppliers and distributors bring to market a portfolio of specialty products as well as commodities. Although specialty products need much effort and attention, commodities sell because of price and distribution. Suppliers have struggled to promote these dual characteristics from the same distributor. The system worked out by Arrow and its suppliers overcomes this critical management problem. The distributor still calls the shots, but on registering its value-adding capability through the design win, it can seek favorable compensation from its suppliers. In this way, suppliers can selectively reward their distributors for their specialist work.

The reward need not always come from the supplier. If the distributor demonstrates the difference in value created, it should be able to seek compensation from customers. Owens & Minor, a leading distributor of medical-surgical supplies ($4.5 billion in sales in 2004), has been at the vanguard of a movement called activity-based pricing.[16] Its customers recognize that Owens & Minor's value added comes mainly from its ability to aggregate individual customers' diverse product requirements and make them conveniently available at a one-stop shop.

Because Owens & Minor holds broad inventory in lot sizes ready to serve customers' immediate requests, its margins are directly related to its management of working capital. Some of its customers demand and receive the highest level of service, whereas others do not. The demanding customers often buy in small lots and seek immediate and frequent availability, compared with the others, which plan carefully and buy in larger assortments. Instead of one delivery per week, Owens & Minor's "stockless" customers demand one or more per day. Stockless customers also want pallets and cases broken up and repacked into smaller units.

Even though suppliers allowed identical product margins, Owens & Minor's cost to serve demanding customers was higher. It was internally known that the cost to serve was related to a complex array of services delivered, but the managers at Owens & Minor developed a matrix based on two major cost drivers: the number of purchase orders per month and the number of lines per purchase order. A customer ordering the highest number of lines as well as cutting the largest number of purchase orders would receive a price almost twice as high as would the customer ordering most efficiently (fewer lines and fewer purchase orders).

The fee-based structure initially seems like an added cost for the customer, but when order quantities start to accumulate, the advantages of a volume discount started to kick in and the efficient and profitable customers began to benefit economically from the arrangement, as shown in figure 8-3. The intermediary has segmented its customers along the value diagonal. Customers seeking a high level of service pay an additional fee, and those buying efficiently from Owens & Minor's perspective are rewarded with a lower price. But when high-cost customers start buying in large volumes, they become eligible for a lower price. Customers are now aligned by the intermediary's value-adding input and cost to serve rather than by a one-size-fits-all pricing formula.

There's yet another reason for seeking differentiated pricing from segmented customers. In certain industries, especially those dealing in commodities, there has been unmistakable price deflation. One study estimated the price drop to be about 2 to 3 percent over the past decade in industries such as rubber and plastic belts; valves and fittings; fasteners

FIGURE 8-3

Owens & Minor: Price based on cost to serve

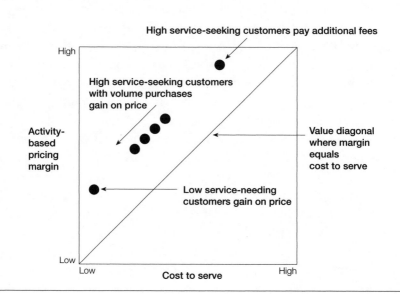

(bolts, nuts, screws, and rivets), and so on.[17] But corresponding operating costs have not gone down proportionately. If anything, U.S. labor costs have steadily trended upward, in part because of inflation in health-care costs. Many of the intermediaries in such industries with restricted opportunities for growth have survived on 1 to 2 percent net margin, and the deflationary effects could put their businesses at risk. In such situations, distributors should charge a fee for service akin to the activity-based pricing model of Owens & Minor. Needless to say, distributors that do not know their cost to serve or do not understand the variations in their customer segments will find it hard to adopt such a pricing model.[18]

Principle 4: Influence Stewardship Through Performance

Although there are many examples of intermediaries as stewards, the vantage position often favors the supplier, especially when the intermediary lacks scale or has no product or branding power. (Retail is the exception to this rule.)

Surprising as it may seem, our concept of stewardship and its disciplines is just as valuable for a small player as a larger, more powerful player (such as Best Buy or H-E-B). By behaving and acting in ways consistent with the disciplines of stewardship, such intermediaries can steer the channel system and its potential steward toward acceptance of such a role, something that benefits everyone in the channel.

Consider the evolution of the relationship between certain General Electric divisions (GE Appliance Control, which made capacitors, transformers, and relays; and GE Motors, which made fractional horsepower motors) and a small distributor called RCI (all the names here, except GE and A.O. Smith, are disguised). In this case, the same stewardship concepts play out. It is value chain performance that enhances the relationship, and the development of trust and commitment moderates the presence of channel power. Even though RCI itself does not have the resources, by carefully building and using the stewardship principles it has thrived in the presence of a large supplier.

RCI was founded by Mark Schwartz as a GE motor repair franchise. In its subsequent role of master distributor, assumed in 1962, RCI sold GE parts to wholesalers, which in turn sold them to thousands of electrical contractors that installed and repaired commercial air conditioning and refrigeration equipment.[19] As shown in figure 8-4, which captures the distribution arrangements in this industry, a master distributor like RCI

FIGURE 8-4

RCI: Overview of industry channel structure

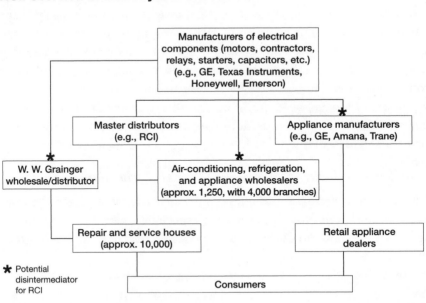

stood a good chance of being potentially disintermediated by any of three alternative channels: a direct supplier channel to the wholesaler; the competing channel from Grainger, which combined the master distributor's and wholesaler's roles; and the OEM channel.

Because few suppliers in the 1960s were capable of manufacturing the quality and range of electrical components for products manufactured by GE's various divisions, the prevailing pattern was for component manufacturers to route products to OEMs. Consequently, if, say, a Trane air-conditioning system failed, Trane's OEM distributors would repair and replace any GE part and component the system might require.

What RCI brought to the relationship was a new, independent contractor channel that a Trane customer could approach for repair and replacement of GE parts and components. Under the prevailing system, independent contractors could not source GE repair parts; this was the gap RCI was attempting to bridge. Whereas GE brought technology, product range, and brand power to the relationship, RCI promised only market access. GE was under no obligation to offer RCI anything except to make its product range available.

Knowing that GE had all the power and that the onus was on RCI, Schwartz went out of his way to demonstrate his firm's value to GE. Much of RCI's success was due to innovations such as a universal mount option that enabled GE engineers to rationalize dozens of models of potential relays to six that Schwartz had personally devised and implemented. Moreover, RCI realized significant price premiums (and thus margins for GE) from after-market GE products. GE rewarded RCI's efforts by granting it after-market product exclusivity. Schwartz continued to add value by breaking bulk and offering small, appropriately packaged and labeled assortments. Moreover, he provided credit to numerous wholesalers that frequently purchased GE products, if only in small quantities.

In developing new markets and introducing product innovations that reduced manufacturing costs for GE, Schwartz routinely exceeded the expectations of GE managers, whose faith was further enhanced by his seeming willingness to operate in the relationship without a lifeline. Schwartz's actions built credibility with these managers, who believed that he identified with their goals and could be relied on to protect their interests. They had begun to trust him. They translated their trust into commitment by making institutional resources available (an action they had been reluctant to take earlier) and eliminating their own alternative distribution options. The two companies agreed on volume quotas and targets by part number, and agreements, albeit informal, began to emerge. RCI, for example, was not to distribute competing products from other suppliers, and GE was to provide RCI exclusivity in the after-market distribution of its components.

This story reinforces a key path we have advocated throughout this book: build channel value through power, but also through performance. RCI's founder was able to do that even in the absence of any significant commitment on GE's part. He gained its trust by delivering results. It was the rapport and confidence built between him and the GE managers that led to escalating commitment on GE's part.

The role of interpersonal trust cannot be overestimated. Across channel boundaries, it is impossible to develop commitment to share information unless there is trust among the key individuals. This critical switch enabled RCI to build its influence even though it could hardly be called a channel steward under the circumstances. GE very much called the shots.

Family circumstances forced an unwilling Danny Schwartz, the twenty-three-year-old son of the founder, to begin to assume ownership responsibilities in 1974. With the demise of Mark Schwartz in 1986, RCI's ownership transition was complete; the younger Schwartz was in charge of all business matters. By then RCI, with annual sales of about $60 million, was among the largest electrical master distributors. GE, with about 30 percent of RCI's share, was the dominant supplier. GE, however, by then was a massive conglomerate. Together, the three GE divisions with which RCI had the most intensive business transactions accounted for $4.7 billion in sales in their product markets.

The next phase of the relationship was characterized by reduced commitment on GE's part. Trust had not transferred with ownership. GE began to withdraw the exclusivity arrangement with RCI for one product after another. GE's search for options clearly signaled that the younger Schwartz had to earn GE managers' confidence before they would renew their company's commitment. At first Danny Schwartz attempted to convince GE that it should continue the exclusive arrangement, but given the vastly changed economic environment and its power in the marketplace, GE did not flinch from seeking alternative distribution.

Consequently the younger Schwartz began to successfully develop alternatives to GE that reduced the disparity in the relationship. For example, he successfully established an alternative source of supply of one component by helping Component Manufacturing, a small supplier, tool up and manufacture the devices at a cost lower than GE's. Schwartz also negotiated with GE competitor A. O. Smith to develop a line of private-label motors to be sold under the RCI brand. Moreover, as GE's largest wholesaler, RCI had the scale to routinely underprice new GE distributors, creating a hostile environment for them.

Faced with Schwartz's success and RCI as its de facto exclusive distributor, GE initiated a new phase in the relationship, this one characterized by a pragmatic acknowledgment that RCI also possessed strengths and alternatives. Rather than have its division managers work independently with RCI, GE appointed a dedicated account manager as the single point of contact on its side. This manager, realizing that GE needed RCI as much as RCI needed GE, made an effort to rebuild trust with Schwartz. Performance replaced emotion as the focus of the relationship, which improved measurably over the next few years. The evolving rapport between these two individuals put the relationship back on an even keel.

RCI's model of gaining influence in the channel is consistent with the virtuous cycle model of alignment. It was a combination of value chain performance and trustworthy dealings that led to commitment on both sides, but RCI had to simultaneously build alternative sources of supply as a visible sign of countervailing power to keep GE honest.

Intermediaries as Channel Stewards

It is easy for channel relationships to be driven by notions of power, whether power is derived from product or brand, market access, or industry structure. But as the examples underlying the four principles demonstrate, other dimensions of expertise—especially the ability to harmonize the demand chain and channel capabilities—can be powerful ways of gaining leverage. These alternative power sources work either by addressing customer needs or by influencing customers and thereby creating value. Such a gain in channel influence is based on performance rather than force.

Ideally, of course, a channel steward will possess a balanced portfolio of performance, power, and a healthy relationship, but assembling such a portfolio takes time and a lot of stewardship. Often, channel members seek more than one source of power to gain tangible leverage in the supply chain. Much research has shown, however, that such systems also display high degrees of dissatisfaction.[20] Some members feel coerced, and when an opportunity presents itself these channel partners often choose to abandon the system or, worse, join ranks with a competitor.

At one time, small channel members like RCI and even somewhat bigger intermediaries like H-E-B did not have the luxury to build up their power source. Value chain performance was the only way they could stay connected to their customers and yet be of value to the supplier. Not only did both companies do a wonderful job of tapping in to that expertise, but also they used that leverage, each in its own way, to build enough sources of power to exert their presence in the value chain.

One cannot overestimate the importance of building alternative sources of product or market, or structural sources of power, to house the hard-earned value a company creates for customers and the channel. The key power source, then, is derived from expertise in the channel value chain. Therein lies the path to long-term calibration among channel partners, and increased success for all.

Intermediaries should see themselves as stewards of the demand chain and evolve with it, leading to the evolution of their own channel value chain, much as Best Buy did. Being at the head of the demand chain calls for a deep understanding of customers' buying behaviors and their underlying profitability. Ultimately, channel stewardship is about enhancing the bottom line. Arrow's approach of getting compensated by the supplier, and Owens & Minor's approach of seeking a fee from high cost-to-serve customers, are only two illustrations of the ways intermediaries can transfer their demand-chain leverage to their own bottom line.

9

Stewarding Multiple Channels

WE HAVE EXPLORED STEWARDSHIP of the channel value chain of a single vertical channel connecting the supplier to its end customers. But suppliers often make several products or product lines and support each of them differently in order to meet the different needs of customers in different market segments. Sometimes suppliers attempt to reach a variety of customers with varying needs. At other times, they focus on covering different geographies. Such strategies call for multiple-channel stewardship.

It would be easier if markets and channels were neatly insulated from one another and each could be optimized as an independent vertical system. Sometimes you can achieve such separation by differentiating the product or brand. But that is not always possible, and therein lies the challenge: if the channels cannot operate as silos, then in addition to managing the appropriate vertical market system for each combination of product, channel, and customer, the supplier must worry about spillover.

Worse, in attempting to best competitors in one channel, suppliers can end up cannibalizing their partners in another channel. Dropping prices or increasing service levels to be competitive in one channel can spark a migration of customers from a neighboring channel if the products are substitutable. That's why channel stewardship cannot be simply about efficiency and effectiveness in vertical systems; it must also encompass the coordination of horizontal spillovers among channels and customer groups. This chapter and chapter 11 describe how channel stewardship works in these more complex circumstances.

A Diagram of Multiple-Channel Situations

Consider the network shown in figure 9-1. For simplicity, we show two competing suppliers (S_1 and S_2) going to market through three distributors (D_1, D_{12}, and D_2). Each of the five buyers in this market (B_1 through B_5) has multiple options for procuring products and services. Distributors D_1 and D_2 are aligned primarily with suppliers S_1 and S_2, respectively, but D_{12} shares its shelf with both suppliers.

How does channel alignment work under these circumstances? For the S_1–D_1 and S_2–D_2 connections, the idea is to convert the vertical hierarchy to a virtually integrated model. This means that the channel steward's policies should promote transparency up and down the value chain and should help motivate the partners to achieve channel goals and targets. Here, because S_1's interests are aligned with D_1's interests and because S_2's interests are aligned with D_2's, there is a good chance of harmony when the system is well designed and governed. The arrival of D_{12} complicates matters.

It is hard to design the network of supplier S_1–D_{12} (connecting to D_{12}'s various customers) as a virtually integrated network, because D_{12}'s loyalties are divided. It also distributes S_2's products to the same customers, so there is a management challenge. The supplier may not be able to gain the same level of transparency and visibility as the one it has with D_1. To maximize its bottom line, D_{12} will certainly attempt to own its customers and

FIGURE 9-1

Aligning and coordinating channels

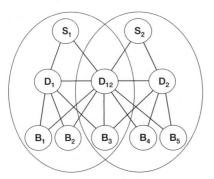

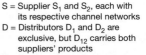

S = Supplier S_1 and S_2, each with its respective channel networks
D = Distributors D_1 and D_2 are exclusive, but D_{12} carries both suppliers' products
B = Buyers or buyer segments

appropriately direct products from either supplier, and this will not perfectly align with the goals of any one supplier.

In this case, S_1 has two options. First, it can construct and implement channel policies so that over time D_{12} will assign primary shelf space to S_1's products. This will happen only if S_1 understands the demand chain and can credibly demonstrate to D_{12} the advantages of falling in line with its requested change. This will involve the kinds of conversations we've described about editing the channel value chain and undertaking the appropriate responsibilities. It's reasonable to assume that S_2 would attempt the same approach.

Ultimately, the supplier with the higher share of D_{12}'s attention has the greater chance of becoming the dominant supplier. Alternatively, S_1 can accept that it may not gain full access to D_{12}'s customers but still needs D_{12} for market coverage. Competitor S_2 may even have the dominant share of D_{12}'s shelf. In that case, S_1 must astutely work through D_{12} to gain customers for itself, even though it might not have the desired level of transparency through the channel. Customers B_1, B_2, and B_3 can be serviced through D_1, but access to B_4 and B_5 can come only through its relationship with D_{12}. Customers B_1, B_2, and B_3 may have different needs than B_4 and B_5; the former might require D_1's added value, whereas the latter set of customers (B_4 and B_5) may simply need product availability and a lower price, which D_{12} provides.

In any case, it is easy to see the emerging battle lines of the horizontal conflict between D_1 and D_{12} over customers B_1, B_2, and B_3. From D_1's perspective, this conflict is a major irritant, especially because it, unlike the disloyal D_{12}, has thrown its lot with supplier S_1. Moreover, D_1 may be right in claiming that D_{12} is taking a free ride on its market development and educational efforts.

Horizontal conflicts can have many nuances. Suppose that customers B_4 and B_5 are served by D_{12}, which is S_1's only access route. What happens if, for example, customer B_4's desired product requirements are in short supply at distributor D_{12} but are available from D_1? Should S_1 encourage D_1 to poach on D_{12}'s customer base? No wonder D_{12} prefers to block end-customer visibility. It can then allocate customer demand to whichever supplier it wishes, without running the risk of losing the order or, worse, the customer.

No matter how S_1 designs its network, it is critical that it attempt to gain visibility of the demand chain, with the ultimate aim of gaining and serving buyers B_1 through B_5 and thereby gain on competitor S_2. Thus, S_1's key focus should be to fulfill as much of the customer demand as possible. To do that, it must coordinate its two distributors so that no customer falls between the cracks and no demand goes unfulfilled.

Intrachannel Conflict

When a channel has far too many dealers, would-be stewards often mistake that for a multiple-channel problem. The two are closely related, but they are not the same. A firm might choose to appoint a large number of dealers in a market area to get its share of shelf space in the face of competition, or to absorb the intense pull created for the product or brand by the firm's reputation and brand-building activities. Regardless of the reason, though, the choice to overdealer in a market area is aimed at reaching greater numbers of *similar* customers. The various dealers may or may not have the same business profile, but their customers do.

Dealer conflicts in such cases are part and parcel of the plan to reach business volume goals. Multiple-channel conflicts are different. At least on paper, the various channels are meant to reach different customer segments with different value propositions. In practice, however, the two occur together, and so for purposes of constructing solutions, we handle them together in this chapter.

Multiple Channels: The Underlying Reasons

Companies create multiple-channel environments for four primary reasons: maturing markets, sales growth goals, evolving customer demands, and, in recent years, the increased availability of the Internet.

Market Maturation

When market growth slows and the fight for market share intensifies, suppliers that have already committed investments in capacity have no choice except to seek fresh pastures. They need the volume to cover their fixed costs and contribute to the bottom line.

They also need lower-cost alternatives to their existing channels. In mature markets, the price pressure felt by suppliers translates into cost pressures on the channels. But many existing channels find it hard to cut costs in line with price compression trends. Just as manufacturers are committed to capacity, channels are committed to product bundles and aspects of service; these are not often easy to decouple in real time with changes in a market environment.

New channels, by contrast, can usually fashion a low-cost approach to customers because they are not beholden to the old service model and because they have access to the latest technologies. The Internet is currently a key driver of this trend, but it is merely the latest in a wave of technology advancements that have guided such evolutions in the past.

Sales Growth Goals

A company might start with a focused definition of the market it wants to serve, but soon it sets growth targets that force it to seek multiple distribution avenues to cover the market. Sometimes a geographical expansion into similar channels seems to address the goals; at other times, the company may need to pursue new types of channels.

Cisco's move into a multiple-channel environment, highlighted in chapter 7, is a good example of how sales goals can push companies to expand their channel systems. Cisco's sales rose from $6 billion in 1997 to nearly $22 billion by 2001, the year its channels proliferated; it was a classic case of a high-tech firm growing quickly with new technologies, new products, and new acquisitions. When a company grows that fast, market coverage and product adoption become key goals, so Cisco made its products available in as many outlets as it could. Note that in high-tech markets, the accelerating life cycle of product technologies feeds the sales-driven need to create multiple channels.

Evolution of Customer Demand

Often, the impetus for a new channel comes from customers. As the product or service works itself through the life cycle, customer needs evolve, and the one closest to the customer—often the dealer or retailer—feels the pull first. Witness how demand has evolved in the personal computer industry. Responding to each wave of change in customer demand, the business model has transformed the shape and character of retail operations—from hobbyist stores to computer specialty stores to computer superstores. In each case, it was an innovative retail entrepreneur who read the consumer environment astutely and constructed a business solution. The entrepreneur's logic is that even if customers have not been clamoring for the new channel's attributes, once they experience the benefits they will switch their store preferences. In other words, a visionary channel may come first, but the demand chain will catch up.

Suppliers, especially incumbents, may initially resist the transition. Others, however, not wanting to miss a possible dominant market trend, will gingerly place their products in the new channel, hoping to buy into an option.[1] The larger incumbents might wait initially, but once the trend begins to solidify they eagerly jump in. The channels, too, advance their own business interests by courting the leading suppliers. The new entrants have nothing to lose and everything to gain by supplying the new channel.

Availability of the Internet

Before the Internet, there were both economic and human costs to adding a new channel. In particular, if such channels involved a third party, the new institution had to buy into the arrangement. All this led to considerable deliberation and delay and even backtracking. Not so in the case of the Internet. As companies are increasingly discovering, particularly since the mid-1990s, the Internet can access hitherto unreachable markets because customers seek it out, rather than the other way around. What's more, the Internet offers customers an "open 24/7" option. And, as you will see in chapter 10, the Internet is a relatively inexpensive way of reaching customers.

For a manufacturer's face-to-face sales organization, the fully loaded costs are about $200 to $250 per call. The same call executed at the next level by a channel partner may cost only about $100 to $150, in part because of the local nature of the costs and in part because of the lower qualifications sought at that level. A telemarketing operation usually costs about $10 to $25 per interaction. The Internet, by contrast, generally clocks in at less than $5 per interaction. These cost numbers are generalizations and differ from context to context, but the approximately 40:20:2:1 ratio is common.[2]

Each of these four reasons is enough to justify pursuit of a multiple-channel environment. When two or more occur at the same time, a multiple-channel environment is often a must for survival. But when new channels overlap with existing channels—that is, when customers have more than one legitimate way to get their desired products and services—it is inevitable that at least some members of the channels will find themselves in conflict.

Simple Problem, Simple Solution

Suppose a company makes two products (1 and 2) for two distinct customer segments (A and B) and sells those products through two distinct channels (X and Y, respectively) and the products cannot be substituted for one another; then there is no channel conflict. As illustrated in figure 9-2, product 1 would go through channel X for customer A, and product 2 would go through channel Y for customer B. It would not matter if the prices were different, the services were different, or the channel costs and return were different.

But when a customer moves from channel to channel for the same product—perhaps seeing an advantage in price in one channel, or an advantage in service in another—channel partners feel threatened and begin to jockey for position. Channel relationships can erode quickly.

The channel steward's goal is to manage the multiple-channel system to engender the channel behavior shown in figure 9-2, even if products and customers overlap.

Coordination Strategies

The first step is to assess whether various channels can claim as their own certain basic characteristics that differentiate them from the other channels in the system. A company acting as channel steward should start figuring

FIGURE 9-2

Channel demarcation

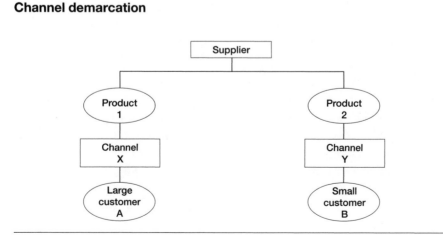

out to what extent it can create boundaries between products and between markets (customers) for each channel.

The idea is that a steward should have a good understanding of the demand chain; with such understanding, the task of constructing unique channels to address specific needs is manageable. Some of the rules we suggest relate to such channel separation policies. If, however, the conflict is caused by intensity issues—two or more intermediaries competing for the same customers—then the rules must change to ensure a level playing field rather than channel separation. We offer those rules as well.

Set Product Boundaries

If clear boundaries exist between products, then delineating and differentiating the supply chain is straightforward. For example, Toro—a $1.5 billion manufacturer of turf maintenance products and equipment (lawn mowers, irrigation products, and snow removal products)—differentiates its channels by product boundaries based on the horsepower, size, and application of the products as well as other product dimensions.

Toro has a residential channel for homeowners serviced by dealers, hardware retailers, home centers, mass merchandisers, and other retailers. Products in this channel include traditional lawn mowers having a range of cutting widths, starters, attachments, and cast aluminum or steel decks. The riding mowers range from a 12hp lawn tractor with a 32-inch deck to a 23hp diesel engine garden tractor with a 60-inch deck.

Products in the professional segment are sold directly to government customers and, through a network of distributors and dealers, to professional users (golf courses, field sports, municipal properties). These products are more specialized, more powerful, larger, and more expensive, making it less likely that homeowner customers will find the products suitable. Although there is the potential for some overlap at the edges of the product lines, the sophistication and size of the product effectively creates the channel boundaries.[3]

At times, the product demarcation approach is a bigger challenge than it appears, especially in business markets, because some customers—usually the bigger ones—buy the entire range of products, whereas the smaller customers may buy only the lower end of the range. From our example at the start of this section, suppose customers in segment A are large and buy products 1 and 2, whereas customers in segment B are smaller and buy only product 2. How is the supplier to design the multiple channels?

The naïve approach would be to route product 1 through channel X, and product 2 through channel Y, asking segment A customers to buy the two products from the respective channels. Such a policy, however, works only when the products are highly specialized or infrequently purchased. For many transactions, segment A customers prefer to have the full range available through one channel, in this case X. But then another problem presents itself: if channel X gets to distribute both products but channel Y gets only product 2, then the design is biased in favor of X, which could undercut Y on product 2 and make it up on product 1. As figure 9-3 illustrates, in this scenario channel X now can snare Y's customers.

Atlas Copco faced this exact dilemma.[4] Its bigger distributors, which served bigger customers, had the distribution rights to a broader range of the company's products than did smaller distributors. These larger players had the distribution rights for both the larger rotary screw compressor and the smaller reciprocating compressor. The larger rotary screw compressors were unique in the market, whereas the smaller reciprocating products were considered commodity products. So the company's smaller distributors had to work hard to close sales and net margins, but its bigger distributors, having the advantage of larger margins on the higher-end proprietary products, potentially could subsidize the lower-end products if they so chose. Unwittingly, the company had created a multiple-channel conflict.

FIGURE 9-3

Channel X interferes with channel Y

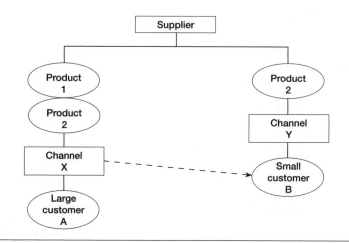

Bigger distributors usually do not encroach on a smaller distributor's small customers; cultivating and maintaining such accounts may not be cost effective. Nevertheless, big distributors may price the harder-to-sell products aggressively, causing grief for smaller distributors that depend on that product range. The latter may be forced to bring down their prices even though customers might not be able to get product at published prices from the alternative (in this case, large) distributor.

The opposite case, however—in which a smaller distributor raids the larger player's customer base—is more common (see figure 9-4). To do that, smaller distributors may have to compromise on margins, but their hope is to gain compensation by selling other services and accessories.

In short, the problem of channel conflict does not go away. When a substitutable product is put in the hands of multiple channels, competition and conflict will follow. That's why product delineation, by itself, may not be effective unless there are boundaries to industry application or customer size.

Set Market (Customer) Boundaries

In the stationary air compressor example, the supplier can set boundaries on the application segments that can be taken by the different channels. Thus, one channel might take the applications directed at manufacturers,

FIGURE 9-4

Channel Y interferes with channel X

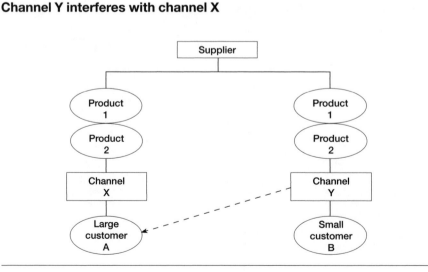

such as automakers, while the other takes on industries needing "clean air" for electronic assembly, pharmaceutical manufacturing, and so on. Many suppliers handle government customers through a separate channel because of their unique competitive bidding requirements.

Depending on the product or service, specifications, and payment terms, a unique buying process may necessitate a dedicated channel. Each channel is likely to be specialized in the kinds of parts, accessories, and services required by each industry and might not be inclined to access customers from the other channels, but that may not always be true. Customer needs could crisscross channels, making it necessary to specify in advance the nature of the end-use customer to be served by each channel member and to monitor and implement the demarcation.

Often, suppliers attempt to delineate channels by account size. Usually, large customers are handled by the supplier's direct channels or by large distributors, and the small and medium-sized accounts are handled by smaller distributors. So the channels are separated implicitly by customer size rather than industry type. It is a challenge to pull off this demarcation even though the logic is straightforward. Large customers (those that buy a larger amount) are more sophisticated in their product needs and therefore require a higher level of service. From a supplier's perspective, a dedicated channel would be worthwhile because of the size of the account and the potential revenues that such a relationship might engender. Even if a customer is not large, if the demand-chain characteristics require sophisticated channel capabilities, a supplier would like to make it available, as long as product margins more than cover the costs of serving that account.

Companies often handle this situation by declaring a "named account" list that only a certain channel is allowed to cultivate. When the channel happens to be the company's own sales force, it is easy to spot and manage potential conflicts by addressing the appropriate distributors. Moreover, because of the size and relationship status of large named accounts, suppliers usually design terms and service offerings that intruders will find hard to match.

However, if the conflicting channels are external, there is an added level of complexity: the need to verify the incursion. Once the encroachment is established, a firm must sooner or later align incentives and impose sanctions to make the system work. For example, it may choose to transfer the appropriate channel margin from the offending channel to the "authorized" one. Occasionally, the firm may need to take more aggressive measures against violators to prevent further erosion and demonstrate its commitment to its authorized channels.

Consider the example of Pfizer's actions with its "gray" channels.[5] Prices of Pfizer's popular prescription drugs like Lipitor and Celebrex are significantly lower in Canada because of government price controls and a socialized health-care system. Pfizer distributed its products in Canada through nearly twenty wholesalers. It suspected two of them of having diverted its products to the United States through unapproved mail-order pharmacies. Because the agreement with these wholesalers prohibited resale outside their home markets, Pfizer cut off supply pending a commitment from the wholesalers to honor the agreed-to territorial domain. According to a Pfizer spokesperson, "We've made certain. We're quite clear that they were in violation. We communicated with all of the distributors on a continuing basis, notifying them of who the approved pharmacies were and those were not approved. It was a matter of unapproved pharmacies that had purchased from them. It's not a permanent action. If they want to notify Pfizer that they will adhere to those terms, we would do business with them."[6]

The Pfizer example draws our attention to yet another mechanism for managing a multiple-channel system, which we discuss next.

Promote Price Convergence

When an effort to establish product and market boundaries is successful, the value bundle is well differentiated in customers' eyes. This is especially true of consumer products, where branding adds another layer of differentiation. Under those circumstances the channels are insulated in a marketing sense and can afford to charge different prices at different terms, because the bundle of products and services is not substitutable.

But when product or market boundaries are blurred in any way—and especially if customers substitute product offerings from different channels—then the channel steward should ensure that all the channels receive products at the same price. The assumption is that as a result of equal prices at the dealer level, there is little scope for price differentials in future sales. In the Pfizer example, the problem originated because of significantly different prices between the United States and Canada. On paper, customer boundaries were in place, but with so much room for arbitraging, certain channel members found the opportunities too tempting to pass up. Such violations are hard to detect, at least initially, because the violators attempt to cover their tracks. The Pfizer case was a gray market violation across national borders, but even within homogenous market areas the principle is the same. When there are price differences among channels for the same products, there is a distinct possibility of channel conflict.

It is standard practice in many businesses to offer quantity discounts to intermediaries that buy in large quantities. This is the economic motivation to boost sales volume. Quantity discounts also reward those intermediaries that take more risks. But the negative consequence is that it is hard to achieve price convergence when suppliers of varying sizes, especially those that add value, compete in the same market.

As a first step, suppliers should credit volume discounts at the end of a purchasing cycle, after a quarter or even two quarters, so that the extra margin is not discounted immediately to customers. A few carefully chosen riders on eligibility requirements can bring discipline to the reselling policies of large intermediaries. When the supplier views smaller channel partners as being valuable and useful to the channel system, it also makes sense to accumulate their value-added discounts and pay them as an overall reward at the end of a sales period. If it is done any other way, an intermediary's top management will lose control of pricing, because an intermediary's operating managers tend to give away the discount ("bleed it to the street," as it is popularly called), and that triggers a further cycle of deteriorating prices.

There is another important reason for price differentials at the dealer level: their operating costs differ. Some dealers simply have a more efficient operating model and a more frugal cost structure, giving them wiggle room in product pricing even if they paid the same price as their multiple-channel competitor. In some industries, such as automobiles, manufacturers' programmed franchising policies minimize these differences. But in most other industries, the operating advantage of a better model can lead to several percentage points in cost saving.

When channel conflicts erupt, low-cost dealers stand to gain customers at the expense of the higher-priced channel. But this is true only of products that are not accompanied by information, education, and service. Often, the high-cost channel has been charged with providing a host of value-adding services that embellish and distinguish the product offering. Customers may use these channels to gain knowledge and then free-ride their services by buying the product from the low-priced channel. For specialty products, this is indeed a huge problem. It undermines the value-added channel and reduces a firm's offering to a commodity status, thus severely damaging its competitive position. That's why price convergence may not be effective without a mechanism to compensate for the higher cost.

Compensate for Cost Differences

Figure 9-5 is based on the assumption that a supplier's customers can be neatly segmented as service seeking or price seeking. Even if the low-price outlets are inconveniently located or poorly stocked, some price-seeking customers will acquire information and service in one channel but buy through the other channel. This often happens in computers, cameras, and other household electronics such as color TVs and camcorders.

Almost inevitably, suppliers separate those channels by product and model, but some products overlap in functionality, resulting in leakages across channels. A supplier can do very little except restrict to a select group the distribution of its products needing the value-added component. It cannot protect its distributors' high margins and gain market coverage at the same time. This is especially true of consumer products, because territorial restrictions may not mean much if customers are willing to travel.

What avenues are open to suppliers that need the coverage without sacrificing the value of the service provided by their selective dealers? Here is an approach used by some astute channel stewards to avoid potential spillovers. In chapter 8 we commented on Intel's support of its distributor Arrow Electronics on design wins.[7] When Arrow worked up a design for a potential customer, it registered the inquiry with Intel, and when it

FIGURE 9-5

Multiple channels: Leaky segmentation

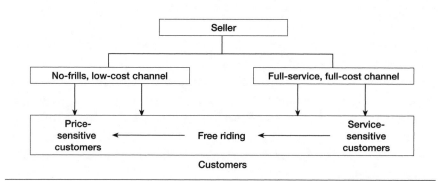

came time to bid on the customer's request, Intel would offer only Arrow a favored pricing scheme in acknowledgment of the effort it had put in. It would be hard for Arrow's rivals to undercut that price.

We call this approach "cost compensation," because that is the intention of the policy. Without such support there would be no incentive for the channel partner to effectively represent the supplier's specialized products in the field.

Another popular variation is a value incentive program. This back-end payment is made at the end of a selling period in recognition of value benchmarks that intermediaries have achieved, such as customer satisfaction, new account activity, new product promotions, and so on. By delaying the award, the supplier curbs a dealer's temptation to pass through the extra margin, instead focusing on enhancing its value-adding capabilities. Consumer goods marketers have found this kind of incentive program easier to implement than the cost compensation alternative.

Calibrating Multiple Channels at Cisco

There is no magic bullet for calibrating multiple channels, especially when they overlap. As channel systems become more complex, channel stewards must implement more complex tactics to keep all channel members as happy as possible. (They must also act on cases in which channel partners would do well to exit the system and ease that transition.)

Cisco again provides a good example of a company dealing with an increasingly complex channel system (see figure 9-6).[8] Cisco's channel partners were required to bring clearly defined capabilities (levels of certification and specialization) to their channel activities and were rewarded accordingly. Cisco implicitly acknowledged the cost differences between the various tiers of partners. The higher level of certification and specialization implied a higher level of expertise and service capabilities, and Cisco's pricing policies rewarded those investments.

Interestingly, because growth and market coverage were at the core of Cisco's model, it did not deny its products, especially at the lower end, to thousands of smaller VARs; only their discount levels were inferior to those of the Gold, Silver, and Premier partners. The price differences sometimes exceeded 15 percent.

Coordinating prices and compensating for value-added costs often serve to insulate the channels sufficiently. But sometimes, channels may

FIGURE 9-6

Multiple channels at Cisco

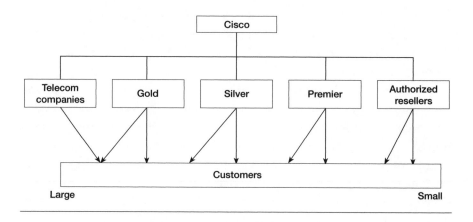

adopt starkly different business models, effectively blunting the basic guides to channel separation we have discussed.

A significant portion of Cisco's sales, for example, went to telecommunications service providers such as Verizon, SBC, and so on. Some of these larger telecoms served the same enterprise accounts as Cisco's large value-added resellers, except that they approached it through telecommunications products and services, whereas the value-added resellers specialized in networking products and services. This was a new market segment that arose as the telecoms themselves chose to enter the Internet service provider (ISP) business after the availability of broadband. Until then, this segment had been mainly the domain of start-ups that leased fixed lines from the service providers. Invariably, these customers purchased the equipment from the VARs. In contrast, telecoms preferred to buy from Cisco. For Cisco, the three tiers of VARs represented one type of channel, and the service providers constituted yet another type of VAR.

By April 2001, as many dot-coms went belly-up, so did many small ISPs that had hosted and managed thousands of Web sites. Telecom companies, which had built excess capacity, saw demand for their services fizzle. As the pie shrank, cross-channel raiding became a problem. Telecoms, which owned the long-haul and local transmission pipes, decided to get into the networking business. This was a logical new source of revenue, as well as a lure to customers choosing carrier services. The telecoms, which owned the wires that connected most companies' WANs (wide area networks), sought to expand beyond the end of the pipe into the solutions game as an additional means of tying customers to their carrier services.

Financially, the telecoms were behemoths compared with most solutions providers. Although reseller discounts went as high as 42 percent for Gold partners, the large telecoms, among them WorldCom and SBC, sometimes offered Cisco gear for 45 percent off (or more) in certain situations.[9] Such service providers controlled the fixed line (copper or fiber optic) as well as the central office switch that facilitated the voice-data-video pipeline that served the information needs of their customers. Some of the service providers themselves were classified as resellers and had the Gold or Silver label.

The heart of the problem, however, lay in their business model. Unlike resellers, which made their money by adding value to networking hardware through installation and integration services, telecommunications service providers marketed an overarching set of products, of which the network gear was only a small part. They could thus afford to price such items aggressively, undercutting the business model of the resellers.

This kind of channel conflict is not amenable to the product-market-customer boundaries demarcation outlined earlier in this section. Here, the customer gets the same product through two different channels and—worse still, from the VAR channel's perspective—at prices that VARs cannot compete on.

How can a company resolve that conflict? There are two options.

Option 1: Construct Penalties or Incentives

As long as the service providers were direct end users of Cisco's networking products, supplying them product for their own use was well within Cisco's stated multiple-channel strategy, and it would have sufficed for Cisco to ensure customer boundaries. That is, Cisco could have served the telecoms directly and let the VARs know that the telecoms were being treated as a house account. But when an end customer also acts as a distributor, it creates cross-channel conflict.

In a similar situation, suppliers in other industries usually address the dilemma by working on the incentive structure. The products are billed and shipped to the end user at full list price, and end-user discounts are provided only for those items where the user provides proof of internal consumption. In that way, the cost of participating in the distribution business is rather steep for the channel aspirant, which then is not eligible for higher levels of discounts.

Alternatively, a supplier bites the bullet and avoids such a relationship, even if it means giving an opening to competitors or forcing customers to receive products and services only from its appointed resellers.

Option 2: Rationalize Distribution Intensity

Cisco's solution took two forms. First, even while tacitly acknowledging the need to have telecom service providers as part of its network, it engaged them in direct conversations to straighten out their end-user pricing policies. Second, it focused on the root cause of incumbent dealers' disaffection: they were losing sales and margins in the new, highly competitive environment.

Cisco adopted policies to reverse those trends. It cut its number of authorized resellers by almost half. Many of the top five hundred Gold, Silver, and Premier distributors continued to hold the Cisco franchise, but beyond that, Cisco was highly selective in choosing those it retained. In the new environment, any general "box-mover" that lacked scale or value-adding expertise was cut.

Moreover, Cisco implemented customized distribution profitability models to help its channel partners manage their working capital, inventory, and other aspects of their business to enhance bottom-line performance. As mentioned in chapter 7, Cisco's certified channel partners improved their return on working capital by 50 percent, return on invested capital by 300 percent, and customer satisfaction scores from an average of 4.0 to 4.5 (on a 5-point scale).

These moves accomplished two important goals. First, they gave Cisco a better handle on its channel partners' business model and their customer service parameters. More importantly, they communicated Cisco's good faith in addressing dealer concerns about the loss of business in a tough competitive environment. Providing qualified leads and assisting dealers in cultivating old and new customers go a long way in redressing a channel's faith in the steward.

Organizing for Multiple Channels

Opportunities for evolving your channel are always available, but you must be skilled in making the transition, constantly attempting to obtain vertical cohesion and horizontal coordination. Moreover, the steps can come one at a time, as long as you're aware of the long-term direction.

It is not an exaggeration to say that most multiple-channel conflicts are caused by the lack of a clear channel strategy. At one extreme, when the channels are designed to get better coverage of similar demand-chain needs, conflicts are inevitable. Instead of drawing strict lines of separation, a better answer is to reduce the intensity of distribution, as Cisco did. At the other extreme, when the channel strategy is designed to reach many different demand-chain segments, then it's best to protect and nurture each channel. Only by knowing why a multiple-channel strategy is desired can a steward calibrate the benchmarks for the cost-benefit trade-off and develop an appropriate response.

Surprising as it may sound, our research indicates that much conflict actually originates at home. As we've discussed in this chapter, there are many good reasons for insulating and segregating multiple channels externally, but it is a mistake to extend those silos into your own organization. If you do, each of the channels will argue the need for dedicated effort to meet volume and revenue goals, but unfortunately such an organization works against the kind of coordination policies we have advocated.

For example, how can you achieve price convergence or cost equalization when the lines of authority go all the way to the top of your organization? The economies associated with mass production or continuous factory operations may tempt a firm's senior management to structure special incentives for certain large-volume intermediaries, while the smaller, more specialized, value-adding dealers, working with the marketing or sales department of the same supplier, must pay a disproportionately higher price.[10] Such a structure not only sets up an uphill battle for the authorized distributors but also leads to price erosion for the supplier. Worse, it damages the profitability and viability of the firm's legitimate channels of distribution.

That's why it is much better to push the management authority down to the level where the channels come together in the field. There will continue to be issues regarding how to coordinate national, regional, and local intermediaries. But even if the administrative structure is compartmentalized, policy making should be coordinated.

There seems to be an easy cure for many multiple-channel conflicts: provide incentives and compensation for all channels that get involved in the sale, and the pain is gone. The complaints stop. The logic of this approach, on the face of it, is simple. Let customers choose which channel they want to be served by, and therefore, the argument goes, every channel that has had a hand in generating or closing the sale should be compensated. In this approach, suppliers usually end up compensating more than one channel for the same sale. In some cases, especially when two internal channels are involved, there is a strong tendency to compensate both sales channels equally. Because quotas and targets become the important hurdles to gaining additional compensation, it minimizes the angst and anger associated with multiple-channel conflict when both routes are rewarded.

Such policies are useful and effective in curbing immediate turf rivalry, but in the long run they are counterproductive. When a supplier is working with big gross margins that dwarf the cost of double incentives, then the policy may work well. But that does not make it right. It is important to structure the finder's fee only for finding and referring the lead, or for performing another specific function. In their anxiety to quell horizontal conflicts, suppliers can be guilty of compensating twice for functions performed by only one channel member. That's when the efficiency equation becomes distorted, and as product margins drop in competitive situations, the horrors of "channel stacking" emerge. That is, channels duplicate each other's functions, escalating costs without improving the effectiveness of the selling effort.

In the early 1990s, for example, IBM was aggressive in commissioning many different routes to market to reach small and medium-sized business users. Often, the channel stacks were three or even four layers deep, with hardware resellers, software vendors, industry specialists, consultants, and agents getting into the picture. Different members would play different roles in different stacks (of the multiple channels). Compensation overlaps were rampant, leading to an unsustainable channel cost. Ultimately, the company had to reengineer and simplify its go-to-market routes, as have many other equipment makers.[11]

Channel stacking is an expedient way to avoid the more challenging job of channel stewardship. With channel stewardship, each channel in the system consists of a team of players coming together to address the demand chain, but they are not stacked on top of each other; rather, they are aligned horizontally to pool their discipline and functional capabilities to construct a channel value chain. Compensation is in keeping with effort.

When the job of stewardship must be repeated over several channels, it is much harder, especially if the channel members overlap across channels or perform different functions in the different channels. It is never a good idea to have the same channel member play two different roles in two different channels of a multiple-channel system. Otherwise, you lose the elegance of fine-tuning channels and must settle for a more aggregate system with fewer multiple routes. Role clarity and consistency go a long way in overcoming the negative consequences of channel conflict.

In chapter 10, we continue our discussion of multiple channels in the unique context of the Internet. Because of the ubiquity of the Internet and the ease of adding it to a channel portfolio, it is a tempting channel possibility. We discuss when and how to accomplish such integration.

10

The Challenges and Opportunities of the Internet as a Channel

IN THE MID-1990S, many businesses jumped online, expecting that the staid brick-and-mortar world would be "Amazon-ed" away.[1] Most of those new-breed companies were intermediaries, and they viewed e-commerce as a silver bullet that would reduce costs and provide unimpeded direct access to customers. In large part, these companies did not fully comprehend the channel value chain they were joining or supplementing. As a result, they focused only on costs rather than considering the benefits that e-commerce could bring to their customers.

Suppliers, of course, soon joined in, many of them with an eye toward eliminating the conventional middleman. Their perspectives were also framed largely in terms of cost: channels, and their many partners, were costly burdens, and the Internet would render them obsolete. So suppliers hedged their bets by including new-breed intermediaries in their channel mix or entering the fray themselves.

Most of the businesses that started operating through the Internet in the 1990s were reacting, in part, to the astounding capabilities of Internet technology. Undoubtedly, some of their actions can also be attributed to an important observation we offered in chapter 1: many businesses were and remain dissatisfied with their channel structures and are frustrated by their inability to effect positive change.

The Internet was seen as a way to effect change. But even though the Internet has been thought of as a tool, it was often applied as a weapon. Witness the auto industry. With the advent of e-commerce and the ability of intermediaries to gather tremendous amounts of information about customers, dealers took protective action, preventing any change that might threaten the status quo. Even useful initiatives that would have advanced the channel value chain were thrown out with the bathwater.

In sum, despite its value as a powerful channel utility, the Internet has complicated the difficult task of stewarding a channel. With more opportunities to bypass channel partners, suppliers' and intermediaries' suspicions about each other's motives have increased. This is unfortunate, because skipping the intermediary level is useful only in limited cases. In most scenarios, it means losing an array of value-added functions that prove difficult to replicate. Channels address customer demand-chain needs, which include product bundles, service bundles, convenience, and so on; often, the infrastructure and administrative costs of replacing these functions are not trivial.

We don't intend to use the benefit of hindsight to critique the channel applications of Internet technology. Rather, we want to understand the power of the technology as a channel (or as a component of a channel value chain) and offer potential channel stewards guidance in its deployment.

How and Where the Internet Works

To gain insight into the role of the Internet, we simplify the world of channels by dividing markets into four types, as shown in figure 10-1.

Quadrant 1 represents a market where a concentrated set of suppliers attempts to sell to a concentrated group of customers. Given a small number of players on both sides, transactions typically are characterized by direct buyer-to-seller interactions. Even if the seller does not use a company-owned sales force, it directs the channel value chain through a set of intermediaries, which are closely, if not exclusively, aligned with itself. Here, the Internet serves merely as an additional utility to serve the same group of customers.

Whether or not there is an intermediary, the primary role of the Internet here is to decrease costs, boost productivity, or better serve customers under the direction of the seller. As you saw in chapter 3, Dell's use of the Internet with its large corporate customers is a good example. It was al-

FIGURE 10-1

Impact of electronic channels

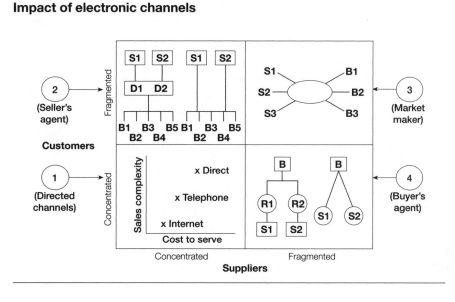

ready going direct to the customer with its own sales force, so Dell introduced and refined its Internet channels so that customers could use the Web to check order status, place reorders, download software, and so on, relieving Dell account managers of the need to shepherd such routine customer inquiries. The freed-up time was now available to Dell's sales force for focusing on value-added activities, perhaps defining and developing new business opportunities.

In quadrant 2, where large suppliers serve fragmented customers, it is seldom possible for the supplier to reach the extensive and dispersed customer base through a direct sales force. When a firm's chosen market has many customers, cost and reach considerations often dictate the use of intermediaries. Here is where the Internet might prove to be a potential force because of its ability to reach small and dispersed customers at a fraction of the cost of existing channels, in some cases with superior information.

The ultimate choice is more complicated and depends on the nature of the product and the balance between demand and supply. When a product is unique or in short supply, the many fragmented customers will find a way to reach the supplier's door. This portal could well be an Internet auction.

It is only when the product is standardized and readily available that channels to market become useful in finding customers and convincing them of the benefits of the product at a cost that affords a profit for the channel members. These channels could be intermediaries, catalogs, or direct channels; regardless of their form, their main role is to match the needs of the demand chain. An Internet channel might serve as a stand-alone matching mechanism with certain segments of previously unreachable customers, or it could be integrated as a utility to complement the work done by existing channels. We explore these options in greater detail in chapter 11.

Quadrant 3 is the space where many sellers meet many buyers. Again, the channels-to-market strategy of any single supplier is determined by its customer selection strategy, the nature of the product, and the demand–supply balance. Nonetheless, the market's many-to-many nature makes it ripe for a marketplace or market exchange to emerge. Such a marketplace might be a traditional market, such as a grain exchange, or it might well be an electronic marketplace. Sellers and buyers exchange information in such markets, leading to the transaction of products and services. Fulfillment happens directly or through a third party.

The market in quadrant 4 has a number of fragmented suppliers attempting to sell their products or services to a concentrated customer market. Sellers prefer to effect sales directly, but customers' demand-chain needs might not support such a focused transaction on the buy side. If the acquisition bundle spans offerings from more than one supplier, the buyer might find it more convenient to buy the product from an aggregator. Even if the quantity brought to market by any one seller is significant, an intermediary might bring scope and assortment through pooling. Alternatively, because the buyer has the buying power in this case, it could well use the Internet as a reverse auction. Its role is that of an efficient sourcing arm and procurement channel.

Channel stewards should note the differing roles of the Internet in each of these quadrants. In quadrant 1 the steward's principal role is to act in consort with the other existing channel partners to enhance effectiveness or reduce costs. In quadrant 2, the Internet primarily supports the role of a seller's agent, be it an electronic catalog or an auction agent. In quadrant 3, the Internet acts as a neutral exchange where many buyers and customers attempt to find a match, and in quadrant 4, the Internet supports the role of buyer's agent.

Creating an Internet Channel

There is no doubt that the Internet changed the equation with respect to the costs of transferring and receiving information. It is common to see a ratio of 40-to-1 when comparing the costs of a face-to-face channel with that of the Internet channel.

Quadrant 1. The directed sales model of quadrant 1 in figure 10-1 mandates the use of the Internet for improving either the effectiveness or the efficiency of the overall value chain. Firm after firm that has integrated the Internet with its direct channels report exactly such gains. At Dell, for example, before the introduction of the Internet, the sales force spent 60 percent of its time on pre-sales and post-sales matters and 40 percent on sales activities. After the development of the Internet interface, especially with respect to key accounts, the allocation was reversed, with 60 percent spent on selling and 40 percent on administrative tasks. There were benefits for customers, too. They were better able to monitor and influence key actions, including purchases, delivery schedules, and budgets.[2]

The challenge for the channel steward in quadrant 1 is to ensure that even though customers want an integrated approach with seamless and costless (from the customer's perspective) transitions back and forth from one channel to the other, the new channel value chain still results in a better bottom line.

What is unique about the Internet is that its effectiveness is not linearly scaled to its costs; it does much better. If we were to label what a channel can do to affect the demand chain as "effectiveness" and map that to the cost dimension, labeled as "efficiency," conventional wisdom suggests that we would have the diagram shown in figure 10-2.[3] This interpretation would be correct if we used the old notion of a channel as an all-encompassing institution that performed a full profile of channel functions. But that definition of a channel is obsolete in most circumstances, and especially under our notion of channel stewardship, which casts the channel value chain as a bundle of capabilities that several channel partners bring together to address a customer's demand.

If each of the channels shown in figure 10-2 were specialized in some aspect of the bundle, then it would be possible to develop a modified representation, shown in figure 10-3, that would have advantages in both effectiveness and efficiency. None of the channels—face-to-face, third-party, telemarketing, and the Internet—would have to be comprehensive and

FIGURE 10-2

Cost and effectiveness of channel alternatives

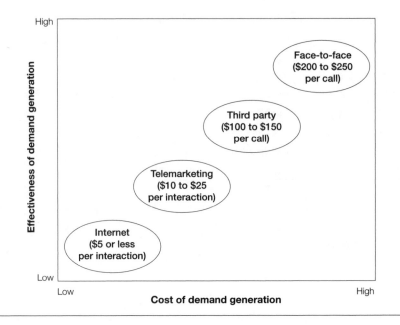

stand-alone. Rather, each would specialize in one or more aspects, and collectively they would deliver customers' requirements.

Quadrant 2. The seller's catalog model in quadrant 2 (figure 10-1) is particularly well suited to reach a dispersed base of potential customers who would otherwise not have access to the products and services of the targeted supplier. When there is more demand than supply, the ability to reach many potential customers enables a seller to adjust prices upward to the market-clearing level.

Eliminating the middleman has its advantages only when the product is standardized enough that the information transaction largely captures the kernel of the exchange. This is true for airline tickets, books, music, and so on, but not for products that require the added-value functions of an intermediary. Under those circumstances, Internet channels can supplement an intermediary's effort but cannot eliminate it.

When products are standardized and markets are fragmented, catalog or Internet buying is facilitated. For example, the average dental office uses fourteen hundred items from one hundred manufacturers, with the dentist ordering five items from eleven suppliers twice a week.[4] Yet competition in these

FIGURE 10-3

Channel integration: Improvement in effectiveness and efficiency

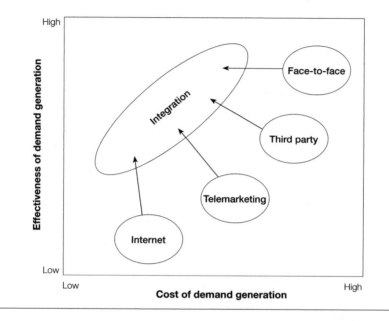

markets is fierce. Pricing is transparent; comparisons between outlets are only a click away. To deal with this reality, Internet retailers will have to create models that go beyond low prices, big selection, availability, convenience, and useful information. Amazon.com, for example, has created a broadened value proposition that includes free shipping based on multiple orders, or a product recommendation based on prior buying or browsing patterns.[5]

Quadrant 3. The fundamental flaw with exchanges of the type described in quadrant 3 is that for most products, they go against the concept of what strategy is all about: to differentiate your offering. After all, manufacturers and distributors and retailers work hard to differentiate their products and services. They attempt to cash in on this unique value, with increased sales or enhanced margins. Exchanges, in contrast, work well when markets are commoditized, but most manufacturers want to avoid that anyway! Even for commodities, criteria—such as delivery reliability, financing flexibility, long-term pricing, and so on—can help differentiate an offer. Odd lots, excess production runs, off-spec items, and a host of other nonstandard (to the producer) items are prime candidates for exchanges. That is because searching for the appropriate customers is expensive. Channel intermediaries that specialize in such markets are sometimes available, but knowing they will attempt to extract their due (or even undue) share of compensation, suppliers and customers prefer a direct link if they can match demand and supply expeditiously. The market exchange makes this process more efficient because the customers who need such items self-select and conduct the search.

The more buyers, the better it is for sellers, and the more sellers, the better it is for buyers. But that is not what a network effect is about. When more buyers benefit even more buyers, and when more sellers benefit even more sellers, we have a network. Telecommunications with open standards is a prime example. Subscribers like to connect to as many others as possible, and when more capacity is added and more subscribers sign up, it increases the value that any one supplier can bring to the market—as long as all these devices can talk to each other. Many of the market exchanges that sprang to life during the Internet boom did not have a strong network effect; rather, their value proposition rested on the efficiencies they gained by providing easily accessible information and reducing transaction costs. Again, the catch was that savings in transaction costs worked for goods characterized by high search or access costs, depending on whose perspective you take, the seller's or the buyer's. But that was not true for all products and services.

Yet at least one exchange understood the power of the network effect. The best-known and most successful market exchange is eBay, with sales of almost $3.3 billion in 2004 and net income of $778 million. eBay intermediates a network where buyers and sellers transact directly. Many of the items are nonstandard and have a unique value for a few potential buyers, who could never have been reached without the eBay network. By making information available, eBay has vastly increased access to customers and suppliers and thus has improved the chances of their finding an acceptable deal.

Moreover, many of the business-to-business (B2B) exchanges that were touted as the next wave of the Internet failed to fully understand the importance of both information and trust in purchasing. Much of the B2B exchange trade, which had been valued at $5.7 trillion across all industries, failed to materialize.[6] The reason? For core inputs, companies preferred to deal with a limited number of companies with which they could build trust and relationships. Moreover, often they were reluctant to make available specifications of their purchasing needs on an open exchange. Rather, private exchanges—firm-based, controlled buying and selling with a limited number of authorized players—have found more traction.

Qudrant 4. As for the buyer's agent model of quadrant 4, for some products—where the definition is almost entirely revealed through information—the Internet serves as a convenient buying mechanism. Many commodities and some engineered products are like that, but not proprietary products. Consider the example of FreeMarkets, now part of Ariba, which was founded in 1995 to take advantage of the $300 billion worth of intermediate raw materials, supplies, and components that go into industrial procurement annually.[7] These are neither commodities nor specialties. The term used at FreeMarkets was *custom components.*

According to FreeMarkets founder Glen Meakem, the Internet as a transaction channel is "most useful when the product is specifiable, when competition among suppliers is sufficient, and when the buyer's purchase is large enough to stimulate that competition."[8] For example, in the $20 billion U.S. market for injection-molded parts, at one time there were three thousand suppliers. The productivity variance between suppliers in the top quartile versus those in the bottom quartile was huge—nearly 100 percent. Even though injection-molding technology was ubiquitous, the customizing of components for unique applications required a considerable amount of organization and administration, which is what FreeMarkets brought to the table. Its role was almost that of an outsourcing consultant. It identified cost-saving opportunities, wrote detailed blueprints for the parts, prepared a request for proposal broken down by lot sizes, developed and screened potential vendor lists, and trained vendors on the use of the bidding software. On the appointed day, it conducted live auctions for each listed item and closed the auction when significant savings were obtained, often far beyond the target price it had set. FreeMarkets offered a customized solution, operating through a network that mirrored a private exchange.

FreeMarkets offered not only the information advantage of the Internet but also, much like an exchange, put the buyers in touch with an array of suppliers. More importantly, through the mechanics of online reverse auctions, it stimulated the competitiveness of the supply-side offer. Of course, such a downward price spiral can work only as long as there is room to squeeze out inefficiencies in the industry, as was the case in FreeMarkets' choice of which verticals to enter. But once the structural costs have been squeezed out, reverse auctions are not very useful in forcing cost reductions. Still, the buyer's agent has a useful information intermediary role to play. The Internet has proven to be an efficient way to collect and process information on commodities, availability, and prices.

The Nuances of Using the Internet as a Channel

Examining the Internet through the lens of channel stewardship, we can identify three significant and common myopias—viewpoints that can result in a distorted view of the Internet's impact and potentially can result in a less than satisfactory channel value chain.

- Myopia 1: viewing the Internet solely as a way to squeeze out channel costs

- Myopia 2: seeing the Internet as an unbounded opportunity to expand revenues

- Myopia 3: banking on a revenue model that focuses solely on the Internet's ability to overcome information asymmetries in the channel

Myopia 1: The Internet Will Surely Reduce Costs

The stated rationale for many Internet initiatives was the purported benefit to customers. With an Internet channel, customers could receive extensive information and access as and when and where they want. It was open for business 24/7. But in reality, the major focus of many early Internet channel initiatives was to squeeze out channel costs in the belief that the demand chain would come along.

But a supplier's or intermediary's perception of the Internet's demand-chain benefits often failed to resonate with customers (or at least a significant number of them). A good example is the online grocery initiative. Beginning in the early 1990s and gathering steam as the decade progressed, this sector became home to several firms. For many traditional supermarket retailers, the idea harked back to the 1950s, when dairies and grocers regularly provided home delivery. Although home delivery had been eliminated with the introduction of the efficient traditional supermarket, supplemented by convenience stores, online grocery firms held fast to different beliefs.[9] They believed that Internet information technology would free time-pressed customers of the need to go to the store, find a parking spot, shop the aisles, stand in line to check out, pack their goods, and drive home. By 2001, after expenditures of more than $1 billion (disproportionately represented by Webvan), only one of the U.S. online grocery companies remained. In the United Kingdom, though, Tesco—a traditional retailer that had adopted a limited online business—was continuing to expand.[10]

Admittedly, there were execution problems as well, but fundamentally online grocers seriously misinterpreted the demand chain for groceries. At least in its earliest forms, the online channel failed to deliver; it entailed high nonpecuniary costs and higher out-of-pocket costs for customers than did the traditional channel. Although many customers did not relish the chore of grocery shopping, they also didn't like to have to pre-plan their grocery purchases. They wanted access to a full product assortment and were skeptical of an agent selecting quality produce on their behalf. Moreover, they were inconvenienced by the wait for home delivery. Customers now had to bear an additional cost, financially as well as one of time and convenience. In addition, there were concerns about e-commerce in general, including data security and information sharing with other vendors. Customers also wanted the lowest prices for certain items—but the lowest prices were to be found at grocery stores. For the general public, online grocery shopping—and especially the start-up time for making the selections—was more costly than a trip to the store.[11]

This is not to say that online grocery service is without a market. In 2002, U.S. online grocery sales were expected to reach $2.4 billion (about 0.4 percent of total grocery sales and the third largest online retail product).[12] Chicago-based Peapod, owned by Royal Ahold, has been only one survivor.[13] Notably, Peapod operates only in selected markets where there is a sufficiently large customer base to support the small segment of customers who want to purchase online. Customers pay for the service, ranging from $4.95 to $9.95 depending on order size, and are required to be home to accept delivery.[14] U.K. retailer Tesco has been one of the few successes in online grocery retailing. It has done so by picking merchandise from its stores during off-peak hours and offering delivery in two fixed time periods in the evening. Recently, however, Albertson's Shaw's supermarkets has announced an entry into the online grocery service, although, as Albertson's CEO noted, "We're not doing this for the 1 or 2 percent of people who might some day want us to deliver groceries to their home. We're doing it because we believe the Internet and a personal portal with your grocery store will be the key catalyst to driving people to change the shopping process in our stores."[15]

The lesson? Many businesses assumed that by connecting sellers and buyers through a seller's agent or a market maker, they would reduce costs and improve convenience, bringing tremendous value to the supply chain. Unfortunately, many of the costs were not really reduced but instead were transferred unwittingly to the demand chain. Customers at the receiving end bore the costs; they had to coordinate information flow with product flow, support, and services. Sometimes customers had to put up with long waits, bear the cost of transportation, and travel to get service support. When all these costs were added up, the Internet channel was not much of a boon.

Much of the infrastructure to support electronic marketplaces was funded by venture capital and, during those exuberant times, was not subject to the discipline of financial returns. In the end, a channel, the Internet or otherwise, must provide a demand-chain benefit if customers are to be influenced to switch. Channel cost savings can be illusory, and, when the gains are real, the steward should find a way to pass on a portion of the benefit to customers in order to promote migration to the channel.

Not every firm (or industry) seeking cost advantages has found the demand chain unresponsive to the Internet. In stark contrast to grocery shoppers' unwillingness to adopt the Internet, airline customers have readily done so. In the case of the discount channel, the adoption has been driven almost entirely by customers seeking a price advantage. The Internet has also been widely accepted for booking traditionally priced fares. Notably, the airlines themselves have accelerated the Internet channel's adoption by making the Internet more attractive than traditional alternatives.

Pioneered by Priceline and imitated by others like Hotwire, the Internet discount channel offered customers some of the lowest prices. These channel intermediaries tapped in to a new market segment: consumers who were unlikely to travel by air because of the relatively high costs. Using the principles of brand masking (discussed in more detail in chapter 11), the Internet channel offered a hitherto unavailable opportunity for air travel. Customers were willing to invest the time to book the flight themselves and accept the inconvenience of not knowing in advance the carrier, the connecting points, or the precise travel times when booking. Demand for the service blossomed as these new travelers entered the market and online agents accessed airline flight inventories. The airlines supported the channel by offering last-minute and weekend travel bargains. Given the potential cost savings and the fact that the airlines made these fares available only online, there was a steady growth of this channel option.

But the Internet channel was not confined to discount buying. Industry research suggests that almost 30 percent of all air travel bookings, about $30 billion, was placed over the Internet in 2003 (including the airlines' own Web sites). Almost all of it was cannibalized from the traditional travel agent channel, whose share slumped from 67 percent to 46 percent of all bookings.[16]

By the time the Internet emerged, the commissions airlines paid to travel agents had ballooned to 11 or 12 percent. Until deregulation in 1978, consumers purchased most airline tickets (approximately 70 percent) directly from the airlines. However, following deregulation and until the arrival of the Internet, travel agents accounted for more than 80 percent of tickets sold. For many travel agents, commissions were their lifeblood, accounting for 65 percent of revenues.[17]

On top of the travel agency commission, another aspect of distribution cost was the booking fee paid by the airline to the computer reservations system (CRS).[18] This amounted to approximately $4 per segment. (A nonstop round trip is two segments; if a plane change is involved en route each way, it is four segments.) The cost of credit card processing was about 2.5 percent, and processing a paper ticket added another 3 percent, leaving the airlines with a total distribution cost of about 20 percent (see figure 10-4). It was this 20 percent that the airlines squeezed down to about 12 percent with the help of the Internet.

Pouncing on the availability of electronic channels, airlines began to reduce commission rates. By 2004 commissions were more or less eliminated, and travel agencies were compensated on the total volume generated for an airline. Such commissions were in the region of 3 percent. Deprived of their major revenue stream, traditional travel agents in turn charged passengers a service fee of $30 to $50. The Internet travel agents charged only $5 to $10. In this dramatic makeover of the travel agent business, there was significant consolidation; nearly five thousand of the twenty-five thousand travel agents have closed since 1995. The larger travel agents (those with more than $50 million in annual revenues) have survived and grown at the expense of the smaller travel agents, accounting for nearly 60 percent of industry revenues in 2004.[19] Those customers that paid the traditional travel agent's fee had a different demand chain and perceived incremental value from that channel's offerings.

The efficiencies of the new electronic channel system were considerable, especially for an industry under duress, where many costs, such as labor, were fixed by union contract. The cost of labor was about 50 percent, fuel about 15 percent, and other variable costs about 15 percent. With increasing fuel costs and a steep fall-off in demand, the airlines

FIGURE 10-4

Evolution of air travel cost

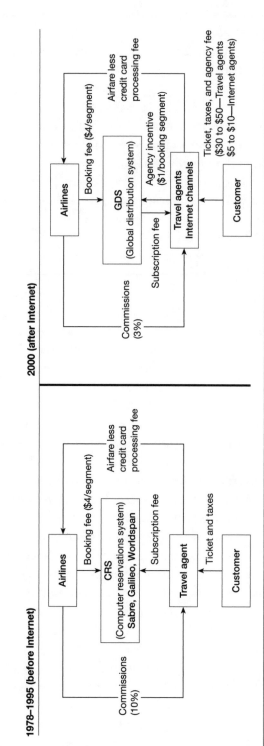

began squeezing distribution cost, perhaps one of the few elements they could control. From a cost perspective, e-tickets were a clear win. The cost to the airline was 50 cents for e-ticketing, compared with $8 for paper. Slowly and almost inevitably, the airlines began to shift to electronic ticketing. The cost of a sale to the airline through an Internet travel agent or the airline's own site was about $10 to $15 per ticket, compared with $30 to deliver the same transaction through a traditional travel agent.

From the airlines' cost perspective, then, it made sense to shift the sale to the less costly channel. Yet from a demand-chain perspective, it was not clear whether customers would choose to invest their time in learning the online booking system when travel agents offered a free service that bundled the transaction, information, and search. The airlines effectively forced the migration by dramatically cutting travel agents' commissions and undercutting their ability to offer the "free" service.

Myopia 2: The Internet Will Easily Expand Revenues

As channel stewards consider the introduction of the Internet, they should carefully assess its impact on the channel value chain. As indicated earlier, without a positive impact on the demand chain, the Internet channel will flounder. The airline example presents a case in point. Travelers gain a clear benefit from online travel service; lowest-priced discount travelers benefit significantly, and business travelers gain access to greatly reduced fares. Also, as we've noted, the airlines have benefited from cost savings associated with reduced commissions.

In many ways, then, with 30 percent of airline bookings made online, it is easy to hold up the airlines as exemplars of channel stewardship. But the situation is more nuanced than it might appear. For example, whether the airlines' use of the Internet has expanded the market or has abetted further price erosion in a competitive industry is an open question. Indeed we may have seen only the first wave, and arguably the easiest wave, of Internet-based channel evolution. What is to come from the next round of innovation may prove more challenging.

Before the use of the Internet for air travel distribution, the airlines had fairly robust customer segmentation.[20] The first group—primarily business travelers and price-insensitive leisure travelers—paid premium prices in exchange for the convenience of popular flight times and flexible travel schedules. The second segment—leisure travelers—was composed of price-sensitive travelers willing to book far in advance and travel at less convenient times in order to access lower-priced fares. The third customer segment—self-managed business travelers—overlapped both segments; depending on the urgency of the business trip and its budget, these travelers might fall into the business or the leisure segment on a given occasion.

Difficult to identify, the self-managed business traveler was usually included in the leisure segment. This segment consisted of people who traveled on their own business, or small- and medium-business travelers who did not have access to corporate travel contracts with travel agents. Through 2002, the business traveler segment was the most profitable, accounting for 37 percent of industry revenues (down from 52 percent in 1981), although accounting for only 20 percent of revenue passenger miles.[21] By contrast, the leisure segment produced 63 percent of industry revenues, although accounting for 80 percent of revenue passenger miles. In 2002, Forrester Research estimated that roughly half of the business travel customers can be classified as "unmanaged [self-managed] business travelers."[22]

This yields a significant share of the business for each market segment. The service requirements and price sensitivities of each sector were vastly different. Whereas "managed" or corporate business travelers emphasized trip convenience (including flight schedules), self-managed business travelers were willing to trade off convenience, to a point, for fares, and the leisure traveler was seeking either price or comfort.

The introduction and adoption of the Internet channel and the dire financial straits faced by the airline industry have blurred the needs of these segments.[23] Given the sharp decline in business travel following the terrorist attacks in New York and Washington on September 11, 2001, airlines reduced fares and relaxed fare restrictions (such as the requirement to stay over a Saturday night) to improve yield. But that has allowed business travelers to seek out low prices without resorting to discount channels. Indeed, a recent study indicates that almost half of all business air travelers personally purchased tickets online in the past year and plan to purchase more online in the future.[24] Another indicates that 37 percent of managed business travelers and 56 percent of self-managed travelers used online channels. That same study suggests that about one-third of the business travelers who book online are mixing business and pleasure and looking for a good deal.[25]

As indicated in figure 10-5, the differences among the channels have blurred. All customers buy from all channels. Whereas at one time the traditional travel agent provided a differentiated service for business travelers,

FIGURE 10-5

Air travel channel structure, 2000

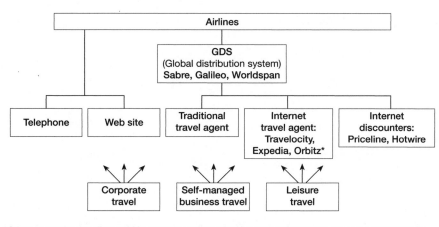

*Orbitz, owned by six airlines in 2004, was attempting to link directly to airline booking systems, bypassing the GDS through "Supplier Link."

its Internet competitors, such as Expedia, have begun to offer similar services. Moreover, because they all access the same booking engine underlying the global distribution system (GDS), there is not much variation in price across the channels. These channels, especially Expedia and Travelocity, have begun to bundle hotel, car, and travel in the same way a traditional travel agent made its value addition felt. As a result, the airlines' most profitable travelers have become conditioned to lower fares.[26]

Initially the Internet travel agents adopted the same model as brick-and-mortar agents, using the GDS to anchor their service. But over time they have evolved a second-generation "merchant" model, whereby they agree to take a certain volume of seats from the airlines for a negotiated price on a "pay or take" (merchant model) basis. Thereafter they are free to mark up the seats for sale to consumers. The airlines cannot control the prices of these seats and the customer segments they are sold to.

When people start traveling more and the load factors improve, one of the biggest advantages that a new channel system could provide is the ability to offer granular segments so that the airlines can exploit different consumers' willingness to pay different prices depending on their travel potential and travel occasions. Table 10-1 shows the steady decline in yield (revenue per passenger mile) since 2000.

TABLE 10-1

Airline industry operations

	Available seat miles U.S. (ASM) millions	Load factor (%)	Break-even (%)	Yield (cents)	Cost per ASM (cents)
1978	299,542	62.1	59.6	8.49	5.65
1983	379,150	61.0	63.2	12.05	7.87
1988	536,663	62.8	61.3	12.31	7.85
1993	571,489	63.6	64.5	13.74	9.17
1998	649,362	70.8	64.9	14.08	9.50
1999	687,502	71.1	66.5	13.96	9.59
2000	714,454	72.4	69.3	14.57	10.31
2001	695,200	70.0	80.9	13.25	10.90
2002	676,949	71.8	84.1	12.00	10.50

Notes: ASM: Standard unit of air transport capacity, defined as one seat transported one mile.
Yield: The price in cents a revenue passenger pays to fly one mile.
Passenger load factor: The percentage of seating capacity that is used.

Source: Air Transport Association, U.S. Airline Cost Index, Nov. 14, 2003, and Air Transport Association, Annual Passenger Prices (yield).

To return to profitability, the airlines must improve capacity utilization without compromising revenue yield per passenger mile flown. That requires matching customer segments with the prices they are willing to pay. Such a segmentation scheme should relate to customers' desired service levels not only when flying but also when buying, starting with their search for information and extending to travel completion.

Airline travel channels are not close to being segmented so cleanly. The channel offerings overlap considerably, and even though the costs to the airlines (and to their customers) are different, the revenue yield is not. The larger national carriers have managed channel evolution with an eye on costs but have yet to optimize revenue yields through better-tuned segmentation and price differentiation. Although they have saved distribution costs by using new channels, perhaps they have compromised revenue yield far more. As one industry observer noted, "Serving customers over the Internet has saved airlines roughly $10–$15 per booking. Nonetheless,

Web-based channels facilitate the price transparency that, at some airlines, makes the average online fare an estimated $50–$100 lower than that of a ticket purchased through other channels."[27]

Focused operators such as Southwest Airlines and JetBlue offer the elements desired by a narrow customer segment: frequent flights (albeit between limited destinations), newer aircraft (with amenities such as satellite television), reasonable comfort, friendly service, and low prices. Moreover, these players have been more successful in the same difficult environment because their low-cost distribution channel (more than 50 percent of sales occur through the Internet) is targeted at tighter customer segments having less scope for price/yield slippage.[28]

Our point here regarding the lack of multiple-channel stewardship by the larger airlines should not be misconstrued. This arrangement is not a silver bullet for such carriers. As we all know, the problem is multidimensional and complex. Channel stewardship is only one of the many levers airlines must press.

Myopia 3: Information Enabled by the Internet Will Be Quickly Monetized

There is no escaping the fact that the Internet provides a more efficient, and often a more effective, way to serve certain customers. Perhaps its most important contribution is its ability to unbundle information from the context of a transaction, thus eliminating the middleman's arbitraging advantages.[29] When asymmetric information is removed from the market, value is created for customers. This has been one of the Internet's key contributions in automobile distribution. In poorly developed markets, the contribution can be even more striking.

A widely cited example is that of eChoupal, an Internet initiative of the International Business division of the India Tobacco Company (ITC).[30] ITC's business unit procures agricultural commodities, buying them from *mandis*, or auctions, and then processes the commodities into value-added goods for a profit. eChoupals were launched in 2000 via ITC's strategic initiative to capture more of the soybean crop, which it turns into oil for domestic sales and into animal feed for export. In purchasing soybeans, ITC had long depended on an inefficient system: farmers sold to village middlemen in *mandis*, with the floor price set by the government. But farmers were forced to accept the price offered by middlemen, because they had already incurred the transaction costs of transporting the produce to market and had no means of storing the crop if there were no buyers. The intermediary, in contrast, having ample storage facilities and market information, bought low and then engineered prices upward for sale to processors like ITC. The traditional intermediary took a disproportionate share of the profits in the channel value chain.

The eChoupal initiative involved setting up Internet kiosks in the house of the village headman, where farmers sought market information on prices, including current world prices, even before leaving their villages. Thus, they could decide whether they were willing to trade at prices guaranteed by ITC. The middleman was bypassed because it performed no useful function. If anything, the intermediary was hoarding information to "buy low and sell high." Armed with information, farmers and buyers like ITC benefited.

To make the business model work, eChoupal combined information with the transaction. The sustainability of the channel comes only from the transaction, and such models must demonstrate their long-term viability.

Consider the role of the Internet in automobile retailing. By making manufacturers' prices—the sticker price as well as the invoice price—visible to consumers, the Internet gives them information that would otherwise have been costly for them to assemble, requiring numerous trips to auto dealers. Autobytel, a pioneer in this business, offered customers online access to model and price information. By linking with local dealers, the site provided availability information and a price offer. Typically, customers searched the site to hone in on a model and place an inquiry. Autobytel forwarded the inquiry to a local dealer, which then phoned or e-mailed the customer with an offer. Customers could close the sale at the dealer's store or use the quote to shop around.

When Autobytel started in 1994, it signed up dealers for a one-time fee of $4,500 to $6,000, plus a monthly fee of $1,250 to $3,000. In its first year it signed up two thousand dealers. Autobytel claimed that about 40 percent of its leads were ultimately converted to sales, but only 17 percent occurred at the recommended Autobytel dealer. With such spillover and the birth of competitive sites, Autobytel's unique "infomediary" model did not convert to commercial success. Until 2002, it had not earned a profit. Subsequently, it repositioned itself as a dealer service site that "help[ed] retailers sell cars and manufacturers build brands through marketing, advertising, data mining and CRM."[31] Under the new structure, dealers paid $9–$25 for every lead directed their way. By 2002, it had about nine thousand dealers paying about $840 annually. Autobytel claimed that it saved dealers about $485 per car in advertising expenses. By moving its revenue model closer to the actual transaction it controlled—lead generation—the company better aligned its information function with the transaction engine. In its previous incarnation there was no way to monetize its value creation. The company saw its net income rise to about $6 million in each of the years 2003 and 2004.

Another company that struggled to break the infomediary jinx was the B2B exchange VerticalNet.[32] By 1999 this Internet company had created fifty industry-specific Web sites in ten sectors, ranging from advanced technologies (such as aerospace) to services (such as property and casualty insurance). Each site offered industry information, discussion forums, news, directories, virtual trade shows, and so on. It also included an electronic store front of suppliers to those industries, which paid a fee to display their stores.

The revenue model was essentially to make a small margin on e-commerce conducted through its B2B exchange. Ultimately, however, the e-commerce revenues remained a small part of VerticalNet's income; its suppliers and buyers used the site to gather information and then connected directly, bypassing VerticalNet's commerce engine. In 2002, the company pretty much disbanded and reorganized itself as a maker of "procurement software."[33]

The Need for Change

The Internet is still viewed by many (customers and companies alike) as something new. The irony is that in the eyes of a channel steward, the way companies use the Internet is as ripe for revision and evolution as any other component of the channel. To take full advantage of all the Internet can offer customers and channel partners alike, the use of the Internet must continually evolve to meet the needs of the demand chains it serves. It must also adapt to take full advantage of ever-changing technological capabilities.

Perhaps the two most significant examples of Internet channel evolution are Amazon.com and eBay, and we use them here as exemplars. We realize that most companies may not have the same high profile as these two stalwarts of the Internet era, but all successful business models, big or small, have one common feature: they have continuously and consciously evolved.

The Amazon.com we log on to today is significantly different from the Amazon.com of the mid-1990s.[34] When Amazon.com first created its business model, book distribution was notorious for having poor supply-chain economics. Retailers carried six to nine months' worth of inventory, and wholesalers another three months' worth. This inventory was abetted by publishers' policy of accepting the return of unsold books from the pipeline. Almost 20 percent of all books were returned and disposed of at a discount. The channel had to bear only the cost, and not the risk, of holding inventory. Nonetheless, the holding cost burdened the channel's profitability, just as the cost of returns hurt publishers' margins.

Amazon.com correctly gambled that publishers and wholesalers would support its electronic channel, which would streamline distribution. Moreover, because fulfillment was driven by actual demand, the initial return rate was only about 2 percent. Amazon.com built its entry on a tangible supply-chain benefit, which was passed on as a price benefit to consumers of 15 to 20 percent. But it did not rest on its initial laurels. It built on the demand-chain needs of its customers.

Amazon.com has continually refined and honed its channel capabilities. For example, at the early site, customers could order only books, and they generally paid for shipping. Internally, the company sought to avoid distribution centers. When a customer placed an order, Amazon.com placed the order with a wholesaler, which shipped it to company headquarters in Seattle. The order was then assembled and shipped to the customer.

Amazon.com has significantly changed the channel from the perspectives of both the demand chain and channel capabilities. On the demand-chain side, it has consistently invested in and leveraged technology to improve the customer experience. In addition to lists and recommendations, customers see customer-specific book recommendations based on past purchases and searches, and they can view selected chapters online. In addition, Amazon.com secures large inventories of the most sought-after books and has made significant changes in its channel capabilities, with six U.S. distribution centers providing expeditious service. Shipping for orders greater than $25 is now free, albeit monitored carefully.

Although the media segment (books, DVDs, videos) continues to account for more than 70 percent of its revenue, Amazon.com has become a vendor of multiple product categories, including electronics, toys, home and garden, and apparel. In addition to the inventory it owns and resells, it has created Merchants@Amazon.com, allowing brand-name vendors to sell their products on the Amazon.com site. It receives commissions and fees depending on the individual contract.

Amazon.com has transformed itself into an e-tailer. Many of the supply-chain cost advantages on which it created its business model have been widely adopted by competitors, especially for books, leaving Amazon.com with no distinctive advantage in any one vertical market. Wisely, therefore, it has allowed selected suppliers access to its customer base, enabling broader fulfillment of its customers' demand-chain needs.

Like Amazon.com, eBay has evolved its channel based on the demand-chain needs of its customers. Recognizing that trust between buyers and sellers is the key to the auction experience, eBay uses technology to establish and build trust. First, it ranks buyers and sellers using direct feedback from individual transactions. Before engaging in an auction, bidders see information on the seller: how long it has been selling and how well it has satisfied customers. When the seller receives payment and when the buyer receives the goods, they are encouraged to provide feedback on the transaction. That feedback log is available in future auctions involving those individuals.

The company encourages the use of PayPal, where auction winners can make electronic payment, which speeds the transaction and offers customers a safe and anonymous way to complete it. eBay's enhancements have increased the security of the transaction. For example, sellers that qualify for buyer protection offer buyers as much as $500 in insurance in the event goods are not delivered or not as represented.[35] For higher-ticket items, eBay offers escrow services; as the name suggests, the payment is held in escrow until the buyer has received, inspected, and accepted the goods. As a last resort, eBay also offers online dispute resolution if the buyer and seller cannot resolve their differences. All these initiatives increase trust between buyers and sellers and, with it, their willingness to enter into a transaction. As a result, the number of registered users has grown from about 1 million in 1998 to almost 95 million in 2003.[36]

The Internet is here, it is important, and it will be integrated into the channel strategies of all businesses. A 2004 *Economist* article noted, "The funny thing is that the wild predictions made at the height of the boom—namely, that vast chunks of the world economy would move into cyberspace—are in one way or another coming true."[37] The article estimated that American consumers would spend more than $120 billion online in 2005. B2B transactions were estimated to reach nearly a trillion dollars that year.

In spite of many individual successes, however, first-generation Internet models are seldom visionary from a channel perspective. Many are based on incorrect perceptions of advantages. Some supposed advantages have proved spurious, because the "eliminated" costs showed up with even more intensity at the customer end. Others have found that the Internet muddies the distinction between customer segments, causing price erosion. Still others have struggled to monetize their Internet business model. All this calls for a high degree of stewardship to hone the channel's capabilities to meet customers' needs.

But the good news is that the race has only begun. It is not too early. There is much to learn from the successes and failures of the first wave. Many businesses have built attractive Internet channels, in part by design and in part through a process of Darwinian evolution.

They are all here and ready to take their business models to the next iteration. In doing so, they should evaluate the Internet as a channel option very much in the frame of the three disciplines of stewardship discussed in this book, especially as an exceptionally attractive utility for building and editing the channel value chain. When incorporated well, this attractive option can enhance channel effectiveness and simultaneously decrease its costs. For those companies that have not yet ventured into the Internet in a big way (other than having a Web site), here is an opportunity to rethink channel strategy. For either set of companies—those into it and those out of it—the Internet is a powerful hook for engaging in serious channel transformation.

11

Integrating the Internet into the Multiple-Channel Solution

THE INTERNET CAN PERFORM a number of the functions of a conventional channel: provide information and education through Web sites, electronic catalogs, and streaming videos; enable transactions through e-commerce engines; make product recommendations through collaborative filtering; negotiate orders through dynamic pricing; up-sell and cross-sell by allowing customers to configure products and product bundles; deliver service via online support systems, and so on.

Having the capability, however, does not mean that these features should be part of every firm's Internet channel design. Even though many firms have added the Internet as an option, not many have worked it carefully enough to understand which aspects of the channel value chain should best be influenced by the Internet. Nor do they understand how to integrate it with the rest of the channel bundle. Most have put out a Web page chock-full of information on the company and its products and services. But few have successfully tapped in to the commercial possibilities and the opportunities for integrating the Internet as part of a multiple-channel solution.

A channel steward must carefully construct the channel value chain and steer customers so that the integration does not negate each channel's specialization and cost advantages. When designed well, a multiple-channel solution is ideally suited to boost loyalty and retention and deepen customer relationships, leading to gains in revenue and profitability.

At the same time, the Internet simply cannot provide some of the important aspects of the buying experience that a human interaction can. A company, through the Internet, can assemble and supply readily available information, but it cannot automate critical judgments, which rely on expertise, knowledge, and strategic customer relationships. Under some scenarios, the Internet works best when it is integrated with a company's existing channels, and in others, it is most effective when it is built as a new stand-alone channel.

Consider, for example, figure 11-1. When it comes to financial investment, studies reveal that consumers are comfortable gathering information on the Web. They do not seem to get much more from interacting with a financial adviser. When it comes to an investment decision, however, many consumers prefer to talk to a person, either on the phone or face to face, even if only to confirm a decision the consumer has made by processing the online research. Yet surprisingly, after consumers have made their investment decisions, many of them are comfortable using the Web to execute the transaction and any necessary follow-up.

This trend suggests that by combining the options in a multiple-channel fashion across the entire process of matching the demand chain to the supply chain, channel stewards can simultaneously reduce costs even while improving their effectiveness and coverage. An article in the *McKinsey Quarterly* claimed that by promoting multiple channels of which the Internet is one, firms can reduce their cost to serve by as much as 10 to 15 percent and increase revenue per customer by as much as 15 to 20 percent.[1]

FIGURE 11-1

Integrated channels

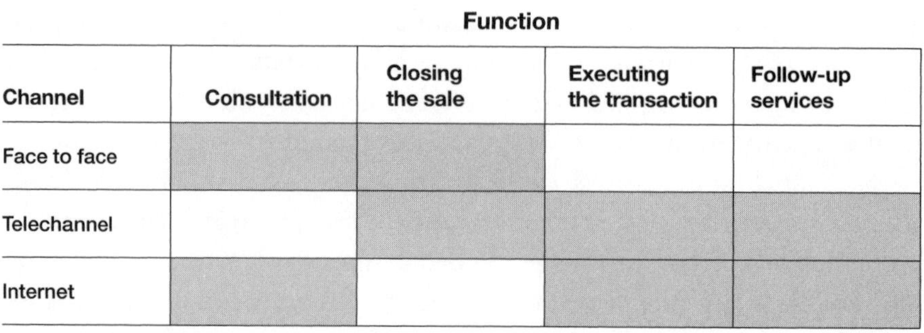

Channel	Function			
	Consultation	Closing the sale	Executing the transaction	Follow-up services
Face to face	▓	▓		
Telechannel		▓	▓	▓
Internet	▓		▓	▓

The Crux of the Problem

Consider a subtle yet important consideration in the construction of a multiple channel such as the one shown in the figure. Here, customers choose how they interface with the provider. It would be almost impossible for the provider—in our example, a bank—to refuse a customer who calls on the account manager (the face-to-face channel) for follow-up services. The account manager may attempt to guide the client to the telephone channel, or in some cases actually provide the services, to keep the customer relationship.

Practically speaking, then, an optimal multiple-channel strategy should be designed to route the bulk of customers' interactions to the most efficient medium, without restricting their choices. Separating channel functions as though they were individual stand-alone channels is fraught with difficulties. Consumers using Web-based services often get frustrated when they need help to complete transactions but have no telephone support person to call. If all that is available is the FAQ (frequently asked questions) button, most consumers will abandon the transaction.

A 1990 HBR article raised exactly that concern in the context of conventional channels.[2] The article cited the example of Wright Line, a company that provided IT storage accessories such as tape drives and cabinets. The company segmented its channels into direct sales, telemarketing, and distribution to cater to large, medium, and small customers, respectively. In reality, however, all three customer segments preferred to use the direct channel for the first buy. When customers first designed their IT systems and needed to buy computer accessories, they preferred the hand-holding and advice that came with the face-to-face channel. But after that, all of them preferred the telemarketing and catalog channels, which they saw as less cumbersome and more efficient. They did not have to wait for the salesperson to call on them; they simply picked up the phone. In effect, all three customer segments bought from all three channels, defeating the company's purpose of setting up multiple channels.

Many companies have yet to fully understand this simple rule of the demand chain, but it is critical for channel stewards: customers choose channels, it is not the other way around. A 2003 HBR article described it thus: "Instead of designing channels to capture targeted demographic segments, you must design them to support unfettered buyers' behaviors. What's crucial is that customers get what they need at each stage of the buying process—through one channel or another."[3]

Such a channel design, however, has one major drawback: it can be very costly. If customers can pick and choose which functions they want fulfilled from which channel, then each channel must be able to deliver a variety of functions on request. The whole point of specialization is to offer customers expertise and, because of that focus, an efficient cost. The composite channel trend is based on exactly that principle: a team of position players that are specialized in one function—information, logistics, service—work together to address a customer's demand-chain needs. Having each specialist double up makes the channel attractive for some customers, but it imposes costs on the system and dilutes its efficiency. A channel steward must build in incentives and disincentives so that customers migrate to the functional specialist, or else the customer should pay a price for going outside the optimal design.

Astute channel stewards do just that. Charles Schwab, for example, makes it easy for its affluent customers to schedule appointments and thus makes it easy to use its branches. These customers can be persuaded to buy other products or increase their share of wallet, and experience has shown Schwab that this happens best at branches. But for those customers who like to manage their own investments, Schwab takes every opportunity to train them on how to use the Web for transactions. By making alternatives to visiting a branch easy, Schwab attempts to steer such customers to its low-cost channel.

W. W. Grainger, the $4.6 billion distributor of electrical components, parts, and supplies is another good example. As an article in the *McKinsey Quarterly* put it,

> The company's 1,200-strong face-to-face sales force visited customers to show them how to order parts using the new Web-based system. Grainger made sure that its salespeople would invest enough energy in these training activities by adjusting its compensation system to give them credit for all sales in their territories regardless of channels. Today the sales reps spend much of their time on higher-value activities, such as finding new prospects and building customer loyalty, while the company has raised its e-commerce sales from less than $100 million in 1999 to nearly $500 million in 2003.[4]

The Internet has often been considered a stand-alone channel, but often its role is more that of a channel utility. It can be designed as a complete channel only for certain products and services: those whose key aspects of demand generation and fulfillment can be accomplished over the Web. In other words, it is suitable for software and e-tickets, along with books, personal computers, and other items, depending on how the channel bundle is designed.

But even in such situations, the crucial role of demand-chain analysis—which accounts for customers' buying and usage behaviors—will determine the Internet's appropriateness. From the supply-chain side, too, the reliability of its logistics and its ability to preserve the integrity of the contract are crucial. Whether the Internet is used as an additional channel utility or a stand-alone channel, each approach requires a different kind of channel management. That's because the designs are based on different assumptions about what the channel is supposed to do.

So even though it may be tempting to call the catalog, the telephone, the fax, and the Internet separate and distinct channels, a steward must interpret their roles in a nuanced way. Often, you need combinations of channels to deliver customers' required bundle of activities. For an air travel e-ticket, all aspects of the search and sale can be conducted on the Internet, so it is a channel; but that is not true, for example, of cars. Consumers looking to buy a car can only get information on the Internet. Price negotiation, delivery, and follow-up services (such as warranties) must happen at the retail channel. The Internet, then, is a utility (much like a telephone or fax machine) and not itself a channel.

The task of a channel strategy is to put together the appropriate combination of intermediaries, including a sales force, to accomplish the various channel activities. Critically, however, these channel flows must originate with the customer.

The Internet as a Stand-Alone Channel

Consider the origin of the discount air travel channels, such as Priceline and Hotwire. Priceline.com was launched in 1998, with budget-minded leisure travelers as target customers. Instead of posting the availability of flights, seats, and their appropriate prices and then letting customers choose the desired combination, Priceline asked potential customers to post an asking price for a travel destination. The Internet site then searched its inventory, which it had acquired from participating airlines. If it could meet the price requested, the customer's credit card was charged and a ticket issued. The routing and the name of the carrier were made known only when the ticket was issued.

In 2002, the airlines, having seen the benefits of this model, launched Hotwire, their own Internet travel agent.[5] Its operating model was a little different from that of Priceline. Here, customers did not input a price; rather, they searched for the lowest price without knowing the routing or the airline. As with Priceline, these became known after the ticket was issued.[6]

As discussed in chapter 10, under the old system, the market could be roughly segmented into two groups: business travel and leisure travel (see figure 11-2). The business traveler was more sensitive to service than price.

In contrast, some leisure travelers were more sensitive to price than service. Before the arrival of the Internet, channels were separated by business versus leisure travel, but there was no way to further differentiate for fear of price seepage. If an airline raised service levels for leisure travelers, the business traveler might switch. If it dropped prices along a "yield" pricing formula, more of its travelers, especially leisure, might wait to take advantage of the lower prices.[7] In an attempt to sell more seats, an airline might end up risking margins.

In addition to business and leisure travelers, the airlines knew there was a third segment—self-managed business travelers—that was almost half of the business segment.[8] As we mentioned in chapter 10, by not

FIGURE 11-2

Priceline: Focus on budget leisure traveler

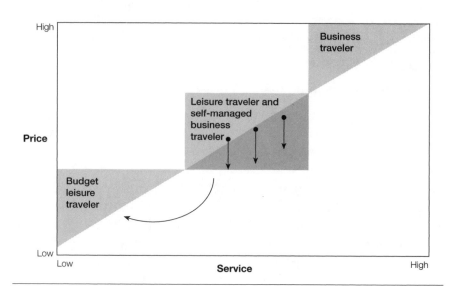

being part of "corporate travel," they could not access special fares, but they were unwilling to totally sacrifice service for price.

When discount operator Priceline emerged, it gave the airlines an opportunity to separate the "budget" leisure travelers from the majority of leisure travelers and the self-managed business travelers. Priceline masked the brand and thus could go further in offering discount tickets to those leisure travelers who were purely price seeking (see figure 11-3). At sites such as Priceline and Hotwire, the only information available before purchase was the price, the number of connections, and the assurance that a major carrier operated the flight. Moreover, the fare had to be paid in advance, and the ticket could not be canceled.

The airlines usually used this channel to offload underutilized capacity in their route structure. So to get from one destination to the other, an airline might route the passenger through its hub, preserving the option of booking a higher-valued seat on its direct flight to the same destination. It was price discrimination, product differentiation, and channel separation all executed in the same package.

Not only did these sites attract a large, untapped discount market, but also the masked booking prevented self-managed business travelers from migrating toward a lower-priced offering. Simultaneously, to better serve these customers, the airlines opened more alternative channels for them. The two leading online travel agencies—Travelocity (established by Sabre)

FIGURE 11-3

Channel masking

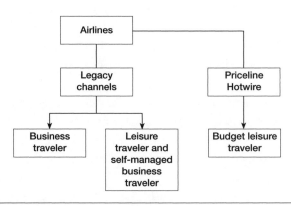

and Expedia (established by Microsoft)—provided 24/7 online access for booking travel (air, hotel, car rental) online.

Principally, then, the Internet as a supplementary stand-alone channel is an excellent way to gain access to previously untapped customer segments. But the design should follow the careful multiple-channel demarcation principles offered in chapter 9 and avoid the pitfalls outlined in chapter 10.

The Internet as Part of an Integrated Channel

The picture looks somewhat different when the Internet is part of an integrated channel. Consider how the printer division of Hewlett-Packard handled the Internet, given that it sold almost entirely through retail channels.[9] Hewlett-Packard is the undoubted market leader in printers. In 1998 it commanded an astonishing retail market share of 85 percent in the higher-priced laser printer category, and a 55 percent share in ink-jets. By then its counterparts, like Dell in the personal computer business, had begun to use the Internet with great success. In a short period, Dell was selling $1 billion per year in personal computers and was expecting to move half its sales ($7 billion by 1999) over the Internet.

There were clear indications that a new generation of consumers was emerging who felt comfortable acquiring products over the Internet. Hewlett-Packard had sold almost its entire volume of printers in the consumer and small-business market through its various channel partners, predominantly computer superstores, consumer electronics superstores, and office product superstores. Retailers' average gross margins on printers were 8 to 14 percent. During their ownership, consumers would buy at least five, and probably more, replacement ink cartridges. Retail margins on these supplies averaged 20 to 25 percent and were quite lucrative.

Large retailers, such as CompUSA and Staples, accounted for almost 90 percent of HP's sales and stood to lose if HP made a large portion of its sales directly. But these retailers had size and market power and perhaps would have offered their shelves to competitive brands had HP chosen to go direct. But at the same time, HP had so much market share and brand recognition that conceivably it could have pulled off a direct Internet channel if it so chose. A classic power struggle could have ensued, but it did not happen.

HP was an astute channel steward. It did not attempt to disintermediate its channel partners. Instead, it used its HP Village Web site to route customers to the nearest retail store. The prices were pegged at retail price points. The Web site was designed to influence the consumer brand choice and drive traffic to stores. Only die-hard Internet buyers would find it advantageous to buy through HP's direct channel. For all practical purposes, the Internet site reinforced existing channels and integrated with their operations.

HP's decision was based on its reading of the demand chain. Consumers did not plan ahead in purchasing replacement cartridges, but rather used their cartridges until they ran out. Thus, convenient availability dictated the cartridge purchase, and retail stores would be critical.

How did HP know that consumers would not flock to the Web to buy printers? The PC market was there for comparison. In spite of Dell's outstanding success with the direct model, most consumers purchased their PCs from a retail store, and it would not be different for printers. The online customer segment was growing but not to the extent that it caused alarm.

So what HP needed was an option to scale up its direct Internet channel if need be, but not a full-fledged offering—in part because of its extraordinary market share and market penetration with leading retailers. HP chose to view the Internet as a utility to reinforce and strengthen existing channels rather than use it as a stand-alone alternative channel. Even though its Internet channel brought in some sales, its main purpose was to provide information on products and retailers and influence brand choice. The idea was that consumers would be predisposed to buy HP printers even before they entered the store.

It is illustrative that HP, in a virtual way, emulated what Dell had done with its vertically integrated channel. Especially for Dell, the Internet provided an opportunity to enhance its effectiveness and improve its efficiency. It was clearly a useful utility to add to its mix in the direct channels. Dell saw the Internet as an opportunity to decrease the cost to serve its existing customers.[10] Customers can buy Dell PCs on the phone or through the Web. The products and prices are identical. They can track order status through whichever channel they prefer, and the information is universal across all the channels. For a Dell corporate customer, the face-to-face channel is yet another option.

The multiple-channel system is designed to encourage customers to use the Web for a number of after-sales activities. It is more efficient from the company's viewpoint, and more effective from the customer's. For example, when a corporate customer identifies itself through the company's Premier Page, the wealth of information that supports the interface is often beyond what a human, even a superb account manager, could retain. This makes it a far more efficient transaction for both the buyer and the seller. The buyer can make an informed decision on purchase and support services without having to wait. The channel components are all integrated and seamless.

The same is true of Talbots, a retailer of women's classic clothing, which also uses the Internet to support its vertically integrated strategy.[11] Suppose a customer chooses a dress at a store but cannot find it in her size. A Talbots associate might assist the customer in using the in-store phone to place an order from the catalog, with the goods delivered free. The objective is to make it a seamless experience for the customer.

Key drivers of such integrated channels are CRM systems that promote transparency across channels and position the various channels to optimize their efficiency. Talbots owns its stores and its catalog operation, making integration easier. The same thinking extends to channels that are owned by third parties, as the HP example illustrates.

It might appear from the examples (printers, computers, and apparel) that integrating the Internet is the only alternative when the product has a significant physical component, but that misses the point. A critical element of the decision is an assessment of the demand chain. When the Internet helps you to reach hitherto untapped market segments by addressing unfulfilled buying behavior, then it becomes a viable alternative (as long as you keep the products and channels well differentiated, like the discount channels in the air travel industry). If, on the other hand, the Internet helps you deepen your relationship with existing or potential customers, it makes sense to roll out the Internet as an added utility to enhance the effectiveness and efficiency of existing channels. The following example provides a look at how and why one business combined the two approaches.

The Internet as a Stand-Alone, Integrated Channel

Multiple channels are confusing when they cross customer segments. Even though, on paper, the multiple combinations are meant to address different customer segments, in practice the same channel may touch different customer segments, and then it is hard to maintain the differentiated marketing policies of the hypothetical design. If the customer segments were neatly aligned by channel type—low-price, low-service seekers preferring the Internet versus high-price, high-service seekers wanting a human interaction—then the problem boils down to differentiating the offering (as Priceline did). The two sets of customers (or customers with different

buying behaviors) use two distinct channels, and the risk of channel conflicts is minimized. But when you attempt to separate customers by function
rather than channel, the task can be challenging. It creates an unintended
problem and requires a nuanced approach.

Merrill Lynch's Internet entry illustrates some of these issues and provides a platform for discussing the potential solutions.[12] The legacy of the
firm's brick-and-mortar sales channel is important to bear in mind throughout this discussion. The company prided itself on exceptional face-to-face
contact and the guidance it provided its clients through its network of
nearly fifteen thousand financial advisers. But in 1998, it found itself under
pressure to offer online Internet trading to its customer base.

Until the late 1990s, firms in this business usually competed against
other firms within its segment. Merrill Lynch competed against other
full-service brokers, while maintaining an awareness of the activities of
discount brokerage leader Charles Schwab. Moreover, brokerage firms
like Merrill Lynch competed with banks by drawing away their affluent
customers' deposit accounts, which formed the entry point for many customers' use of securities firms. Facilitated by advances in technology, the
differentiation between the segments began to blur and there was increased competition between the segments for affluent investors.

The average Merrill Lynch private client was age fifty or older, with an
annual income of about $80,000 and assets of nearly $500,000; the Schwab
profile, in contrast, skewed much younger. Its customers were about forty
years old, earned about $95,000 a year, and had assets of less than $200,000
under investment. The biggest threat faced by full-service brokers like
Merrill Lynch was the possibility that when discount brokers like Schwab
acquired a customer, he would have no incentive to switch as his assets
grew. Thus, having an online channel became a critical growth vehicle.

In the late 1990s, a group of electronic brokerage firms, including
E*TRADE and Ameritrade, dramatically reduced transaction costs by leveraging technology not only in the back office but also in the customer interface. These electronic firms typically did not have branch offices and
relied solely on electronic order entry. E*TRADE and Ameritrade performed
basic trades for as little as $8 per trade and charged extra for additional ser-
vices. By 1999, nearly one-third of all retail trades were conducted online,
and it was expected that this portion would increase to two-thirds by 2003.
Clearly, customers were willing to change their behavior to suit the new
channels.

Soon leading discounters such as Charles Schwab, always known for technological innovation, began to offer their customers the option of trading online. Schwab charged its customers $29.95 per electronic trade. As a result, Schwab saw the online share of its total account base jump from 5 percent in 1994 to 60 percent in 1999.

Merrill Lynch's internal analysis had revealed that many of its customers had transferred a portion of their assets to an online channel, be it Schwab or E*TRADE, just to have the ability to experiment. Customers seemed confident of their new channels and, in a bull market, came to believe that their investment choices were astute. This trend was worrisome for Merrill Lynch, because customers usually invested their wealth in more than one account; any leakage from the primary account could be a forerunner of things to come, especially if the customer found that the new host was adding value and enhancing portfolio performance.

Merrill Lynch announced its multiple-channel strategy in the middle of 1999. The idea was to blanket the market with a wide variety of channels to cover the various buying needs. Merrill went from three to five channels. As shown in figure 11-4, it added an online channel, ML Direct, to attract first-time investors, pricing it on par with Schwab at $29.95 a trade. For its existing customers, Merrill created a fee-based, integrated channel option, Total Merrill (then called Unlimited Advantage). For a percentage of their assets (1 percent at the time of launch), these customers received the services of a financial consultant, and they could also trade online as often as they wished. These, combined with the existing traditional channel and the telephone channel—Financial Advisory Center (called Investor Services at that time)—provided broad coverage of Merrill Lynch's various market segments.

Called Integrated Choice, Merrill Lynch clients were offered a continuum of channels from the fully self-directed (ML Direct) to the fully delegated (discretionary). Based on their individual needs and preferences, clients could opt for single or multiple accounts.

Not wanting to limit client choices, Merrill Lynch gave its clients the option of maintaining more than one type of account. Thus, clients could have some of their assets in ML Direct and the rest in Unlimited Advantage or a traditional account, and they could choose whether to let their financial consultant view their ML Direct account.

What is unique about the approach that Merrill Lynch took was that it adopted both forms, one with the Internet as a stand-alone and the other

FIGURE 11-4

Merrill Lynch: Integrated choice

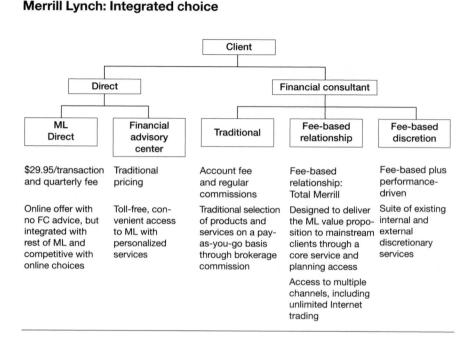

ML Direct	**Financial advisory center**	**Traditional**	**Fee-based relationship**	**Fee-based discretion**
$29.95/transaction and quarterly fee	Traditional pricing	Account fee and regular commissions	Fee-based relationship: Total Merrill	Fee-based plus performance-driven
Online offer with no FC advice, but integrated with rest of ML and competitive with online choices	Toll-free, convenient access to ML with personalized services	Traditional selection of products and services on a pay-as-you-go basis through brokerage commission	Designed to deliver the ML value proposition to mainstream clients through a core service and planning access	Suite of existing internal and external discretionary services
			Access to multiple channels, including unlimited Internet trading	

with the Internet as part of an integrated offering. ML Direct was a stand-alone channel and Total Merrill was an Internet-integrated channel.

There was compelling evidence to suggest that the new wave of customers initially choosing Schwab would one day grow to have high levels of assets. If Merrill failed to capture them now, it would miss out on their future, especially when new competitors like Schwab had broadened their capabilities to include full service. This meant that Merrill Lynch had to make a concerted attempt to enlist these customers. But its current face-to-face channel was inappropriate, only in part for reasons of cost. Merrill Lynch's reputation was built on its full service and hand-holding—precisely the features that the new breed of young investors wished to avoid. To this group of customers, Merrill Lynch was seen as a high-cost service aimed at people quite unlike themselves. These technology-savvy customers wanted readily accessible research information on the Web. They had the confidence and inclination to make the investments themselves. For these customers, the Merrill Lynch brand was baggage. If Merrill Lynch wanted to target these customers, it needed to demarcate the new channel and perhaps create a new service with a new brand. In short, Merrill Lynch would have to build a completely new channel capability to address a completely new (to it) demand chain.

Although this analysis suggests that ML Direct would be the centerpiece of Merrill Lynch's strategy, its core asset was the $1 trillion left in its hands by nearly 250,000 priority clients. These customers had been loyal to Merrill Lynch over the years and had valued the advice offered by its financial advisers; but in the Internet era, they wished to have the added utility to play a bit with their investments. It was the absence of this feature that drove them to competitors like Schwab. Even then, they did not take all their assets, only a portion. It would have been too risky otherwise.

Thus, Merrill Lynch created "Unlimited Advantage," an integrated channel that let customers conduct their inquiries and transactions any time through any channel, at their convenience. For one common fee, they could choose how they wanted to do business. They could seek advice through one channel and transact through the other, or any combination. It didn't make sense to price brokerage transactions at one fee and Internet transactions at another, so Merrill Lynch changed the fee structure to represent a percentage of assets, regardless of transaction mode.

Thus, Merrill Lynch developed two new channels—one primarily to defend and enhance its existing business model, and the other to attract customers from a newly developing segment with whom it had not traditionally done business. When you attempt to enter a new market segment, the Internet can serve (if need be) as the centerpiece of the new channel. But if you're defending and deepening relationships with existing customers, you must integrate the Internet with the existing channels.

The New Wrinkle

When developing multiple-channel systems that span the customer life cycle (or buying cycle), you need to build systems that engineer cross-channel migration. ML Direct was created to attract emerging new customers, and "Unlimited Advantage" was created to retain Merrill's existing customers. Different product bundles, prices, and brand positions characterized the two channels—one a no-frills, low-service, low-price channel, and the other full-service, with unlimited trading access and an asset-based pricing structure.

Merrill Lynch did not seek an independent identity for the direct channel, perhaps because the ultimate plan was to transition customers to the sweet spot of its business model, its full-service channel. That is where its key competitive advantages and its core competencies lay. But this meant that the multiple-channel strategy needed to include a strategy for migrating customers across the channels. The company realized that a significant number of its traditional brokerage customers preferred the services of its telephone channel. This was true especially of people with smaller assets at Merrill, who did not get the same attention from the company's financial consultants as did their larger counterparts.

Here's how it worked. First, a telephone representative was always available to assist larger clients, providing them with the desired information and completing any trades. Such customers also could choose between a transaction-based fee or an asset-based fee. To a great extent, this was a way to align customers by channels that Merrill Lynch viewed as optimal.

Although this channel was designed in 1997 to serve clients with assets of about $100,000 or less invested at Merrill Lynch, experience showed that some clients with substantially larger assets preferred to be served this way. These clients usually did not like to trade much and sought help selectively, but when they did so, they liked a prompt, knowledgeable response rather than a personal but delayed response. Their notion of relationship was based on service speed. Careful account analysis at Merrill Lynch led to this channel swelling fivefold, to more than a million customers, by 2004.

As in the framework of figure 10-3 from chapter 10, Merrill's approach was an attempt to align customers along a frontier of effectiveness and efficiency so that different customer segments were served by different channels, each being the most optimal channel from the customer's as well as the company's perspective. Customers could then migrate up and down the various channels depending on the best fit.

This is clearly a new wrinkle in multiple-channel management, where channels are meant to capture the life-cycle movements of customers. Proactively designing and managing that evolution are the tasks of a channel steward. In fact, different channel combinations must facilitate not only the life cycle but also a customer's different purchasing behaviors. The Internet has made it entirely possible to do so.

Integrated, Coordinated, and Competitive

The problem of multiple-channel management is not new, but technology, especially the Internet, has served up variations that call for creative

FIGURE 11-5

Multiple channels come in different flavors

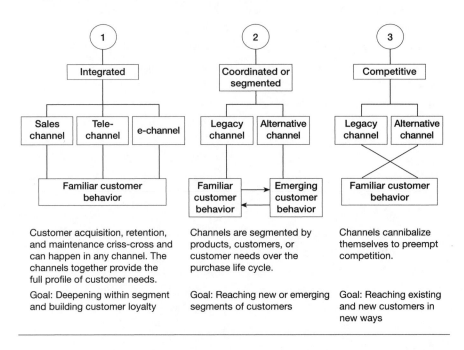

Customer acquisition, retention, and maintenance criss-cross and can happen in any channel. The channels together provide the full profile of customer needs.

Channels are segmented by products, customers, or customer needs over the purchase life cycle.

Channels cannibalize themselves to preempt competition.

Goal: Deepening within segment and building customer loyalty

Goal: Reaching new or emerging segments of customers

Goal: Reaching existing and new customers in new ways

new ways of coordinating a multiple-channel system. These approaches include the time-tested rules of constructing channel separations that have demonstrated their value in conventional multiple-channel systems. To discuss how they should be coordinated, we classify these systems into three broad categories: integrated, coordinated (segmented), and competitive (see figure 11-5). Our view of the conflict management challenges is summarized in figure 11-6.

In integrated systems, all the channels work together to give customers various avenues for search, acquisition, and support. The key coordination task is to create a seamless way for customers to weave through the maze and give them transparency across the various channel media. Customers should have the option of searching on one channel, ordering on another, and following up on a third, with the system providing full information about what transpired in earlier steps in any of the channels.

Tools like CRM (customer relationship management) are useful because they integrate the customer experience. Although new customers will be

FIGURE 11-6

Conflict management challenges

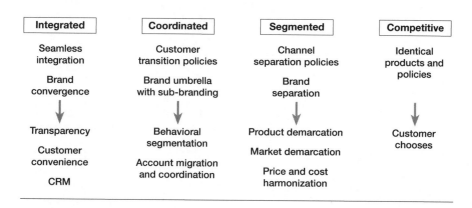

added to the fold, in terms of their buying behavior the channel designer need only deal with what is known. This calls for a deepening within the known segment rather than reaching out to new pastures. The idea of integration is to provide a unified platform for acquiring and retaining customers and sustaining the relationship by developing a lifelong loyalty to the supplier's value proposition. An integrated system is more costly than one that is specialized by function, because each component of the integrated channel performs multiple functions. But the key design criterion is to focus on how much more value such an integrated approach will create for customers, especially known customers.

In coordinated systems, the channels are indeed separated and are aimed at addressing the demand-chain needs of various customer segments, or even differing behaviors of the same customer on different purchase occasions or through changes in the life cycle. Although the demand side is segmented, such systems call for considerable coordination to ensure the fidelity of the channel separation. It should be difficult for customers to substitute any part of the entire value bundle from an alternate channel. Each match between their demand chain needs and channels would be the most appropriate fit for the purchase occasion.

Here is where a coordinated channel differs from an integrated channel. There must be subtle variations in your brand representation to reflect the differing value propositions of the channels. Should the differing brands be united under an overarching brand umbrella? That depends on how you plan to migrate customers. Merrill Lynch, for example, positioned ML Direct as a sub-brand, because it expected to transition a portion of that customer base within a few years of entering that channel. That is also the case with ING Direct and ING Bank. Even though the two channels are separated and targeted at different customer segments, the bank has ambitions to cross-sell. But in other cases, where the migration is not expected soon, a separate brand franchise may help to further distinguish the two offerings.

Where you lack such clear differentiation, you need judicious rules and incentives to ensure separation of the customer pools served by the separate channels. These rules ensure that the channels are segmented by products, customers, or customer needs over the purchase life cycle. The idea is to reach out and cover new markets or segments of buying behavior, and that is the reason to have a differentiated channel structure to sensibly coordinate the overlaps.

In a multiple-channel structure where emerging channels are set up as competing options, there is no need for channel separation. The idea is to let the channels compete and then transition to the winning bandwagon. Thus, although the supplier may not differentiate on products, product quality, or prices offered to the multiple channel partners, the extent of value addition in each channel will differ, and therefore customers will get a differentiated product bundle from the different channels. Not all the options will survive, and that is to be expected. The key motivation for the channel designer here is to ensure that it is not left out of a potential market opportunity or left napping as the industry undergoes change.

As we have said, a channel steward needs to have a clearly articulated channel strategy before launching an effort to manage its multiple channels. In some cases, management might involve setting rules and boundaries and even pruning channel partners that do not fit the logic. At other times, it might involve a more laissez-faire approach backed up by clear account migration and transition paths, or stepping back and letting the most effective and efficient channels win. The best approach depends on what your channel goals are to start with and why you embarked on the multiple-channel venture. These decisions must be made at a senior level, where the oversight of the entire channel strategy is vested.

12

Strategy and
Implementation of
Channel Stewardship

THROUGHOUT MUCH OF THIS BOOK, we have approached the concept of stewardship from the standpoint of channel strategy, focusing on issues and solutions within and close to channels of distribution. The key idea is to understand and harmonize the forces of the demand chain and your own channel capabilities while recognizing and calibrating the distribution of power throughout the channel. Ultimately, the goal of stewardship is to align and influence the channel system to address customer needs, while delivering appropriate financial returns to channel partners that contribute to achieving system goals.

Until now, we have stayed at the level of channel strategy. For channel stewards to perform to their fullest potential, however, the approach we advocate must be accepted as an essential part of business strategy. Many executives we have worked with make the mistake of viewing channel strategy as the implementation arm of business strategy. But it is at least an integral element, and sometimes it resides at the heart of business strategy. In effect, then, channel stewardship must permeate top management's awareness and decision making.

Our goal here is to frame the ideas in this book in a context aimed at giving top managers a working rationale for moving toward a stewardship model, and we offer a framework for building the business case for stewardship. We begin by sketching the actions of three pharmaceutical companies that attempted to vertically integrate their channels of distribution. Using the stewardship lens and elevating channel strategy to the level of business strategy, you'll see that they could have achieved their goals without having to integrate structurally. Building on the pharmaceutical examples and others, we build our case for drawing top management's attention to the discipline of channel stewardship. We close the chapter with some thoughts for managers on initiating the process.

Pharmaceuticals: The Strategy of Channel Acquisition

In the past ten years or so, three major pharmaceutical manufacturers acquired their respective distribution intermediaries (called pharmacy benefit managers, or PBMs). During 1993 and 1994, Merck acquired Medco, which served about 38 million individuals; SmithKline (now part of Glaxo Wellcome) acquired DPS (Diversified Pharmaceutical Services), serving about 11 million individuals; and Eli Lilly acquired PCS Health Systems, serving about 50 million people.[1] Shortly thereafter, each of these companies divested its acquisitions—Eli Lilly in 1998, SmithKline in 1999, and Merck in 2003.[2]

Why acquire a downstream channel partner? Why divest that same partner shortly thereafter? The rationale behind these manufacturers' actions provides a good backdrop against which to outline the inexorable links between channel strategy and overall business strategy and stress the importance of channel stewardship.

The Role of PBMs

Pharmacy benefit managers typically offer a range of services to large, self-insured employers, insurance carriers, managed care organizations, and government health plans that provide prescription drug coverage to their employees, retirees, or members.

PBMs first took shape in the mid-1960s but emerged as a major force only toward the middle of the 1980s. Before the arrival of PBMs, two parallel channels existed in the industry—one for the information and financial flow of pharmaceuticals, characterizing much of the demand-chain dynamics, and the other for the distribution of products, characterizing much of the action on the supply-chain side. There was no contact between the buyer (the insurance company or self-insured employer) and the seller (the pharmaceutical company).

On the financial and information side, employers contracted with a managed care plan or insurer to provide employee health benefits. Pharmaceutical needs were determined by doctors, who wrote prescriptions that were filled by pharmacies. Costs were either paid by patients or reimbursed by the insurance company. On the distribution side, manufacturers distributed their products through wholesalers to retail pharmacies, which made them available to patients. Because these channels were separated, there was little awareness of and no ability to control the costs of medications.

As shown in figure 12-1, PBMs quickly became the glue that connected buyers and sellers. Working on behalf of its customers, typically corporations, insurers, or managed care organizations (such as health maintenance organizations), a PBM aimed to reduce costs and optimize the use of medications. Initially, PBMs focused on claims processing.[3] But with the rise of managed care, PBMs grew in scope and by the mid-1990s had developed mechanisms to control drug costs: negotiated discounts with pharmacy networks, formulary development and management, and rebates from brand-name drug manufacturers. It was a classic case of reading the gaps in the demand chain and stepping in with new dimensions of service in the channel value chain.

FIGURE 12-1

Role of PBM in pharmaceutical flows

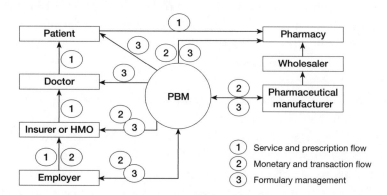

Source: V. Rangan and Marie Bell, "Merck-Medco: Vertical Integration in the Pharmaceutical Industry," Case 598-091 (Boston: Harvard Business School, 1998). Used with permission.

The Shifting Environment

Unsurprisingly, these intermediaries began to look attractive to the pharmaceutical companies. The acquisitions in question had much to do with the manufacturers' reading of the channel environment. In chapter 2, under our discussion of the mapping discipline, we identified a broader set of forces that impact channel strategy. Among these are macroeconomic trends and changes in the regulatory framework. These forces came into play in the pharmaceutical industry, driving manufacturers' actions.

In the early 1990s, the health-care industry was under attack. Health-care spending had grown to nearly 12 percent of GNP. The $100 billion pharmaceutical industry, traditionally removed from scrutiny because it represented only about 8 percent of health-care costs, found itself increasingly in the spotlight over the rising cost of its products as well as the margins it earned.

The health-care industry began moving from one environment—a traditional fee-for-service arrangement dominated by individual physicians and specialists referring patients to hospitals—to one that increasingly emphasized managed care organizations such as HMOs. In 1995, managed care organizations accounted for nearly 53 percent of total pharmaceutical sales, and many observers expected that managed care's share of the market would reach 90 percent by 2000.[4]

Under the changed environment, PBMs would be effective influences on the pharmaceutical companies because of their control of formularies as a major tool in influencing drug use.[5] PBMs offered to control their customers' drug costs by selecting certain drugs to be on the formulary and developing financial incentives to encourage the use of formulary products. In developing the formulary, PBMs used pharmacy and therapeutic (P&T) committees consisting of pharmacists and physicians to analyze the safety, efficacy, and substitutability of prescription drugs. PBMs took the recommendations of the P&T committee to develop a formulary listing a sufficient number of drugs to give physicians a number of treatment options. If an equivalent low-cost drug was available, it was inevitably included in the formulary and sometimes was highly recommended.

In this environment, pharmaceutical companies saw the PBMs as a key ally in getting their proprietary drugs, developed at great cost, on the formularies of the drug benefit providers, and hence the acquisitions.[6]

However, when three significant industry players integrated downstream for roughly the same reason, it caused another shift in the environment. The Federal Trade Commission feared that the industry giants would lock up their respective distribution channels with proprietary drugs, thus promoting a monopoly supply chain, which in turn could potentially affect consumer welfare by restricting choices. To discourage such practices, the FTC sought sanctions and agreements that required PBMs to install impartial committees to determine formularies, accept and pass on drug discounts offered by rival manufacturers, and protect the confidentiality of competitor data from their pharmaceutical company owners.[7] Under the new scenario, ownership of the channel was unnecessary, so it made perfect sense for the manufacturers to divest their holdings. Eli Lilly signed a consent decree and subsequently divested itself of PCS Health Systems. SmithKline soon followed suit.

Merck attempted to erect an arm's-length relationship with Medco, giving it independence and freedom to structure policies (especially the formularies), with a view to maximizing value to clients.[8] Merck continued to own Medco for several years, attempting to shift Medco's focus to mining downstream patient information on disease states, drug usage, compliance, and other data that would benefit the health-care provider as well as the pharmaceutical companies. Ultimately, though, Merck was unable to demonstrate to its shareholders the synergistic advantages of the vertical integration, and it divested in 2003.

The Channel Stewardship Challenge

The challenge faced by the pharmaceutical companies was how to influence their customers (end users) and channel partners to give them a disproportionate share of their wallets in the market for "approximately equivalent" drugs. Here is where our principles of channel stewardship could usefully come into play. The challenge of having to work through a powerful intermediary that shares shelf space with competitors is not new to channel managers. Downstream vertical integration is one structural solution, which Merck and others in the industry took. Our discussions in chapters 4, 5, and 6 offered alternative approaches to the same problem.

Consider this: the maker of the drugs does not possess any information on drug usage and compliance. The efficacy of a drug in real use can be compromised by interaction with other drugs or even patients' dietary habits and lifestyles. Drug companies may spend nearly $1 billion to discover a drug and take it through three phases of clinical trial before seeking the FDA's approval, but they are cut off from customer usage data, which only the PBMs possess. Such data could be crucial for the treatment of chronic illnesses and further development of new drugs and regimens.

This is the gap that Merck tried to bridge through its attempts at health management programs when it owned Medco. A typical program targeted a disease, such as asthma or diabetes, and worked through a care and treatment regimen starting with lifestyle habits (exercise, diet), medications, and so on. The focus would be on a patient's health and whether or not its management warranted medications. After the program was fully developed and validated, Medco educated those enrolled in the plan and their physicians about the more cost-effective treatment programs and monitored the rate of compliance all the way down to drug usage by patients.

It is precisely this information gap that our idea of alignment attempts to bridge. To do so, ownership is not always necessary. As long as the channel system is appropriately stewarded, it can function as a virtually integrated channel. Thus, what the three industry participants approached as a channel structure decision could well have been tackled as a channel stewardship challenge.

As discussed earlier, particularly in chapter 6, a key to gathering the kind of information that closes the end-user loop is to build a deeper partnership with intermediaries and, by gaining their confidence, to boost your presence in their product and service portfolio. Indeed, our ideas on channel stewardship lend themselves to application of a full range of channel decisions that shape a firm's business strategy. Top managers should leverage this opportunity when it comes to engaging in channel strategy.

Other Channel Challenges Calling for Strategic Action

Contrast the channel strategy challenges of the pharmaceutical industry with those of the airline industry. Whereas the top pharmaceutical managers saw the higher-level strategic possibilities without necessarily taking advantage of the operational ways of getting there, the airlines took the opposite tack. On the one hand, they showed great alacrity in seizing the operational advantages offered by new technology to migrate their channels away from travel agents to the Internet. On the other hand, they have only begun to harness the strategic possibilities of the Internet in addressing the core imbalance of supply and demand and the opportunity to align prices with fine-grained customer segmentation and channel demarcation. What now appears to be a multiple-channel strategy, with the Internet playing an increasingly important role, is only the tip of the iceberg. The payoff for the airlines will come when these channels are aligned with the various customer buying behaviors and with customers' willingness to pay a price conditional on the value they receive. When properly conceived and integrated as part of a firm's business strategy, what might initially appear to be a channel innovation has fundamental implications for business strategy.

The U.S. entertainment industry provides a good example of this last point. About five hundred movies were released in 2003, nearly 40 percent by the large studios such as Disney and the remainder by independent producers, some big (such as DreamWorks) and others small.[9] In 2003, it cost about $64 million, on average, to make a movie, and another $39 million to market, promote, and distribute it. Only about 60 percent of movies made a profit at the box office, and only about 10 percent were considered box-office blockbusters (having revenues exceeding $100 million).[10] Considering that most of these blockbusters are produced at a much higher cost than an average movie, their profitability is severely squeezed, assuming there is any at all. Movies are distributed through channels known as windows in a sequential pattern that can last as long as two years (see figure 12-2).

FIGURE 12-2

Channel windows for filmed entertainment

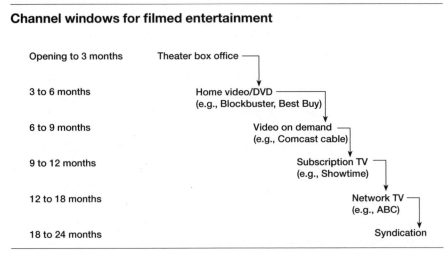

So a blockbuster makes money every time it cascades through the channel windows. Prudently holding it at the box office to optimize the initial spurt is part of channel management. In the view of some industry leaders, the industry "may have gone too far with moving up DVD releases."[11] But if a movie is a flop—at least 40 percent are, to some degree—careful management of the channel windows adds an incremental contribution to the sunk costs. If the movie has only a brief exposure at the box office, it may achieve a cultlike fan following if later released in a handful of exclusive channels. Alternatively, it might go into the home video market sooner than the usual six months; some in the industry not only support shortening the channel windows but even advocate releasing certain movies to theaters, DVDs, and video on demand all on the same day.[12] In fact, only about 30 percent of a movie's revenues come from the box office; videos and DVDs contribute nearly 40 percent, and broadcast channels account for the other 30 percent.[13]

The point is that different channel windows have different profit potential for different movies. By carefully integrating the product design (in this case, the creative content) with channel rollout strategies, an astute business can enhance the profit potential of its portfolio. These decisions are overseen by operational managers but have enormous strategic consequences for company profitability.

As with the pharmaceutical manufacturers, here too there is obviously the temptation to own the channels. Conventional thinking says that the more channel property you own, the higher the chances of leveraging the one in two successful products that come your way and of minimizing the losses of the failing one. That is one reason Disney owns the ABC TV network.[14] But here is the catch. If ABC were to broadcast a disproportionate number of Disney movies, for example, it is not hard to see why it might be a flawed proposition for itself and its viewers, who span a broader demographic group than those who would relate to Disney's offerings alone. ABC would need to broadcast successful content from other producers to keep its broader viewership happy and its profits healthy, just as it would need the reach of its competitors' channels to flog its own broad product line.

All this calls for a system of management that has a high degree of interdependency without vertical ownership, and that takes us back to channel stewardship. When channel strategy plays out as business strategy, the task of channel stewardship coincides with the role of steering a firm's destiny. It involves using and collaborating with competitors and their channels, and it necessitates senior management's attention and involvement.

Starting at the Top

An organization will find opportunities to evolve its channels at any number of interfaces. To guide the company's future, members of top management who are charged with charting a strategy are usually the ones who attempt to track changes in the environment. Thus, members of that team should also undertake the kind of mapping we have advocated, charting the movement of the demand chain, the capabilities and power positions of the various channel partners, and the nature of competitive actions. It is crucial that such analysis be conducted systematically and objectively to avoid blind spots and entrenched assumptions. A credible analysis is essential to sell the idea of channel evolution to both internal and external stakeholders.

It was a similar mapping exercise that alerted the pharmaceutical companies to pay closer attention to potential acquisitions. Your analysis should go further, mapping the effects of external forces on the demand chain and channel capabilities. These forces include changes in trade practices or regulation, technological innovations in production and the supply chain, macroeconomic trends, and so on, all of which influence customers' buying patterns and the channels they choose.

A valuable lesson can be learned from the pharmaceutical industry. These channel determinants are influenced by what seem to be independent outside forces but sometimes are themselves the consequence of actions by industry players. The FTC, for example, constrained potential actions by the vertically integrating suppliers. So the mapping discipline should include contingency planning and "what if" exercises. War games and other simulations are also useful in helping you understand the impact of your own and competitors' moves.

Many firms routinely conduct strategic analysis and construct future scenarios, but rarely do they translate their projections to the level of the core forces that determine channel strategy: the demand chain, channel capability, channel power, and competitive actions. When such high-level analyses are triggered by pain points in a channels-to-market strategy, top managers become receptive to evolving the firm's distribution channels. Absent such triggers, channel strategy usually gets short shrift.

Our channel stewardship approach calls for proactive leadership from top managers as well as from operational managers, resulting in a thoughtful and practical path toward channel transformation through active stewardship. It is the operational managers who face the pain points.

Starting in the Field

A straightforward way to get attention is to focus on areas of immediate importance and consequence, which manifest themselves in one of several forms. Sales or margin performance, or the lack of it, is often a good starting point. Whatever the reasons, when a company's sales and marketing systems do not generate a target volume, there is reason to review the go-to-market strategy. Before you begin transforming your channels, you must identify the problems, determine where they are located in the channel value chain, and assess how they affect channel performance.

Conflict with or between channel members, especially when a significant customer or prominent channel member is involved, is another important alert. Specific problems in the alignment of your channel often provide an excellent opportunity to ask the deeper questions implied by the three disciplines of stewardship.

The trick, however, is to not yield to the temptation to try a quick fix. Instead, what is called for is a thoughtful analysis of the underlying issues. Here is where the framework of channel stewardship becomes a useful starting point for management action. Although the following does not summarize the many ideas advanced in this book, it provides two useful perspectives that convey the strategic implications of the channel stewardship framework.

Top Managers: Channels as a Collection of Capabilities

Instead of viewing the channel design problem as one of finding the right channel partner to get products to market, our framework suggests viewing the problem as one of constructing the appropriate set of capabilities to get the product from manufacturer to consumer.

Figure 12-3 shows the perspective of a supplier's two customer segments, each with its own set of needs. The demand chain for segment 1 requires the channel value chain to construct the composite capabilities shown: capabilities A, B, and C are taken from the supplier's reserve, and capability Z

FIGURE 12-3

Channels as capabilities

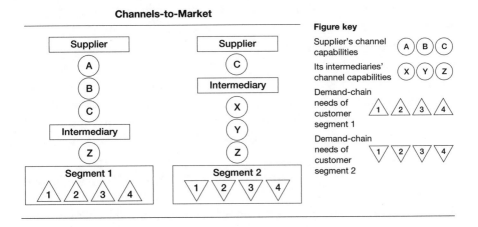

from the intermediary's reserve. Collectively, these four capabilities address the customer segments' demand-chain needs.

For customer segment 2, however, the composite is somewhat different, with the intermediary providing capabilities X, Y, and Z and the supplier pitching in with capability C. It is the capability pipe from supplier to customer that determines the nature of the channel value chain, and not the structure of the institutions and intermediaries that mediate this link.

So under the new mind-set we propose, suppliers and intermediaries develop the appropriate capabilities and, under the watchful eye of the channel steward, put together the appropriate combination to address customer needs. The capability pipe will evolve with the evolution of customers' demand-chain needs, the capabilities of the suppliers and their intermediaries, and the effectiveness and efficiency of deploying these capabilities. The key idea is that the capability pipes are dynamic and should respond to the environment. Occasionally there may be a perfect match between capabilities and the institutions that have them, but channel stewardship aims to put aside the channel structure idea and bring to the forefront a flexible combination of channel value chain components.

In the figure 12-3 scenario, for segment 1, the channel steward is likely the supplier itself, which must ensure that its intermediary is adequately compensated for the one key capability it brings to bear. For segment 2, it is the intermediary that is likely the steward. Being closer to that customer, perhaps it has a better sense of customers' needs and knows how to structure the composite capabilities. This closeness naturally translates into more power and profits, but channel stewardship means that the partner, in this case the supplier, must also get adequate returns for its efforts. Otherwise, it may have no incentive to perpetuate the current system.

These are the same ideas we espoused earlier, but now we present them from the perspective of top management. In leading their organizations, senior managers must dynamically manage the consequences of developing, building, and editing the channel value chain. They must invest in resources, both capital and human, to realize the full potential indicated in the figure.

Having urged top managers to view channels as collections of capabilities, we recognize that many of these capabilities reside with channel partners that must be motivated to act in the interests of the channel value chain. That task, as we have advocated, is best performed by a team of specialists, all working on a common, multidimensional goal: customer satisfaction, partner satisfaction, and fair profits for all those involved in adding channel value.

To promote this complex coordination, channel systems must promote transparency in the channel value chain and trust among the managers of the various organizations. Such behaviors solidify the mutual commitment to enhance channel performance. But what is commitment, if not top management's promise to commit organizational resources? Much channel conflict is the result of a breakdown in the crucial process of team building, and top management must realize its critical role in promoting the culture in which this team spirit takes root and flourishes in the stewardship of its channels.

From the perspective of the core forces described in chapter 2, multiple channels are a manifestation of the jockeying that characterizes the forces of the demand chain versus the capabilities of the channel. It indicates that the environment is forcing a channel's evolution. Either the supplier's customers have changed their buying practices and are buying from a different channel, or significant new market opportunities have emerged that are forcing the supplier to consider alternative channels. Whatever the reason, when demand-chain needs are different for different sets of customers (or for different buying behaviors of existing customers), either existing channels must evolve or new channels must be added.

At least for the next several years, if not longer, multiple channels are a way of life. They are a leading indicator of the need to carefully navigate the natural forces in the market, but, in doing so, managers must carefully construct rules and boundaries after they have defined the goals of the strategy.

As an extension of a multiple-channel strategy, the Internet must find a prominent position in a firm's channel portfolio, either as an integrated or a stand-alone channel. As we have discussed, this new channel has the unique capability of enhancing effectiveness as well as efficiency. Top management cannot afford to let this opportunity slip, because winning business models are being shaped now that can have long-term effects on the nature and shape of competition. Being out of sync now means being out of the race forever.

Operational Managers: A Balanced View of Channel Alignment

Impending conflicts with important channel partners and customers quickly get the attention of operational managers because of their potential impact on revenues and the bottom line. Because managers often cannot predict the real outcome on the bottom line, channel systems tend to fall back on the status quo. This is especially true of suppliers. Another reason for this reaction is that individuals in the two firms have invested years in developing relationships. These relationships often predate the tenure of the current managers of the function, especially at the supplier end.

But conflicts occur because the supplier and its channel partner disagree about the match between customers' needs and the capabilities of the channel system that serves them. That's why such situations provide another opportunity to go beyond the human emotions and bring to bear the logic and analysis underlying the arguments laid out here. As described earlier, such operational issues often are a sign of poor alignment and faulty channel design. But operational managers may not perceive it that way, or, even when they do, they incorrectly assume that they are helpless to effect change. Under the principles of channel stewardship, we urge operational managers to press on with the analysis and build the bigger picture for the attention of senior management.

In doing so, operational managers must carefully balance three important considerations. The first is the trust and rapport that exist between the key individuals in both organizations, followed by the commitment demonstrated by the two organizations. The second consideration is the parties' respective power positions and the posturing that might follow. Third and most important, from the perspective of the channel steward-ship ideas proposed here, managers must carefully develop a blueprint of each organization's contributions in addressing customers' needs.

The heart of this analysis is proposed in chapter 6, and you should not flinch from integrating it into your analysis of the underlying causes of the channel's performance. Management's role is to bring a balanced view of the conflict, incorporating all three legs: trust and transparency; power and control; and channel value chain performance. Anything else is only a bandage solution to a deeper problem.

This recommendation should not be misconstrued to mean that a firm should inevitably choose the disintermediating option. Far from it. Often, the tough option leads you to the humbling realization that the channel partner (either upstream or downstream) is the one that brings the bulk of the value to customers. But if that is the case, you must assess how you can be productive in contributing to the channel steward's vision and goals in serving the demand chain. Is this an acceptable position, or would it be better to build power sources so as to gain better control and leverage, especially in a poorly led channel? The answer has implications for long-term channel strategy.

With the availability of IT solutions, you have an opportunity to redefine relationships with your customers and channel partners. As we have argued, these solutions are only the building blocks of an overall technical architecture that can be a powerful platform for stewarding a channel in the interests of customers. Knowing this, operational managers should attempt to extend the boundaries of IT initiatives to understand the broader logic of what these solutions can do for a channel strategy.

Many products find a circuitous path to end users. A supplier might try to gain business leverage by treating the intermediary like a customer. That is a serious mistake. Even if the supply chain stops at the intermediary, the supplier should extend its information chain all the way to the end customer. This need not be done surreptitiously, working around the channel partner, but should be done in a sharing way.

A supplier must be astute in converting upstream sources of power, such as product or technology advantages, into a lasting channel advantage. Unless such advantages are concretely protected, they are likely to be dissipated by actions of downstream channel players, which themselves may be in a position to take advantage of the product's value-adding capabilities.

The real question, then, is how you participate in the profit pool that results from your upstream technology. More often than not, such issues show up on the operational side, where middle managers may not perceive the strategic aspects of a channel policy or may not be confident that top management will perceive it that way. The alternative path—going around current channels—often requires policy approvals and investment decisions that could delay and even reverse performance trajectories, so operational managers tend to settle for the status quo. As a result, they handle structural issues in a transaction mode, ignoring the variety of stewardship approaches that can address issues central to their firms' strategies. Channel stewardship is about gaining the leverage to track and allocate the profit pool. Management should not shy away from it.

The Channel Stewardship Process

Surely there are many more opportunities than the handful sampled here for managers to forge a channel strategy that integrates with the firm's overall strategy. Nonetheless, our purpose is to underscore a key lever of channel stewardship: finding a match for customers' demand-chain requirements.

Such a vision must permeate the organization. Senior managers as well as operational managers must recognize that, in one way or another, the chronic and persistent problems they face have a common origin: a lack of channel stewardship. Whether it is confusion regarding channel roles and responsibilities, vertical conflict with a distribution partner, horizontal conflict among the distributors, a channel compensation problem, or a lack of performance, they are all interconnected in our channel stewardship framework. It is important for operational managers to draw the attention of top managers, if only to educate them on the ground-level realities, all of which have a bearing on the firm's overall strategy.

The three disciplines of channel stewardship—mapping; building and editing the channel value chain; and aligning and influencing the channel system—go hand in hand. Top managers are usually quite cognizant of the mapping discipline, although they might not know it by that name. Their leadership in plotting and navigating a winning path through the maze of environmental and competitive forces is at the core of their function. It is central to strategy formulation. When it comes to channel stewardship, however, top managers must delve deeper into the three disciplines of channel stewardship.

As in our illustration of the pharmaceutical and entertainment industries, the answer to the stewardship question lies in channel design and management through the editing and the alignment disciplines. Acquisition may be effective for other business reasons, but in a channel context, the other aspects should be considered as part of the strategy. This calls for a proactive stance by top managers in calling for the kind of analysis we recommend.

In a sense, channel stewardship requires two independent processes to come together (see figure 12-4). One process, shown at the bottom, is the continuous process of channel management, with its day-to-day management challenges. We urge operating managers to view this as an opportunity to continuously tune the aligning and influencing discipline. They have much to gain by rising above the day-to-day issues of managing channel conflicts, whether vertical or horizontal. The job calls for more than simply keeping the channel members happy. It calls for assessing system performance at least once a year. The day-to-day then becomes a part of the larger blueprint.

This cycle should intersect and influence, but also be informed by, the longer cycle of strategy setting. Here, top management scans the environ-

FIGURE 12-4

Channel stewardship as strategy

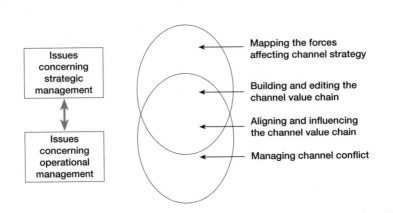

ment and anticipates changes in the business environment, a process we call the mapping discipline. Mapping should happen at least once every three years, or whenever major shifts in the environment occur or are anticipated.

When such an intersection happens regularly in a decision-making context—instead of an obligatory annual appearance before the corporate planning committee—much good can happen. Now the critical bridging discipline—building and editing—comes into play. In most companies, this is where the gap lies, because no one owns this function. Top managers often view this issue as insufficiently strategic to draw their attention, and operational managers often find themselves constrained for time and resources and without the authority to tackle what they consider a strategic issue. At times, the marketing function, which prepares annual plans for products and markets, may raise the key questions about channel capability and costs; but even then, sales budgets and targets take the limelight, and the critical channel questions are raised but never answered.

We have observed that in those companies that are committed to their channel stewardship role, usually there is a group of channel marketing managers who take on this role. They are the ones willing to break away from the old paradigms associated with channel management and embrace the new paradigm of channel stewardship. (See table 12-1 for a summary of the key attributes.) But it does not have to be that way. It is not the position that matters, but that some group of managers takes the responsibility for integrating the key disciplines of channel stewardship.

TABLE 12-1

Management implications

Old paradigm	New paradigm
1. Channel value chain: a vertical system	1. Channel value chain: a horizontal collaboration
2. Incentive system: relay race	2. Incentive system: team sport
3. Channel value chain somewhat of a black box	3. Channel value chain increasingly transparent
4. Profit pool not always within reach	4. Increasing access to profit pool

This is neither a day-to-day activity nor an occasional exercise. It is the platform that brings a strategic perspective and welds the needs of channel management with the longer-term frame of channel design. When that approach is further embedded within the larger vision of where the business should be headed, you have the ideal conditions for channel stewardship to flourish.

Notes

Introduction

1. These managers included John Stempeck, John Kavazanjian, Ranjit Singh, and Michael Ruffolo. See V. Kasturi Rangan, "Xerox: Book-In-Time," Case 599-119 (Boston: Harvard Business School, 1999, revised 2002).

2. "Annual Benchmark Report for Retail Trade and Food Services: January 1992 through February 2005," U. S. Census Bureau, March 2005, 5. Significant components of the $3.9 trillion in retail trade include motor vehicles and parts dealers ($882 billion), furniture, home furnishings and electronics, and appliance stores ($198 billion), building materials and garden equipment and supplies dealers ($303 billion), food and beverage stores ($498 billion), health and personal care stores ($205 billion), gasoline stations ($320 billion), clothing and clothing accessories stores ($190 billion), sporting goods, hobby, book, and music stores ($80 billion), general merchandise stores ($503 billion), nonstore retailers ($233 billion), and food services and drinking places ($380 billion).

3. "Annual Benchmark Report for Wholesale Trade: January 1992 through February 2005," March 2005, vi.

Chapter 1

1. Discussion of Rohm and Haas is drawn from V. Kasturi Rangan and Susan Lasley, "Rohm and Haas (A) New Product Marketing Strategy," Case 587-055 (Boston: Harvard Business School, 1986, revised 1993).

2. At this time, Compaq and Hewlett-Packard were independent entities. In 2002, Compaq was absorbed into Hewlett-Packard as part of a merger.

3. In the mid-1990s, IBM began an Authorized Assembler Program designed to make "channel assembly one of the cornerstones of its strategy to reduce inventory and help the channel better compete against direct marketers" (*Computer Reseller News*, November 18, 1996). In 1997, Compaq created a Channel Configuration Program to sell build-to-order products using channel assembly through its major resellers. During the same period, Hewlett-Packard announced its Extended Solutions Partnership, which had similar objectives. Although build-to-order through channel intermediaries was withdrawn, ultimately Compaq, Hewlett-Packard, and IBM created a build-to-order option through a direct channel. See Craig Zarley and Edward F. Moltzen, "IBM Beefs Up Channel Final-Assembly Plan," *Computer Reseller News*, January 27, 1997, 5; and Andy Shaw, "Building Your Own

Systems (Computer Suppliers' Relations with Resellers)," *Computer Dealer News*, June 2, 1997, 20.

4. John Pletz, "Dell Turns Productivity Gains into Market Share," *Austin American-Statesman*, August 26, 2002. The importance of scale in manufacturing was also seen after Hewlett-Packard's merger with Compaq. Within a year of the merger, Hewlett-Packard claimed $1.5 billion in savings from supply-chain operations. Darrell Dunn and Beth Bacheldor, "HP Faces Questions as Rivals Cut Prices," *InformationWeek*, August 25, 2003.

5. Discussion of Callaway Golf is drawn from Rajiv Lal and Edith D. Prescott, "Callaway Golf Co.," Case 501-019 (Boston: Harvard Business School, 2000, revised 2005).

6. Telephone interview with Callaway's then president, Patrice Hutin, October 26, 2004.

7. Discussion of Goodyear is drawn from John Quelch and Bruce Isaacson, "Goodyear: The Acquatred Launch," Case 594-106 (Boston: Harvard Business School, 1993, revised 1994).

8. Diane Clarkson, "Market Forecast Report, Travel 2004," Jupiter Research, October 9, 2004. The study estimates the size of the U.S. air travel market based on passenger tickets sold on scheduled airlines operating in the United States and international flights operating outside the United States.

9. "Airline Ticketing," GAO-03-749 (Washington, DC: U.S. General Accounting Office, 2003), 21.

10. Telephone conversations with Dave Edwards, vice president, Termiticide, Dow AgriBusiness, November 19, 2004.

11. Glover T. Ferguson, Anatole V. Gershman, Lucian P. Hughes, and Stanton J. Taylor, "Reality Online: The Business Impact of a Virtual World," *Outlook Special Edition*, Accenture, September 2002.

12. See, for example, Douglas M. Lambert, ed., *Supply Chain Management: Processes, Partnerships, Performance* (Sarasota, FL: Supply Chain Management Institute, 2004), 1–27, 123–164; and John T. Mentzer, *Fundamentals of Supply Chain Management: Twelve Drivers of Competitive Advantage* (Thousand Oaks, CA: Sage Publications, 2004): 1–23, 59–76.

13. The concept of the value chain is discussed in detail in Michael Porter, *Competitive Advantage: Creating and Sustaining Superior Performance* (New York: Free Press, 1985), 30–33.

14. The notion of "channel captain" has existed in the marketing literature since 1970. See Robert Little, "The Marketing Channel: Who Should Lead This Extra-corporate Organization," *Journal of Marketing* 34 (January 1970): 31–38. Its interpretation, however, has been equated to having the most power [see, for example, discussion in A. Coughlan, E. Anderson, L. W. Stern, and A. El-Ansary, *Marketing Channels*, sixth edition (Upper Saddle River, NJ: Prentice Hall, 2001), 36] to force the other channel members to implement the captain's agenda. Our notion of stewardship is quite different. Channel power may or may not be the driving force for a channel steward. Having the influence to effect channel performance is. Moreover, a channel steward is concerned not only with its returns but also that of other channel partners, and, most importantly, the channel steward aims to address customers' channel requirements (demand chain).

Chapter 2

1. Discussion of Snapple is drawn from John Deighton, "Snapple," Case 599-126 (Boston: Harvard Business School, 1999, revised 2003).

2. For a good description of the five forces framework and its embellishments, see Pankaj Ghemawat, *Strategy and the Business Landscape* (New York: Addison Wesley Longman, 1999), 19–48. The original framework in all its detail is available in Michael Porter, *Competitive Advantage: Creating and Sustaining Superior Performance* (New York: Free Press, 1985).

3. Paul Taylor, "NADA 2005 Data, Economic Impact of America's New-Car and New-Truck Dealers," *AutoExec Magazine*, May 2005, 41.

4. Ibid., 49.

5. Ibid., 45; and "Mega Dealer 100," *Ward's Dealer Business*, May 2005.

6. Julie Ask, "U.S. Automotive Consumer Survey," Jupiter Research, 2005, http://www.jupiterresearch.com/bin/item.pl/research:vision_print/93/83-96133/.

7. Richard Smith, "Franchise Regulation," *Journal of Law and Economics* (April 1982): 131.

8. Ibid., 131–132.

9. Greg Gardner, "Government Assault," *Ward's Auto World*, May 1996.

10. Robert McGarvey, "Car Chase," *Upside*, December 1999, 156–164, cited in Garth Saloner, A. Michael Spence, and Eric Marti, "Disintermediation in the U.S. Auto Industry," Case EC-10 (Stanford, CA: Stanford Business School), 20. Supported by a sampling of Massachusetts and Texas revenues. Based on 2002 state budgets, sales tax is 5 percent of Massachusetts revenues and 3 percent of Texas revenues.

11. Jonathan Fahey, "Dealers 1 Internet 0," *Forbes*, April 29, 2002.

12. Richard Smith, "Franchise Regulation," *Journal of Law and Economics* (April 1982): 133. Further detail is in "Franchise Laws in the Age of the Internet," NADA White Paper, January 2001. For example, to obtain a license, candidates had to have a contract with a manufacturer authorizing the dealer to sell a specific line of new cars and only those cars. Additionally, most states required that the dealer operate a facility in an established place of business, with many states specifying the size of the building, the capacity of the repair department, and so on.

13. When Ford launched a used-car site, legal action was taken in North Carolina, Arizona, and Florida, with these states passing regulations against manufacturer ownership of dealerships. In 1999, the U.S. District Court for the Western District of Texas in Austin upheld a state law that barred Ford from selling cars over the Internet even though sales went through licensed dealers, noting, "The plaintiff is prohibited from selling motor vehicles to consumers by mail, phone calls, leafleting, skywriting or drum signals, as well as on a plane, on a train, in a house or with a mouse." See "Franchise Laws in the Age of the Internet," NADA White Paper, January 2001, citing *Ford Motor Co. v Texas Department of Transportation, et al.*, U.S. District Court, Western District of Texas, July 20, 2000.

14. Paul Taylor, "NADA 2005 Data, Economic Impact of America's New-Car and New-Truck Dealers," *AutoExec Magazine*, May 2005, 45.

15. The networks of vendors and parts suppliers that supply the automobile factories are an integral part of the supply chain. Because of this chapter's downstream channels perspective, the linkages and networks extending from the supplier to the customer are focused in figure 2-5.

16. Taylor, "NADA 2005 Data," 43.

17. Lee Hawkins, Jr., "GM May Close at Least 3 Plants, Placing Further Pressure on UAW," *Wall Street Journal*, November 21, 2005.

18. "OEM Order to Delivery Process," CapGemini Ernst & Young, 2001, 39. Cited in *Goldman Sachs eAutomotive Report*, January 2000.

19. CapGemini, "Accelerating the Original Equipment Manufacturer Order-to-Delivery Process Through the Connected Automotive Value Chain," 2001, 39, itself citing *Goldman Sachs eAutomotive Report*, January 2000.

20. C. D. Bohon, "Survival and Triumph," *Ward's Dealer Business*, April 1996, 28.

21. Charles A. Synder, "Playing by the Rules," *Automotive Executive*, May 1992, 70.

22. "GM's New Chief Sets Management Agenda," *Reuters News*, August 1, 1990.

23. Saloner, Spence, and Marti, "Disintermediation in the U.S. Auto Industry," 11.

24. Keith Naughton, "Revolution in the Showroom," *BusinessWeek*, February 19, 1996, cited in Yankelovich Partners study.

25. "Ford Wins Most Categories in Polk Loyalty Study," *Automotive News*, December 15, 1997, 10; R. S. Sisodia and J. N. Sheth, "Car Retailing Needs a Tune-Up," *Wall Street Journal*, December 20, 1999, A26; and "Changing Channels in the Automotive Industry," *Strategy & Business*, First Quarter 1999, 44, all cited in Saloner, Spence, and Marti, "Disintermediation in the U.S. Auto Industry."

26. CapGemini, "Accelerating the Original Equipment Manufacturer Order-to-Delivery Process," 39.

27. "'Fewer but Larger' Trend Slashes US Dealer Totals," *Automotive News*, April 24, 1996.

28. Jan Muller, "Meet Your Local GM Dealer: GM—The Big Three Are Trying New Schemes to Combat Net Invaders," *BusinessWeek*, October 11, 1999.

29. Jeff Kurowski, "Retail Revolution Planned by Ford in Indianapolis," *Tribune Business Weekly*, June 19, 1997.

30. Mary Connelly, "Ford Dealers Repurchase Stores," *Automotive News*, November 19, 2001.

31. Saloner, Spence, and Marti, "Disintermediation in the U.S. Auto Industry"; and further in Robertson Stephens, *The eAuto Report*, January 11, 2000.

32. CarMax is unique among the public dealers. Primarily a used-car dealership, CarMax retooled its concept to include both large-scale and small dealership lots supported by satellite locations. Net income in fiscal 2002 and 2003 was $90 million and $94 million, respectively. The other public dealerships sell primarily new cars. By 2001, all the public dealerships were profitable. Analysis has suggested that the promise of the public dealerships was yet to be fulfilled. Without purchase advantages and with limited flexibility in locating new dealerships, scale economies proved somewhat limited. Acquisitions always ran the risk of losing local ownership presence, and dealer acquisition prices proved higher than expected, effectively dampening return on net operating assets.

33. Muller, "Meet Your Local GM Dealer."

34. Stefan M. Knupfer, Russell K. Richmond, and Johnathan D. Vander Ark, "Making the Most of U.S. Auto Distribution," *McKinsey Quarterly* no. 1 (2003).

35. Mark Cooper, "A Roadblock on the Information Superhighway: Anticompetitive Restrictions on Automotive Markets," Consumer Federation of America, February 2001, iv.

Chapter 3

1. Andy Serwer, "The Education of Michael Dell," *Fortune*, March 7, 2005, 73.

2. For example, in 1975, a computer chip had 65,000 transistors. By 1989, with the 486 processor, the number had risen to 1.4 million, and the newest Intel 0.13-micron technology had 55 million transistors on a fingernail-sized piece of silicon. When Moore's Law was first stated, a single transistor cost about $5. In 2004, that same $5 would purchase 5 million transistors. "Expanding Moore's Law," Intel Corporation, Product TL_002, 2002.

3. Data drawn from annual reports. The figures quoted for Hewlett-Packard include sales from HP and the former Compaq. On September 4, 2001, HP and Compaq announced a merger agreement to create an $87 billion technology leader under the HP name. The merger was narrowly approved by the HP board in March 2002.

4. Dell discussion is drawn from V. Kasturi Rangan and Marie Bell, "Dell New Horizons Teaching Note," Case 503-040 (Boston: Harvard Business School, 2002); Das Narayandas and V. Kasturi Rangan, "Dell Computer Corporation," Case 596-058 (Boston: Harvard Business School, 1995, revised 1996); V. Kasturi Rangan and Marie Bell, "Dell Online," Case 598-116 (Boston: Harvard Business School, 1998, revised 1999); and V. Kasturi Rangan and Marie Bell, "Dell—New Horizons," Case 502-022 (Boston: Harvard Business School, 2002).

5. Daniel Fisher, "Dell's Next Game," *Forbes Investment Guide*, Special Issue, June 10, 2002, 104.

6. Michael Dell with Catherine Fredman, *Direct from Dell* (New York: Harper Collins, 1999), 13.

7. Ibid.

8. Ibid., 159.

9. Ibid., 161.

10. Ibid., 204.

11. Drawn from Dell, Inc. Analyst Meeting Presentation, April 8, 2004, http://www .dell.com/downloads/global/corporate/sec/20040408_analyst.pdf.

12. Michael Dell, quoted in Narayandas and Rangan, "Dell Computer Corporation," 11.

13. Dell's entry into retail not only forced it to manufacture product to stock retail shelves, but also took away its biggest advantage: customization. Additionally, going through the trade meant that Dell had to provide it with an incentive. The Dell retail price index equaled 88 percent, compared with 100 percent for the Dell direct model. Dell also incurred expenses in support of the channel (training costs, replacement costs, and costs of obsolescence). The net effect was that Dell's operating expense went from 10 percent to 14 percent. All in all, Dell got lower gross margins going through the retail channel, but its operating expenses remained high. See Narayandas and Rangan, "Dell Computer Corporation," 11.

14. Adam Lashinsky, "Where Dell Is Going Next," *Fortune*, October 18, 2004, 115.

15. Serwer, "The Education of Michael Dell."

16. Michael Dell with Catherine Fredman, *Direct from Dell*, 26.

17. Ibid., 14–15. The technology combined the two hundred chips required to make a PC based on a 286 microprocessor into five or six ASIC (application specific integrated circuit) chips.

18. Bruce Einhorn, "Your Next TV: It Will Be Flat, Ultra High-Tech and Made in Asia," *BusinessWeek*, April 4, 2004, 32.

19. Serwer, "The Education of Michael Dell," 73.

20. Inferred from Michael Dell with Catherine Fredman, *Direct from Dell*, 14.

21. Joseph Maglitta, "Special Dell-ivery," *Electronic Business*, 1997, 44.

22. From 1998 to 2004, Dell's R&D expense as a percentage of net sales ranged from 1.0 percent to 2.3 percent; selling, general, and administrative (SGA) expenses ranged from 8.5 percent to 9.8 percent, respectively. By contrast, over the same period, HP's R&D as a percentage of product revenue was about 15 times that of Dell, and SGA as a percentage of net revenue was about 4 times that of Dell. Comparable figures for Compaq as an independent company were about 1.6 times for R&D and 7 times for SGA.

Chapter 4

1. At first glance, our six-step framework may resemble an eight-step procedure offered by Louis W. Stern and Frederick D. Sturdivant in an important *Harvard Business Review* article, "Customer-Driven Distribution Systems," July–August 1987. Indeed, the notion of service output levels offered in that article (based on Louis Bucklin's 1966 thesis, "A Theory of Distribution Channel Structure") is the key building block of our concept of the demand chain. Our framework, however, is anchored on the channel value chain principle and the role of the intermediary as a consequence of demand-chain requirements. Here is where the difference lies. We determine the nature of the intermediary combination in the last step of the model after thoroughly assessing and evaluating the customer's demand chain, whereas the Stern and Sturdivant framework is based on the institutional paradigm, driving the choice of the intermediary in the second step.

2. For a more elaborate analysis see: V. Kasturi Rangan, Melvyn A. J. Menezes, and E. P. Maier, "Channel Selection for New Industrial Products: A Framework, Method, and Application," *Journal of Marketing* 56 (July 1992): 69–82; and V. Kasturi Rangan, "The Channel Design Decision: A Model and an Application," *Marketing Science* 6 (Spring 1987): 156–178.

3. For insight into quantitative analysis associated with the consideration of the options, see ibid.

4. Much work exists in the institutional economics domain, especially in the realm of transaction cost theory, which at one time was interpreted by scholars and marketing academics as providing the defining framework on ownership versus delegation of channel tasks. But now it is widely accepted that such an interpretation is grossly incomplete. It is understood that channels are strategic investments and often the end result of a variety of analyses, of which short-term economics is only one component. This work can be found in Erin Anderson, George S. Day, and V. Kasturi Rangan, "Strategic Channel Design," *Sloan Management Review* (Summer 1997); and V. Kasturi Rangan, E. Raymond Corey, and F. Cespedes, "Transaction Cost Theory: Inferences from Clinical Field Research on Downstream Vertical Integration," *Organization Science* (August 1993).

5. A related term, *hybrid*, has been used by some management writers to describe such composite arrangements. But to be clear, *hybrid* has also been used to refer to situations in which multiple channels serve multiple customer segments. We use the term *composite* exclusively in the context of a single team in which members divide up responsibility for different functions within a single channel value chain serving a common customer.

Chapter 5

1. Much of the application of the theory of power in marketing channels can be traced to Richard Emerson, "Power-Dependence Relations," *American Sociological Review* 27, no. 1 (1962): 31–41. According to Emerson, power is a dyadic concept; it rests on the ability of actor A to elicit action from actor B. Much of that capability, Emerson argued, rests on the mutual dependence of actors A and B and the critical resources each controls to enable the other's actions.

2. The subject of channel power is discussed extensively in A. Coughlan, E. Anderson, L. W. Stern, and A. El-Ansary, *Marketing Channels*, sixth edition (Upper Saddle River, NJ: Prentice Hall, 2001), 199–235. For a discussion of power and how it is used to influence, see Jeffery Pfeffer, "Understanding Power in Organizations," *California Management Review* (Winter 1992): 29.

3. In the marketing literature, several sources of power have been identified, such as reward power (the ability to reward), coercive power (the ability to punish), expert power (product or market expertise), referent power (the desire of others to associate), and legitimate power (legal authority). See Coughlan et al., *Marketing Channels*, sixth edition, 206–214.

4. Louis W. Stern, Adel I. El-Ansary, and Anne T. Coughlan, *Marketing Channels*, fifth edition (Upper Saddle River, NJ: Prentice Hall, 1996), 287.

5. Jerry Useem, "One Nation Under Wal-Mart," *Fortune*, March 3, 2003; and Anthony Blanco and Wendy Zellner, "Low Prices Are Great, but Wal-Mart's Dominance Creates Problems," *BusinessWeek*, October 6, 2003.

6. Andrew Ross Sorkin and Steve Lohr, "Procter Closes $57 Billion Deal to Buy Gillette," *New York Times*, January 28, 2005, A1.

7. Mark Wigfield, "Appeals Court Orders FCC to Rewrite Media Rules," *Dow Jones News Service*, June 24, 2004.

8. The discussion of television channel systems has been drawn from V. Kasturi Rangan and Scott Lathrop, "Sunbeam Television (A)," Case 596-956 (Boston: Harvard Business School, 1995, revised 1996).

9. Marc Beauchamp, "Sticks and Stones," *Forbes*, May 5, 1986; and Jeffrey F. Rayport and Cathy Olofson, "Marshall Industries," Case 899-239 (Boston: Harvard Business School, 1999, revised 2001).

10. Beauchamp, "Sticks and Stones."

11. Ibid.

12. To the best of our knowledge, this trade practice was never taken up for consideration by the FTC as a potential unfair trading practice. At the time, there was ongoing litigation regarding antidumping charges that ultimately led to tariffs against Japan.

13. Share of Nike's domestic revenue from Christopher Lawton and Maureen Tkacik, "Foot Locker Changes Mix of Sneakers," *Wall Street Journal*, July 22, 2002; and Suzanne Kapner, "Sneaker Cease Fire: Nike, Foot Locker Near End to Painful Dispute," *New York Post*, July 24, 2003.

14. Kapner, "Sneaker Cease Fire."

15. Foot Locker has approximately 3,600 stores worldwide, encompassing Foot Locker, Lady Foot Locker, Kids Foot Locker, and Champs Sports. Foot Locker had five times as many stores as its closest competitor.

16. Isadore Barmash, "Foot Locker Chain of Athletic Shoes Is One of the Most Rapidly Expanding," *New York Times*, March 25, 1982.

17. Bill Saporito, "Woolworth to Rule the Malls, *Fortune*, June 5, 1989.

18. Maureen Tkacik, "Rubber Match: In Clash of Sneaker Titans, Nike Gets Leg Up on Foot Locker," *Wall Street Journal*, May 13, 2003.

19. Kevin Lane Keller, *Strategic Brand Management* (Upper Saddle River, NJ: Prentice Hall, 1998). Per the Keller book (E3), Prefontaine was the first athlete to be paid to wear Nike.

20. Robin Schatz, "Sneaker Wars," *Newsday*, November 22, 1987.

21. Nike, http://www.nike.com/nike/biz/media/nike_timeline/nike_timeline.pdf.

22. Keller, *Strategic Brand Management*, E5.

23. Inferred from Geraldine E. Willigan, "High-Performance Marketing: An Interview with Nike's Phil Knight," *Harvard Business Review*, July–August 1992, 91–100.

24. Nike, http://www.nike.com/nike/biz/media/nike_timeline/nike_timeline.pdf.

25. Keller, *Strategic Brand Management*, E9.

26. Tkacik, "Rubber Match."

27. Christopher Lawton and Maureen Tkacik, "Foot Locker Changes Mix of Sneakers," *Wall Street Journal*, July 22, 2002.

28. Thomas Ryan, "Foot Locker Steps Toward Greater Profits," *Sporting Goods Business*, February 2003.

29. Discussion on the dispute resolution drawn from Stanley Holmes, "Nike's Upward Swoosh," *BusinessWeek Online*, June 25, 2004; Amy Reeves, "Foot Locker Inc.," *Investor's Business Daily*, December 31, 2003; and Stephanie Kang, "Foot Locker Profit Jumps 25%, Boosted by Influx of Nike Shoes," *Wall Street Journal*, March 3, 2004.

30. For further discussion, see John F. Gaski, "The Theory of Power and Conflict in Channels of Distribution," *Journal of Marketing* 48 (Summer 1984): 9–29; John F. Gaski and John R. Nevin, "The Differential Effects of Exercised and Unexercised Power Sources in a Marketing Channel," *Journal of Marketing Research* 22, no. 2 (May 1985): 130–142; and Nirmalya Kumar, Lisa K. Scheer, and Jan-Benedict E. M. Steenkamp, "Interdependence, Punitive Capability and the Reciprocation of Punitive Actions in Channel Relationships," *Journal of Marketing Research* 35 (May 1998): 225–235.

Chapter 6

1. This example is drawn from V. Kasturi Rangan and Marie Bell, "Comergent Technologies Inc.: Enterprise E-Commerce," Case 505-016 (Boston: Harvard Business School, 2005).

2. This concept is further developed in Benson P. Shapiro, V. Kasturi Rangan, and John J. Sviokla, "Staple Yourself to an Order," *Harvard Business Review*, July–August 1992, 113.

3. A *Harvard Business Review* article identified four perils that CRM implementations should avoid; primary among them is a lack of vision on what it is supposed to do for and

regarding customers. Darrell K. Rigby, Frederick F. Reichheld, and Phil Schefter, "Avoid the Four Perils of CRM," *Harvard Business Review*, February 2002, 101–109.

4. Stuart Derrick, "The Foreseeable Future," *Revolution*, October 2003.

5. With the CPFR tool, manufacturers and suppliers exchange internal demand data and jointly come to decisions regarding production and purchase planning, demand fore-casting, and inventory replenishment between the partners in the supply chain. The value of the CPFR model is that it allows manufacturers and their partners to gain visibility into each other's demand chain, order forecasts, and promotional plans through a standardized, systematic process of shared brand and category planning.

6. Douglas Lambert suggests that supply-chain management is a composite of cus-tomer relationship management and supplier relationship management. He proposes eight processes that underlie supply-chain management, of which the first four (customer rela-tionship management, customer service management, demand management, and order ful-fillment) reside in the front end of the process we call channel value chain. Douglas M. Lambert, ed., *Supply Chain Management: Processes, Partnerships, Performance* (Sarasota, FL: Supply Chain Management Institute, 2004). Similarly, John Mentzer proposes a vision of supply-chain management that lies at the heart of competitive strategy and therefore a firm's bottom line. See John T. Mentzer, *Fundamentals of Supply Chain Management: Twelve Drivers of Competitive Advantage* (Thousand Oaks, CA: Sage Publications, 2004).

7. There is considerable coverage of trust and commitment in the marketing litera-ture. A comprehensive review is provided by Robert M. Morgan and Shelby D. Hunt, "The Commitment-Trust Theory of Relationship Marketing," *Journal of Marketing* 58 (July 1994): 20–38. Also see Patricia M. Doney and Joseph P. Cannon, "An Examination of the Nature of Trust in Buyer-Seller Relationships, *Journal of Marketing* 61 (April 1997): 35–51. Much of the marketing literature fails to distinguish interpersonal from interorganizational effects, most of it focusing on the constructs themselves rather than the levels at which they operate. In research undertaken with Das Narayandas, I have found that trust and commit-ment operate at distinct levels. See Das Narayandas and V. Kasturi Rangan, "Building and Sustaining Buyer-Seller Relationships in Mature Industrial Markets," *Journal of Marketing* 68, no. 3 (July 2004): 63–77.

8. In a comprehensive *Harvard Business Review* article based on surveys of thousands of dealers, Nirmalya Kumar showed that partners that trust each other generate greater profits, serve customers better, and are more adaptive. See Nirmalya Kumar, "The Power of Trust in Manufacturer-Retailer Relationships," *Harvard Business Review*, November–December 1996, 92–106.

9. There are many approaches to measure these constructs, but ultimately they must be driven by context. At times researchers have used measures of outcomes, such as level of conflict, satisfaction or dissatisfaction, and other affective measures. These measures pro-vide a clue about the health of the interactions in the channel, but for the purposes of align-ment, it is better to seek direct measures of power, trust, and commitment. In "The Power of Trust in Manufacturer-Retail Relationships," Nirmalya Kumar offers the following di-mensions of trust. *Distributive justice* deals with how profits are divided and how responsibil-ities and rewards are shared. *Procedural justice* refers to the framework (or otherwise) of the steward's procedures and policies for dealing with its vulnerable partners. *Communications* refers to the willingness of the partners to engage in dialogue. *Impartiality* is the dimension of trust that reflects how partners are dealt with equitably. *Refutability* means that vulnerable partners have a process for participating in or appealing channel policy decisions. Also see, for example, Gary L. Frazier, "On the Measurement of Interfirm Power in Channels of Distribution," *Journal of Marketing Research* 20 (May 1983): 158–166; and Adel El-Ansary and Louis W. Stern, "Power Measurement in the Distribution Channel," *Journal of Market-ing Research* 9 (February 1972): 47–52.

10. Lisa K. Scheer and Louis W. Stern, "The Effect of Influence Type and Perfor-mance Outcomes on Attitudes Toward the Influencer," *Journal of Marketing Research* 29

(February 1992): 128–142, demonstrated that a less dominant influence approach engendered more positive attitudes, which is a core theme of this chapter.

11. Jerry Useem, "One Nation Under Wal-Mart," *Fortune*, March 3, 2003, 64.

12. These concepts are discussed in Nirmalya Kumar, Louis W. Stern, and Ravi S. Achrol, "Assessing Reseller Performance from the Perspective of the Supplier," *Journal of Marketing Research* 29 (May 1992): 238–253.

13. Much of the background for this relational governance is based on Ian R. MacNeil, *The New Social Contract* (New Haven, CT: Yale University Press, 1980). For important marketing channel papers derived from that framework, see Jan B. Heide and George John, "Do Norms Matter in Marketing Relationships?" *Journal of Marketing* 56 (April 1992): 32–44; and F. Robert Dwyer, Paul H. Schurr, and Sejo Oh, "Developing Buyer-Seller Relationships," *Journal of Marketing* 51 (April 1987): 11–27.

Chapter 7

1. Discussion drawn from Pankaj Ghemawat and Jose Luis Nueno, "Zara: Fast Fashion," Case 703-497 (Boston: Harvard Business School, 2003); and Andrew McAfee, Vincent Dessain, and Anders Sjoman, "Zara: IT for Fast Fashion," Case 604-081 (Boston: Harvard Business School, 2004).

2. Discussion is drawn from V. Kasturi Rangan, "Cisco Systems: Managing the Go-to-Market Evolution," Case 505-006 (Boston: Harvard Business School, 2005).

3. Larry Hooper, "Cisco Certified Ranks Halved," *Computer Reseller News*, December 6, 2002.

4. Discussion drawn from V. Kasturi Rangan, "Atlas Copco (A)," Case 588-004 (Boston: Harvard Business School, 1987, revised 1993).

5. Discussion drawn from V. Kasturi Rangan and E. Raymond Corey, "Ingersoll Rand (A)," Case 589-121 (Boston: Harvard Business School, 1992).

6. Interview with Ray Löfgren, president, Atlas Copco Compressors, Inc., August 17, 2005.

7. Discussion drawn from Frank V. Cespedes and V. Kasturi Rangan, "Becton Dickinson & Co.: Vacutainer Systems Division," Case 592-037 (Boston: Harvard Business School, 1991, revised 2000).

8. In a 1998 interview with the *Harvard Business Review*, Michael Dell said, "Virtual integration means you basically stick together a business with partners that are treated as if they're inside the company . . . Most important the direct model has allowed us to leverage our relationships with both suppliers and customers to such an extent that I believe it's fair to think of our companies as being virtually integrated. That allows us to focus on where we add value and to build a much larger firm more quickly." See J. Magretta, "The Power of Virtual Integration: An Interview with Dell Computer's Michael Dell," *Harvard Business Review*, March–April 1998, 72.

9. This discussion has been drawn from V. Kasturi Rangan and Marie Bell, "Comergent Technologies: Enterprise E-Commerce," Case 505-016 (Boston: Harvard Business School, 2005) and author interviews at Haworth.

Chapter 8

1. Adam Fein, "Facing the Forces of Change: The Road to Opportunity," National Association of Wholesaler-Distributors, 2004.

2. Adam J. Fein and Sandy D. Jap, "Manage Consolidation in the Distribution Channel," *Sloan Management Review* (Fall 1999): 61.

3. This description is drawn from W. W. Grainger, 10K, filed December 31, 2003.

4. Jerry Useem, "One Nation Under Wal-Mart," *Fortune*, March 3, 2003, 65.

5. Michael Garry and Sarah Mulholland, "Master of Its Supply Chain to Keep Its Inventory Costs Low and Its Shelves Fully Stocked, Wal-Mart Has Invested Extensively—and First—in Technology for the Supply Chain," *Supermarket News*, December 2, 2002.

6. Ibid.

7. Charles Fishman, "The Wal-Mart You Don't Know," *Fast Company*, December 2003, 68.

8. Discussion drawn from Balaji Chakravarthy and V. Kasturi Rangan, "Best Buy," Case 598-016 (Boston: Harvard Business School, 1997); and Balaji Chakravarthy, "Best Buy: Staying at the Top," Case IMD-3-1430 (Lausanne: Switzerland, IMD, 2004).

9. Chakravarthy, "Best Buy: Staying at the Top."

10. Discussion drawn from V. Kasturi Rangan and Marie Bell, "H-E-B Own Brands," Case 502-053 (Boston: Harvard Business School, 2002, revised 2003); and supplemented by interview notes.

11. David O. Williams, "Lessons in Private Label," *Supermarket Business*, June 1996.

12. V. Kasturi Rangan and Marie Bell, "H-E-B Own Brands."

13. Supercenters averaged 100,000 to 200,000 square feet and contained not only the thirty-six general merchandise departments found in a traditional Wal-Mart discount store but also traditional grocery products such as frozen foods, bakery, fresh produce, meat, and dairy.

14. Discussion drawn from Das Narayandas, "Arrow Electronics, Inc.," Case 598-022 (Boston: Harvard Business School, 1998, revised 2003).

15. Ibid., 5.

16. The discussion of Owens & Minor is drawn from V. G. Narayanan and Lisa Brem, "Owens & Minor (A)," Case 100-055 (Boston: Harvard Business School, 2000, revised 2002); and V. G. Narayanan and Lisa Brem, "Owens & Minor (B)," Case 100-079 (Boston: Harvard Business School, 2000).

17. Adam Fein, "Deflation's Profit Squeeze," *Modern Distribution Management*, 2004, http://www.mdm.com/stores/fein3311.html, accessed November 5, 2004.

18. For more information on the importance of knowing cost to serve, see Benson P. Shapiro, V. Kasturi Rangan, Rowland T. Moriarty, and Elliot B. Ross, "Manage Customers for Profits (Not Just Sales)," *Harvard Business Review*, September–October 1987, 101–108.

19. This discussion is drawn from V. Kasturi Rangan et al., "RCI Master Distributor: Evolution of Supplier Relationships," Case 595-001 (Boston: Harvard Business School, 1994, revised 1995).

20. For further discussion, see John F. Gaski, "The Theory of Power and Conflict in Channels of Distribution," *Journal of Marketing* 48 (Summer 1984), 9–29; John F. Gaski and John R. Nevin, "The Differential Effects of Exercised and Unexercised Power Sources in a Marketing Channel," *Journal of Marketing Research* 22, no. 2 (May 1985): 130–142; and Nirmalya Kumar, Lisa K. Scheer, and Jan-Benedict E. M. Steenkamp, "Interdependence, Punitive Capability and the Reciprocation of Punitive Actions in Channel Relationships," *Journal of Marketing Research* 35 (May 1998): 225–235.

Chapter 9

1. Erin Anderson, George S. Day, and V. Kasturi Rangan, "Strategic Channel Design," *Sloan Management Review* 38, no. 4 (1997): 59.

2. Lawrence Friedman and Timothy Furey, *The Channel Advantage* (Oxford: Butterworth-Heinemann, 1999): 153.

3. This discussion of Toro is drawn from Toro Co., 10K, filed January 14, 2004.

4. This discussion is drawn from V. Kasturi Rangan, "Atlas Copco (B)," Case 588-020 (Boston: Harvard Business School, 1987, revised 1992).

5. Christopher Rowland, "Pfizer Targets Canadian Pipeline, Cuts Supply of Drugs to Wholesalers It Links to US Mail Order Deals," *Boston Globe*, February 28, 2004.

6. Ibid.

7. Das Narayandas, "Arrow Electronics, Inc.," Case 598-022 (Boston: Harvard Business School, 1998, revised 2003).

8. This discussion is drawn from V. Kasturi Rangan, "Cisco Systems: Managing the Go-to-Market Evolution," Case 505-006 (Boston: Harvard Business School, 2005).

9. T. C. Doyle, "John Chambers and You," *VAR Business*, August 5, 2002.

10. Frank Cespedes, E. Raymond Corey, and V. Kasturi Rangan, "Gray Markets," *Harvard Business Review*, July–August 1988, 75–82. The authors cite the case of the disk drive industry, where, to keep factory output high, volume incentives were offered to end users, large or small, encouraging many small end users to buy in volumes. But then, unable to consume the entire quantity, they sell the excess to the dealer channel, causing severe price erosion for the authorized dealers, which get the product from the producer at a higher price.

11. The practice of channel stacking at IBM is noted in Craig Zarley, "XChanging for the Better," *Computer Reseller News*, August 16, 2004, 84.

Chapter 10

1. These terms became part of the Internet lexicon based on the success of the pioneering Amazon.com, which appeared to take the staid book retailing business by storm. Note, though, that not everyone greeted the Internet with such enthusiasm. For example, others offered caution: "Caught up in the general fervor, many have assumed that the Internet changes everything, rendering all the old rules about companies and competition obsolete. That may be a natural reaction, but it is a dangerous one." See Michael Porter, "Strategy and the Internet," *Harvard Business Review*, March 2001, 63.

2. V. Kasturi Rangan and Marie Bell, "Dell—New Horizons," Case 502-022 (Boston: Harvard Business School, 2002).

3. Several articles and books have used diagrams such as this to present the cost advantages of Internet channels. See, for example, Lawrence G. Friedman and Timothy Furey, *The Channel Advantage* (Oxford: Butterworth-Heinemann, 1999), 153.

4. Clare Ansberry, "Let's Build an Online Supply Network! As the Trend Grips Industries, Some Big Hurdles Loom: Logistics, Antitrust, Culture," *Wall Street Journal*, April 17, 2000, B1.

5. "Santa's Helpers: A Survey of E-Commerce," *Economist*, May 15, 2004, 5.

6. Nicole Harris, "'Private Exchanges' May Allow B-to-B Commerce to Thrive After All," *Wall Street Journal*, March 16, 2001.

7. In June 2004, Ariba, a procurement software company, acquired FreeMarkets in a cash and stock transaction valued at about $500 million. At the time of the announcement (January 2004), the merged company was expected to have revenues of about $350 million. See Corilyn Stropshire, "Competitor Purchasing Freemarkets," *Pittsburgh Post Gazette*, January 24, 2004. Discussion drawn from V. Kasturi Rangan, "FreeMarkets OnLine," Case 598-109 (Boston: Harvard Business School, 1998, revised 1999).

8. Rangan, "FreeMarkets OnLine."

9. By the 1990s, supermarkets accounted for more than 70 percent of grocery sales, earning gross margins of about 24 percent and net operating margins of 1 to 2 percent. Statistics drawn from Paul R. Messinger and Chakravarthi Narasimhan, "Has Power Shifted in the Grocery Channel?" *Marketing Science* 14, no. 2 (1995).

10. U.S. critics of Tesco's online model suggested that its survival was based on a higher structural industry net income (8 percent in the United Kingdom versus 1 to 2 percent in the United States) rather than a superior online grocery business model. Christopher T. Huen, "Delivery Anyone?" *Information Week*, July 16, 2001, 22.

11. Ken Partch, "The Trouble with Online Grocery," *Supermarket Business*, August 15, 2001.

12. Bruce Mohl, "Shaw's Plans to Leap Online; New Service Part of Net Strategy," *Boston Globe*, October 13, 2004.

13. Earlier players—Webvan, HomeRuns, Streamline, and Shoplink—all exited the business.

14. Mohl, "Shaw's Plans to Leap Online."

15. Ibid.

16. "Airline Ticketing: Impact of Changes in the Airline Ticket Distribution Industry," GAO-03-749 (Washington, DC: United States General Accounting Office, July 2003), 21. The U.S. airline industry was estimated at $118 billion in 2003. Jim Corridone, "Airlines Industry Survey," Standard & Poor's, November 14, 2005, 9.

17. "Online Travel Distribution," Credit Suisse First Boston, February 27, 2002, 82–83. In 1995, air travel accounted for 65 percent of average travel agency business. By 2002, that figure had fallen to 44 percent.

18. A little before, but mostly after the airlines were deregulated in 1978, the major airlines invested heavily in their own computer reservations systems (CRS). American Airlines owned Sabre; Delta, through a series of acquisitions, ended up owning Worldspan; and United Airlines owned Apollo (which became Galileo). The CRS, as its name suggests, was a central reservation system—a software program run on mainframes that travel agents accessed and used to make bookings. These CRS systems ultimately became known as global distribution systems (GDS). Airline ownership of the GDS continued through the mid-1990s, when the airlines lost their competitive advantage associated with owning this aspect of the channel value chain. U.S. Department of Transportation rules formulated in 1997 eliminated any advantage that an owner airline had with its GDS, such as preferential display of flight schedules. As a result, the airline owners of the GDS, Sabre, Galileo, and Worldspan have all divested their respective stakes, leaving them completely independent of airline influence. See "Airline Ticketing: Impact of Changes in the Airline Ticket Distribution Industry," GAO-03-749.

19. Ibid., 25.

20. Yield management created an ever-changing array of prices designed to maximize the revenue yield per mile of every flight. It was in this era that the fourteen-day advance and required Saturday night stay emerged to price-discriminate and segment the less price-sensitive, more time-sensitive travel occasion from the more price-sensitive, less time-sensitive travel occasion, broken down into the characteristics of business travel and leisure travel.

21. Jim Corridone, "Airlines," Industry Survey, Standard & Poor's, May 20, 2004, 18.

22. Henry H. Harteveldt, "Business Travel on the Web: A Work in Progress," Forrester Research Inc., January 15, 2003. Based on these proportions, we estimate that the air travel market is approximately 20 percent managed business travelers, 20 percent self-managed business travelers, and 60 percent leisure travelers. Online, 33 percent are managed business travelers, 27 percent are self-managed business travelers, and 40 percent are leisure travelers. See also, "Expedia Corporate Travel Offers Exclusive Deals for Small Business," Expedia press release, November 16, 2004; and Travel Market Forecast Report, Jupiter Research, vol. 2, 2004.

23. The combination of a poor economy following the April 2001 stock market crash and the September 11, 2001, terrorist attacks led to a downturn in that industry from which it has yet to recover. In 2002, the top ten airlines lost $11.3 billion on revenues of $81 billion, having lost $7.6 billion on revenues of $87 billion the year before. In 2000 these airlines had been profitable, with operating income of $5.8 billion. "Airlines," Standards & Poor's.

24. "Air Travel Survey Finds 30% of Business Travelers Flew Less Last Year," press release, Travel Industry Association of America, December 20, 2002.

25. Harteveldt, "Business Travel on the Web: A Work in Progress."

26. Scott McCartney, "The Middle Seat: Web Effect Is Greater on Airline Revenue than Costs," *Wall Street Journal*, October 17, 2002, D2.

27. Joseph B. Myers, Andrew D. Pickersgill, and Evan S. Van Metre, "Steering Customers to the Right Channels," *McKinsey Quarterly*, issue 4 (2004).

28. Jim Corridone, "Airlines Industry Survey," Standard & Poor's, May 20, 2004, 3. Indeed, Southwest Airlines, JetBlue, and AirTran Holdings were all profitable in 2003, whereas the major airlines have struggled to survive. Southwest had profits of $442 million in 2003 (although profits were approximately half that figure after accounting for government aid).

29. Jeffrey F. Rayport and John J. Sviokla, "Exploiting the Virtual Value Chain," *Harvard Business Review*, November–December 1995, 75.

30. The discussion of eChoupal has been drawn from David M. Upton and Virginia A. Fuller, "The ITC eChoupal Initiative," Case 604-016 (Boston: Harvard Business School, 2003, revised 2004).

31. This discussion has been drawn from Autobytel, 10K, filed December 31, 2003.

32. Discussion of VerticalNet has been drawn from Das Narayandas, "VerticalNet (www.verticalnet.com)," Case 500-041 (Boston: Harvard Business School, 1999, revised 2000).

33. Paulette Thomas, "Case Study: Another Look Saves Firm from the Heap," *Wall Street Journal*, September 28, 2004.

34. Discussion of Amazon.com is drawn from Stig Leschly, Michael Roberts, and William A. Sahlman, "Amazon.com—2002," Case 803-098 (Boston: Harvard Business School, 2002, revised 2003).

35. Sellers qualify for buyer protection when they maintain 98 percent positive feedback ratings, have at least 50 feedback points, and use PayPal as the method of payment. "eBay Inc., Bidding on the Future of e-Commerce," Bear Stearns, January 28, 2004.

36. Data culled from ibid.

37. "A Perfect Market: A Survey of E-commerce," *Economist*, May 15, 2004, 3. Also noted in the article is the size of several e-commerce channels: $55 billion in online retail sales, $10 billion in travel through InterActiveCorp. alone, and $24 billion in auction trade on eBay alone.

Chapter 11

1. Joseph P. Myers, Andrew D. Pickersgill, and Evan S. Van Metre, "Steering Customers to the Right Channels," *McKinsey Quarterly*, issue 4 (2004).

2. Rowland T. Moriarty and Ursula Moran, "Managing Hybrid Marketing Systems," *Harvard Business Review*, November–December 1990, 146–155.

3. Paul F. Nunes and Frank V. Cespedes, "The Customer Has Escaped," *Harvard Business Review*, November 2003, 96.

4. Myers et al., "Steering Customers to the Right Channels."

5. The site was founded by Texas Pacific Group, a private-equity group, and six major airline companies: American Airlines, United Airlines, Continental Airlines, Northwest Airlines, US Airways, and America West. Later, Delta joined as an investor. In 2003, Hotwire was sold to IAC, which also owned Expedia.

6. These pricing mechanisms are discussed further in Robert J. Dolan, "Priceline.com: Name Your Own Price," Case 500-070 (Boston: Harvard Business School, 2000); and Robert J. Dolan and Youngme Moon, "Pricing and Market Making on the Internet," Case 500-065 (Boston: Harvard Business School, 1999, revised 2000).

7. One of Europe's new discount airlines, EasyJet, maintains an active pricing model. Passengers logging on to the site see prices change daily or even more frequently, depending on sales volumes.

8. Henry H. Harteveldt, "Business Travel on the Web: A Work in Progress," Forrester Research Inc., January 15, 2003. Generally, managed travelers are business travelers bound by company travel policy regarding booking. They may be required to book at corporate rates, go through specified travel agencies, and so on. By contrast, unmanaged travelers have unlimited choices in making travel arrangements.

9. Discussion drawn from Rajiv Lal, Edith D. Prescott, and Kirthi Kalyanam, "HP Consumer Products Business Organization: Distributing Printers via the Internet," Case 500-021 (Boston: Harvard Business School, 1999, revised 2000).

10. Examples of this are seen in V. Kasturi Rangan and Marie Bell, "Talbots: A Classic," Case 500-082 (Boston: Harvard Business School, 2000); and V. Kasturi Rangan and Marie Bell, "Merrill Lynch: Integrated Choice," Case 500-090 (Boston: Harvard Business School, 2000, revised 2001).

11. Discussion of Talbots is drawn from V. Kasturi Rangan and Marie Bell, "Talbots: A Classic."

12. Discussion of Merrill Lynch is drawn from V. Kasturi Rangan and Marie Bell, "Merrill Lynch: Integrated Choice."

Chapter 12

1. Discussion of PBMs is drawn from V. Kasturi Rangan and Marie Bell, "Merck-Medco: Vertical Integration in the Pharmaceutical Industry," Case 598-091 (Boston: Harvard Business School, 1998); and V. Kasturi Rangan, "Merck-Medco (B)," Case 500-078 (Boston: Harvard Business School, 2000).

2. In 1998, Eli Lilly sold its PBM, PCS, to Rite-Aid Corporation for $1.5 billion, at a significant discount from the $4.1 billion it had paid for the business in 1994. A year later, SmithKline sold its PBM, DPS, to Express Scripts, which paid $700 million for the acquisition, considerably less than the $2.4 billion SmithKline had paid in 1994. Several years later, in 2003, Merck spun off its Medco PBM to Merck shareholders, who received 0.1206 shares of Medco for every share of Merck common stock. "PBMs Undergo Transition as Industry Matures," *Chain Drug Review*, April 26, 1999; and Linda Lloyd, "Merck & Co. to Spin Off Prescription Drug Benefits Manager," *Philadelphia Inquirer*, August 6, 2003.

3. PBMs like Medco and PCS typically had about 50,000 participating retail pharmacies in their retail networks.

4. "About 95% of US workers with health insurance were covered under managed care plans in 2002, with conventional fee for services representing only 5%. This represents a marked change in a relatively short period: in 1988 managed care represented about 27% and fee for service, 73%." "Healthcare Pharmaceuticals," Industry Survey, Standard & Poor's, December 11, 2003, 16.

5. A formulary is a listing of preferred drugs by therapeutic class, often with cost designations. Formularies are designed to limit the number of medications covered by a plan. Often they have copayment tiers to encourage the use of preferred medicines. Three-tiered formularies have become the most prevalent; the copay is lowest for generic drugs, higher for preferred brand-name products, and highest for nonpreferred brand-name medications. In addition to restraining costs, formularies can minimize drug interactions and ensure that consumers receive safe and effective medications. *Biotech Business Week*, February 2004.

6. Some of the drugs that were at the heart of the formulary battles, each category worth about $10 billion a year, included *ulcer*: Zantac (Glaxo Wellcome), Pepcid (Merck), Axid (Eli Lilly), and Tagamet (SmithKline); *cholesterol lowering*: Lipitor (Pfizer), Zocor (Merck), and Pravachol (Bristol-Myers Squibb); *depression*: Prozac (Eli Lilly), Zoloft (Pfizer), and Paxil (SmithKline).

7. The FTC review of the Lilly PCS merger resulted in a consent agreement. The FTC determined that safeguards were necessary to ensure that Lilly and PCS maintained a competitive practice for determining which drugs were on PCS's formulary. It required that (1) PCS maintain an open formulary, (2) PCS appoint an independent committee composed of non-Lilly and PCS personnel to oversee the formulary, (3) Lilly and PCS establish safeguards to prevent each from sharing nonpublic information concerning other drug manufacturers, other PBM bid proposals, and the like, and (4) PCS accept all the discounts,

rebates, and other concessions offered by the manufacturers and reflect them when determining the ranking of products on the open formulary. M. Howard Morse, "Vertical Mergers: Recent Learnings," *Business Lawyer*, August 1998, 1217.

8. Medco's mail-service operation was the largest in the industry, fulfilling more than 50,000 prescriptions per week by 2000. Because of the time lag between receiving a prescription and order fulfillment, there was the opportunity to effect "therapeutic substitution," especially with drugs for chronic illnesses, such as hypertension, high cholesterol, and so on. Substitution required the approval of the prescribing physician, and Medco had implemented a superb physician contact telephone and Web capability [Rangan, "Merck-Medco (B)," 4]. In spite of this capability, industry studies have shown that little or no substitution actually took place at Medco. Marta Wosinska and Robert S. Huckman, "Generic Dispensing and Substitution in Mail and Retail Pharmacies," *Health Affairs*, July 28, 2004.

9. Melissa Marr, "Now Playing: Expensive Movies," *Wall Street Journal*, March 27, 2004, B4. This article also provides the reference for production and marketing costs. The major studios were Disney Studios, Paramount Studios, Columbia Studios, Warner Brothers, 20th Century Fox, and Universal Studios.

10. The number of blockbusters varied from year to year. In 2002, 15 percent of films were consider blockbusters. In 2003, only 9 percent achieved that status. U.S. Entertainment Industry: MPA Statistics, MPA Worldwide Market Research, 2002, 2003.

11. Ronald Grover, "What's Driving the Box Office Batty," *BusinessWeek Online*, July 11, 2005.

12. Grover, "What's Driving the Box Office Batty." This article provides an estimate of retailer DVD sales for 2005 of $18 billion, compared with $10 billion in box-office sales.

13. Melissa Marr, "Warner's 'Event' Movie Bet," *Wall Street Journal*, June 1, 2004, B1. More recent data suggests further erosion in revenues from box-office releases. Edward Jay Epstein (http://www.edwardjayepstein.com/mpa2004.htm) cites a Motion Picture Association market research report that indicates worldwide box-office revenues accounting for 17 percent, video and DVD 47 percent, and television 36 percent.

14. For example, Sony owns Columbia Studios and Sony theaters; Viacom owns CBS and Showtime (and until recently owned the Blockbuster retail chain as well); Fox owns Fox network and 20th Century Fox studios; NBC owns Universal Studios; and Time Warner AOL owns HBO, Warner Brothers, and Turner Broadcasting.

Selected Bibliography

Books

Corey, E. Raymond, Frank V. Cespedes, and V. Kasturi Rangan. *Going to Market: Distribution Systems for Industrial Products*. Boston: Harvard Business School Press, 1989.

Coughlan, Anne, Erin Anderson, Louis W. Stern, and Adel I. El-Ansary. *Marketing Channels*. Upper Saddle River, NJ: Prentice Hall, 2001.

Articles

Ailawadi, Kusum, Norm Borin, and Paul W. Farris. "Market Power and Performance: A Cross-Industry Analysis of Manufacturers and Retailers." *Journal of Retailing* 71, no. 3 (1995): 211–248.

Anderson, Erin. "The Salesperson as Outside Agent or Employee: A Transaction Cost Analysis." *Marketing Science* 4, no. 3 (1985): 234–254.

Anderson, Erin, George S. Day, and V. Kasturi Rangan. "Strategic Channel Design." *Sloan Management Review* (Summer 1997): 59–69.

Bradach, Jeffrey L., and Robert G. Eccles. "Price, Authority and Trust: From Ideal Types to Plural Forms." *Annual Review Sociology* 15 (1989): 97–118.

Buzzell, Robert. "Is Vertical Integration Possible?" *Harvard Business Review*, January–February 1983, 92–102.

Cespedes, Frank V., and E. Raymond Corey. "Managing Multiple Channels." *Business Horizons* 33, no. 4 (1990): 67–78.

Cespedes, Frank V., E. Raymond Corey, and V. Kasturi Rangan. "Gray Markets: Causes and Cures." *Harvard Business Review*, July–August 1988, 75–82.

Dwyer, F. Robert, Paul H. Schurr, and Sejo Oh. "Developing Buyer-Seller Relationships." *Journal of Marketing* 51 (April 1987): 11–27.

Dwyer, F. Robert, and M. Ann Welsh. "Environmental Relationships of the Internal Political Economy of Marketing Channels." *Journal of Marketing Research* 22, no. 4 (1985): 397–414.

Economist, "A Survey of E-commerce," May 15, 2004.

El-Ansary, Adel I., and Louis W. Stern. "Power Measurement in the Distribution Channel." *Journal of Marketing Research* 9 (1972): 47–52.

Emerson, Richard M. "Power-Dependence Relations." *American Sociological Review* 27, no. 1 (1962): 31–41.

Fine, Adam J., and Sandy D. Jap. "Manage Consolidation in the Distribution Channel." *Sloan Management Review* (Fall 1999): 61.

Frazier, Gary L. "On the Measurement of Interfirm Power in Channels of Distribution." *Journal of Marketing Research* 20 (1983): 158–166.

Gadiesh, Orit, and James J. Gilbert. "Profit Pools: A Fresh Look at Strategy," *Harvard Business Review*, May–June 1998, 139–147.

Gaski, John F. "The Theory of Power and Conflict in Channels of Distribution." *Journal of Marketing* 48 (Summer 1984): 9–29.

Heide, Jan B., and George John. "Do Norms Matter in Marketing Relationships?" *Journal of Marketing* 56 (April 1992): 32–44.

Klein, Saul, Gary L. Frazier, and Victor J. Roth. "A Transaction Cost Analysis Model of Channel Integration in International Markets." *Journal of Marketing Research* 27, no. 2 (1990): 196–208.

Kulp, Susan Cohen, Hau L. Lee, and Elie Ofek. "Manufacturer Benefits from Information Integration with Retail Customers." *Management Science* 50, no. 4 (2004): 431–444.

Kumar, Nirmalya. "The Power of Trust in Manufacturer-Retailer Relationships." *Harvard Business Review*, November–December 1996, 92–103.

Kumar, Nirmalya, Lisa K. Scheer, and Jan-Benedict E. M. Steenkamp. "The Effects of Perceived Interdependence on Dealer Attitudes." *Journal of Marketing Research* 32 (1995): 348–356.

Kumar, Nirmalya, Louis W. Stern, and Ravi S. Achrol. "Assessing Reseller Performance from the Perspective of the Supplier." *Journal of Marketing Research* 29 (1992): 238–253.

Lee, Hau L. "Creating Value through Supply Chain Integration." *Supply Chain Management Review* (September 1, 2000).

Little, Robert W. "The Marketing Channel: Who Should Lead This Extra-corporate Organization?" *Journal of Marketing* 34, no. 1 (1970): 31–38.

Messinger, Paul R., and Chakravarthi Narasimhan. "Has Power Shifted in the Grocery Channel?" *Marketing Science* 14, no. 2 (1995): 189–223.

Moriarty, Rowland, and Ursula Moran. "Managing Hybrid Marketing Systems." *Harvard Business Review*, November–December 1990, 146–155.

Narayandas, Das, and V. Kasturi Rangan. "Building and Sustaining Buyer-Seller Relationships in Mature Industrial Markets." *Journal of Marketing* 68, no. 3 (2004): 63–77.

Narus, James A., and James C. Anderson. "Turn Your Industrial Distributors into Partners." *Harvard Business Review*, March–April 1986, 66–71.

Nunes, Paul, and Frank V. Cespedes, "The Customer Has Escaped." *Harvard Business Review*, November 2003, 96–105.

Porter, Michael. "Strategy and the Internet." *Harvard Business Review*, March 2001, 63–78.

Rangan, V. Kasturi, Melvyn A. J. Menezes, and E. P. Maier. "Channel Selection for New Industrial Products: A Framework, Method, and Application." *Journal of Marketing* 56 (1992): 69–82.

Rangan, V. Kasturi. "The Channel Design Decision: A Model and an Application." *Marketing Science* 6, no. 2 (1987): 156–181.

Rangan, V. Kasturi, E. Raymond Corey, and Frank V. Cespedes. "Transaction Cost Theory: Inferences from Clinical Field Research on Downstream Vertical Integration." *Organization Science* 4, no. 3 (1993): 454–477.

Rayport, Jeffrey F., and John J. Sviokla. "Exploiting the Virtual Value Chain." *Harvard Business Review*, November–December 1995, 76.

Rayport, Jeffrey F., and John J. Sviokla. "Managing in the Marketspace." *Harvard Business Review*, November–December 1994, 141–150.

Ross, William T., Jr., Erin Anderson, and Barton Weitz. "Performance in Principal-Agent Dyads: The Causes and Consequences of Perceived Asymmetry of Commitment to the Relationship." *Management Science* 43, no. 5 (1997): 680–700.

Scheer, Lisa K., and Louis W. Stern. "The Effect of Influence Type and Performance Outcomes on Attitude Toward the Influencer." *Journal of Marketing Research* 29 (1992):
128–142.

Shapiro, Benson P., V. Kasturi Rangan, Rowland T. Moriarty, and Elliot B. Ross. "Manage
Customers for Profits (Not Just Sales)." *Harvard Business Review*, September–October
1987, 101–108.

Shapiro, Benson P., V. Kasturi Rangan, and John J. Sviokla. "Staple Yourself to an Order."
Harvard Business Review, July–August 1992, 114–122.

Stern, Louis W., and Torger Reve. "Distribution Channel as Political Economies: A Framework for Comparative Analysis." *Journal of Marketing* 44, no. 3 (1980): 52–64.

Stern, Louis W., and Frederick D. Sturdivant. "Customer-Driven Distribution Systems."
Harvard Business Review, July–August 1987, 34–39.

Case Studies

Bell, David E., and Ann K. Leamon. "Eddie Bauer, Inc." Case 500-034. Boston: Harvard
Business School, 1999, revised 2005.

Bradley, Stephen B., and Kelley Porter. "eBay, Inc." Case 700-007. Boston: Harvard Business School, 1999, revised 2001.

Bradley, Stephen B., and Erin E. Sullivan. "eBay, Inc. (B)." Case 703-499. Boston: Harvard
Business School, 2003.

Burgelman, Robert A., and Philip Meza. "Amazon.com: Evolution of the E-tailer." Case
SM-83. Stanford: Stanford Graduate School of Business, 2001.

Cespedes, Frank V., and V. Kasturi Rangan. "Becton Dickinson & Company: Vacutainer
Systems Division (Condensed)." Case 592-037. Boston: Harvard Business School, 1991,
revised 2000.

Chakravarthy, Balaji. "Best Buy: Staying at the Top." Case IMD-3-1430. Lausanne: Switzerland: IMD, 2000, revised 2005.

Chakravarthy, Balaji, and V. Kasturi Rangan. "Best Buy." Case 598-016. Boston: Harvard
Business School, 1997.

Dolan, Robert J. "Priceline.com: Name Your Own Price." Case 500-070. Boston: Harvard
Business School, 1999, revised 2000.

Ghemawat, Pankaj, and Jose Luis Nueno. "Zara: Fast Fashion." Case 703-497. Boston:
Harvard Business School, 2003.

Lal, Rajiv, and Edith D. Prescott. "Callaway Golf Company." Case 501-019. Boston: Harvard Business School, 2000, revised 2005.

Lal, Rajiv, Kirthi Kalyanam, and Edith D. Prescott. "HP Consumer Products Business Organization: Distributing Printers via the Internet." Case 500-021. Boston: Harvard
Business School, 1999, revised 2000.

Leschly, Stig, Michael J. Roberts, and William A. Sahlman. "Amazon.com—2002." Case
803-098. Boston: Harvard Business School, 2002, revised 2003.

McAfee, Andrew, Vincent Dessain, and Anders Sjoman. "Zara: IT for Fast Fashion." Case
604-081. Boston: Harvard Business School, 2004.

McFarlan, F. Warren, and Nicole Tempest. "Charles Schwab Corporation (A)." Case 300-
024. Boston: Harvard Business School, 1999, revised 2001.

Narayanan, V. G., and Lisa Brem. "Owens & Minor, Inc. (A)." Case 100-055. Boston: Harvard Business School, 2000, revised 2002.

Narayanan, V. G., and Lisa Brem. "Owens & Minor, Inc. (B)." Case 100-079. Boston: Harvard Business School, 2000.

Narayandas, Das. "Arrow Electronics." Case 598-022. Boston: Harvard Business School,
1998, revised 2003.

Narayandas, Das. "VerticalNet (www.verticalnet.com)." Case 500-041. Boston: Harvard Business School, 1999, revised 2000.

Quelch, John, and Bruce Isaacson. "Goodyear: The Aquatred Launch." Case 594-106. Boston: Harvard Business School, 1993, revised 1994.

Rangan, V. Kasturi. "Atlas Copco (B): Gaining and Building Distribution Channels." Case 588-020. Boston: Harvard Business School, 1987, revised 1992.

Rangan, V. Kasturi. "Atlas Copco (A): Gaining and Building Distribution Channels." Case 588-004. Boston: Harvard Business School, 1987, revised 1993.

Rangan, V. Kasturi. "Cisco Systems: Managing the Go-to-Market Evolution." Case 505-006. Boston: Harvard Business School, 2005.

Rangan, V. Kasturi. "FreeMarkets OnLine." Case 598-109. Boston: Harvard Business School, 1998, revised 1999.

Rangan, V. Kasturi, and E. Raymond Corey. "Ingersoll-Rand (A)." Case 589-121. Boston: Harvard Business School, 1989, revised 1992.

Rangan, V. Kasturi, and E. Scott Lathrop. "Sunbeam Television (A)." Case 596-056. Boston: Harvard Business School, 1995, revised 1996.

Rangan, V. Kasturi, and Jay Sinah. "Xerox: Book-in-Time." Case 599-119. Boston: Harvard Business School, 1999, revised 2002.

Rangan, V. Kasturi, and Marie Bell. "Comergent Technologies Inc.: Enterprise E-Commerce." Case 505-016. Boston: Harvard Business School, 2005.

Rangan, V. Kasturi, and Marie Bell. "Dell—New Horizons." Case 502-022. Boston: Harvard Business School, 2002.

Rangan, V. Kasturi, and Marie Bell. "Dell Online." Case 598-116. Boston: Harvard Business School, 1998, revised 1999.

Rangan, V. Kasturi, and Marie Bell. "H-E-B Own Brands." Case 502-053. Boston: Harvard Business School, 2003.

Rangan, V. Kasturi, and Marie Bell. "Merck-Medco: Vertical Integration in the Pharmaceutical Industry." Case 598-091. Boston: Harvard Business School, 1998.

Rangan, V. Kasturi, and Marie Bell. "Merrill Lynch: Integrated Choice." Case 500-090. Boston: Harvard Business School, 2000, revised 2001.

Rangan, V. Kasturi, and Marie Bell. "Talbots: A Classic." Case 500-082. Boston: Harvard Business School, 2000.

Rangan, V. Kasturi, and Marie Bell, Paresh Shah, and Mihir Desai. "RCI Master Distributor: Evolution of Supplier Relationships." Case 595-001. Boston: Harvard Business School, 1994, revised 1995.

Rangan, V. Kasturi, and Susan Lasley. "Rohm and Haas (A) New Product Marketing Strategy." Case 587-055. Boston: Harvard Business School, 1986, revised 1993.

Rayport, Jeffrey F., and Cathy Olofson. "Marshall Industries." Case 899-239. Boston: Harvard Business School, 1999, revised 2001.

Upton, David, and Virginia Fuller. "The ITC eChoupal Initiative." Case 604-016. Boston: Harvard Business School, 2003, revised 2004.

Index

About the Authors

V. Kasturi (Kash) Rangan is the Malcolm P. McNair Professor of Marketing at the Harvard Business School. He has an engineering degree from I.I.T (Madras), a business degree from I.I.M (Ahmedabad), and a doctorate from Northwestern University's Kellogg School of Management. Professor Rangan's business marketing and channels research has appeared in management journals such as the *Journal of Marketing, Harvard Business Review, Sloan Management Review, Journal of Retailing, Management Science, Marketing Science,* and *Organization Science.* Rangan has authored such books as *Going to Market,* which deals with distribution systems for industrial products (coauthored with E. Raymond Corey and Frank V. Cespedes), and *Business Marketing Strategy,* which presents approaches for managing industrial products and markets over their life cycle (coauthored with Benson P. Shapiro and Rowland T. Moriarty). Rangan currently serves on the editorial boards of the *Journal of Retailing* and the *Journal of Business-to-Business Marketing.* He has also served on the editorial board of the *Journal of Marketing.* His most recent research on "channel stewardship," presented in this book, advances concepts and methods by which firms may transform their go-to-market strategy. Rangan is also actively involved in studying the role of businesses, nonprofits, and NGOs in addressing the needs and wants of lower-income consumers. He has written a number of case studies and articles on the topic and serves as one of the founding cochairs of the Social Enterprise Initiative at Harvard, whose faculty study and teach the challenges of nonprofit management. Prior to moving to the United States, Rangan held several sales and marketing positions for a large multinational company in India. He has been on the faculty of the Harvard Business School since 1983 and lives in the Boston area.

Marie Bell has been a Research Associate at the Harvard Business School since 1993, where she has contributed to the development of more than twenty cases. She has also worked extensively in the hospitality and executive education sectors. She received her MBA from Harvard Business School in 1989 and also resides in the Boston area.